CW00418843

Parentcraft

ParentCraft

A practical guide to raising children well

2nd edition

Ken & Elizabeth Mellor

FINCH PUBLISHING
SYDNEY

ParentCraft: A practical guide to raising children well

This second edition first published in 2001 in Australia and New Zealand by Finch Publishing Pty Limited, ABN 49 057 285 248, PO Box 120, Lane Cove, NSW, 1595, Australia.

03 8 7 6 5 4 3 2

Copyright © 2001 Ken Mellor and Elizabeth Mellor

The authors assert their moral rights in this work throughout the world without waiver. All rights reserved. No part of this publication may be reproduced, stored in a retrieval system or transmitted in any form or by any means (electronic or mechanical, through reprography, digital transmission, recording or otherwise) without the prior written permission of the publisher.

National Library of Australia Cataloguing-in-Publication entry:

Mellor, Ken.
    ParentCraft: a practical guide to raising children well.

    2nd ed.
    Bibliography.
    Includes index.
    ISBN 1 876451 19 X.

    1. Parenting. 2. Child rearing. 3. Parent and child.
    I. Mellor, Elizabeth, 1938–. II. Title.

    649.1

Edited by Shelley Kenigsberg
Text designed and typeset by *DiÄgn*
Cover design by *DiÄgn*
Internal photographs by Skeet Booth
Illustrations by Phil Somerville
Printed by Brown Prior Anderson

Notes The 'Notes and references' section at the back of this book contains useful additional information and references to quoted material in the text. Each reference is linked to the text by its relevant page number and an identifying line entry.

Other Finch titles can be viewed at **www.finch.com.au**

Contents

Introduction   vi

I Your role

1   Your job as a parent   2
2   Being a successful parent   15

II Your family

3   Your experience of families   30
4   Your own family patterns   36
5   Family dynamics   43
6   Balancing work and family life   51

III Some important skills

7   Working as a team   60
8   Handling parental conflict   66
9   Parenting with love   74
10   The discipline sequence   84
11   Standing to decide   96
12   Knowing when and how to act   107
13   Communicating clearly   120
14   Paying active attention   131
15   Repeating ourselves   137

16   Developing self-esteem   141
17   Managing brothers and sisters   149

IV Patterns in childhood

18   Natural transitions   160
19   A second chance   169
20   Four births, four bonds   176

V Ages and stages

21   Phases of childhood   192

VI Tools

22   Grounding   212
23   Relaxation   218
24   Family meetings   221
25   Couple time   223

A final word   226
Acknowledgements   227
Recommended reading   228
Biame Network   230
Notes and references   231
Index   245

Introduction

We are delighted with the response to the first edition of **ParentCraft**, which far exceeded our expectations. Many parents, teachers and childcare workers say that the book fills a significant gap in what was previously available. They particularly liked the unusually helpful ways of approaching children and the specific suggestions on how to handle common issues that arise either at certain ages or over extended periods. A mother of five, Adrienne's response was typical: 'What a great book. Congratulations! It is so readable, and full of wisdom and solid commonsense – profound stuff made simple'.

Our goal was to produce a book that is understandable, easy to learn from and useful for people with different backgrounds, values and expectations. That this has worked is clear from the complimentary international response to the book. It is currently being translated into several languages.

The developmental information in the Ages and Stages section describes what happens at different ages and lists useful parental responses at each stage. Many people breathed a sigh of relief when they discovered how normal their children were and how they could handle them.

Throughout the book we urge balance and suggest ways of achieving this. We need to learn to balance love and discipline, permissiveness and limits, and our support for individuality with the needs of the family as a whole. Also, somehow we need to balance the demands of home and work, something that is a real test for many of us these days. And through everything, we need to keep affirming and strengthening our children's senses of themselves as loving, creative, assertive, thinking, feeling and capable people.

Of course, raising children is a hands-on affair, and all our suggestions assume this. They are specific and practical, and usable in the midst of ordinary family life. Our goal was to collect the wisdom of many parents we have known over the years and share it, both to offer encouragement from those with experience and to give specific advice that really works.

And there may be an unexpected benefit. Many people have read and reread the book because each time they did, it helped them to heal their own pasts by filling in important gaps in the parenting they got as they grew up.

Your part

As you use what we have suggested, you may need to adapt what you read. Your family as a whole, each of your children and the situations in which you are living are unique. It is more than okay to experiment. It will often be necessary. Reshape our suggestions in whatever ways you think will make them work better in your family.

Our backgrounds

We have been involved with parenting and childcare in a variety of ways for more than thirty years. Our work during this time has included various forms of social work, psychotherapy, parent education, childcare worker training, marriage guidance counselling, family therapy, and involvement in custodial and institutional care. Most important of all, we have had lots of contact with children of all ages.

Our own daughter is close to adulthood as we write this. Also, we have each helped in raising hundreds of other children. These children were near and distant relatives, and the children of our clients, colleagues, trainees, friends and others. At one stage, while heading up a spiritual community for eight years, we had general responsibility for as many as twelve children at a time.

Our sources

Many hundreds of people have contributed. Some were acknowledged experts. Many were parents who taught us by telling us what they did. Our best sources were parents who had raised or were raising their children successfully. Often what they showed us and said was pure gold. We also learned enormously from discussions with other parents. Sharing successes and failures, our trials and errors, and our feelings of confidence and uncertainty with other parents was a tremendously important part of this learning.

> If you want to succeed at something, copy the people who have already succeeded.

Let's get on with it

We think that parents have the most important job of anyone anywhere. Everything we do as parents influences the lives of our children and helps to shape them for the years to come. Through them, the future of the world is also shaped. So let's do a good job. Let's get it right. Let's do it together when that will help. And let's enjoy the process.

YOUR ROLE

This section is designed to help you understand your role as a parent. Many parents give lots of thought to their roles, while others don't. In our experience, those who understand what they need to be doing at home are much more likely to do it and do it well.

Section I

Chapter 1

Your job as a parent

This chapter is a short job description for parents. The main idea is to let you know what is to come in the rest of the book and to highlight several things that give important context to much of the content.

The main jobs

Our two main jobs as parents are caring for our children and running our families. There are many joys and delights involved, and many challenges. We savour the delights and meet the challenges. As you will already know if you are a parent, there are many rewards of parenthood. They are both wonderful in themselves and add to our incentives to do the best we can. It is worth noticing them and remembering them.

- 'I love it when they come up to me with a smile and want a cuddle.'
- 'Looking at him from the door as he sleeps is always a special treat.'
- 'When she tells me excitedly about her day, I get just as excited.'
- 'My special treat is seeing her all dressed up ready to go out with her boyfriend.'

Just about all that we do each day is part of the job. Adding it up, there are certainly hundreds and possibly thousands of things a day. Think of what you have done already today:

- bathed, dressed and fed the children
- taken them to school or picked them up afterwards
- paid some bills, done the banking
- done the washing, vacuum cleaning, shopping, prepared for dinner
- travelled to and from work, and worked all day
- helped with or checked homework
- played with the younger children, talked to the older ones

- fixed a broken toy or bike
- discussed the children with your partner

All of these activities divide into six basic jobs that all parents need to do.
1. Keep our children safe.
2. Help them live well.
3. Train them to live in the world.
4. Persevere for as long as it takes.
5. Care for ourselves.
6. Take charge of our families.

Protecting our children

Safety is *always* important. We need to think of the possible dangers wherever our children are and take practical steps to deal with them in advance.

A young mother pedalled her bike to the shops with her toddler in an add-on seat behind hers. She leaned the bike against a shop window and went inside, leaving her thirteen-month-old on the back of the bike. Quite predictably, within minutes, screams of alarm and pain erupted as the bike hit the pavement. The baby's arm was broken. This was completely avoidable.

Keeping children safe

A little thought can avoid unnecessary tragedies like babies hanging themselves on curtain cords, toddlers being run over when the family car is being backed in the driveway, children drowning in backyard pools, or other accidents in which children are hurt, maimed, or killed.

It is worth sitting down and listing everything in your home and around where you live that poses a threat. Then you can protect your children appropriately and teach them how to manage these things safely.

Generally, our responsibilities are clear. When our children are babies, their safety is totally up to us. As they get older, they can take increasing responsibility for this, but our job remains. Even as they approach adulthood and we can reasonably expect them to act sensibly and carefully, we still need to be alert and offer guidance when necessary.

The need to be alert seems completely obvious to many parents. Yet it is not to lots of others. In our contacts with people over many years, we have often noticed that significant numbers of parents don't know the basics about safety. When we checked with them, their replies were a surprise.

- 'Before the kids arrived, I thought I knew what to do. After they arrived, I was right out of my depth.'
- 'I used to pretend I knew what I was doing. But I didn't really have a clue.'

Here is a brief list of some of the elementary things we need to do to ensure our children are safe.

- When they are young, keep them within eyesight, whenever they **could** get into trouble.
- Teach them about fires, stoves, heaters, electricity, knives, guns and other dangers, and guard them well until they are completely safe with them.
- Make sure they can cross roads safely (usually not alone before nine or ten years of age).
- Teach them how to protect themselves from sexual predators.
- See to it that they know the safe use of rollerblades, bikes, skateboards and other recreational vehicles.
- Educate them in how to deal with environmental dangers, such as snakes, spiders, bush fires, water hazards, sun, ice and snow.
- Ensure you know where they are and what arrangements are in place for them returning home safely when they go to visit friends, to parties and on other outings.
- Help them to say 'No', and to set limits with themselves and with others who would put them at risk.
- Inform them of the risks of various activities like drug use, driving dangerously, drinking alcohol and driving, and swimming and diving in unsafe places.

> It is our job to teach children what they need to know to live safely in the world. To do this well, we have to provide whatever protection they need, until they are fully capable of protecting themselves.

(See Chapter 12, 'Knowing when and how to act', and Chapter 18, 'Natural transitions' for more on safety issues.)

Helping them live well

Living well is important and parents generally do all they can to help their children do so. Dividing this into three parts helps us see clearly what is involved: health, happiness and fulfilment.

Health

Children's health is supported initially by all those things we do to feed, bathe, clothe, shelter and keep them healthy. As they get older, they increasingly take over the responsibility. By the time they are in late adolescence, they need to be managing all of their health requirements routinely. Providing their basic education about health and ensuring that they live healthily is included in our job.

As with safety, we have found many parents are either unaware of, or they are poorly educated in, how to live healthily. This automatically means that they cannot pass on to their children even the basics about living healthily. Children need to learn things such as:

- what to eat, when to eat, and what not to eat
- to keep warm when it is cold and to keep cool when it is hot
- to exercise and rest in a right balance
- the value of health practitioners like doctors, dentists and homeopaths
- to live actively
- to take care in the sun and the extreme cold
- to get as much fresh air as possible
- how to care for themselves when ill or injured
- how to take responsibility for their own health care

We also have the responsibility to stay alert for signs that specific things are not working out well. If we suspect this, we need to investigate what is going on, survey options for dealing with any problems, and do what is necessary. A short checklist is: problems with any of the five senses, particularly eyesight and hearing; distorted growth of feet or limbs; minimal brain damage causing dyslexia and other problems; and the development of crooked teeth.

> Bill seemed to cry incessantly, even scream in pain at times. His distressed parents were at their wits end. Medical investigations showed nothing. Advised to go to a cranial osteopath to have his head and neck checked for possible birth injuries, they were delighted with the results. Only a few sessions transformed him into a calm, happy, normal baby.

Mary and Angus began to suspect that their daughter had a problem after she started school. She had always seemed slow to learn and respond, and did not speak until late, but they thought nothing of this until she began coming home upset from school. The other children kept calling her 'dumb'. When asked, the teachers said that she did not pay attention in class. Upon investigation, they discovered that she had very reduced hearing. As soon as she was fitted with hearing aids, she improved dramatically and, far from 'being dumb', proved herself highly intelligent and quick.

Salli-Marie had repeated headaches when her reading load increased half-way through high school. An eye test revealed that she had been short-sighted for most of her life and no-one had noticed. When asked, she said that everything had always looked blurry and she had never thought anything more of it. Her study became much easier after glasses were fitted, and she did much better at school.

Happiness

Feelings and attitudes are closely tied to our own interpretations of things. We learn very early that we cannot 'make our children happy'. Children are very much in control of this. However, we can deliberately do lots that we think will stimulate them to feel happy, confident and capable of managing what they face in their lives.

Perhaps not surprisingly, our parental attitudes, feelings and actions make the biggest contribution here. The reason is that the children absorb both what we do with them and the way we do it. They then do within themselves exactly as we have done with them, particularly those things that we repeat. So, for example, if we have loved them, they will love themselves; if we have scolded them, they will scold themselves; and if we have ignored them, they will ignore themselves.

As well as absorbing our actions, they learn from our direct teaching. Part of our job is to teach the practical wisdom that we have gathered over the years. Some examples of both are:

Loving them with complete acceptance of who they are as people from their conception onwards: cuddling them, smiling at them and laughing with them, regularly telling them we love them, and enjoying the person in each of them. (In Chapter 9, 'Parenting with love' we make some suggestions about what to do when this isn't easy.)

Setting standards for them to strive for and keeping on helping them to achieve these standards until they do it routinely. Examples include politeness, caring about others, doing jobs well, telling the truth, and 'listening to me when I talk to you!' (See Chapter 10, 'The discipline sequence'.)

Setting limits so they know what is acceptable and what will get them into trouble both inside and outside the home. Some examples are violence – like hitting, kicking or biting; lying and stealing; not following through on promises; and swearing. (See Chapter 10, 'The discipline sequence'.)

Helping them learn how to relate to others: how to join a 'group of kids' in school, to stand firm when others disagree, or to control their own actions when they are causing problems.

Giving them practice at solving their own problems by walking them through ways that work often enough for them to do it easily for themselves. Help them practise what to do when feeling strongly about something (see Chapter 22, 'Grounding'); how to keep going when they want to give up; ways they can talk to others who have problems with them; and how to keep trying new things when their first efforts don't work.

Teaching them how to keep their attention on what they want rather than waste their energies on what they don't want. Happiness and the things we want in life come from what we concentrate on and we can teach our children this 'gem of an idea' from an early age.

Fulfilment

As parents we want our children to find deep satisfaction in life. This usually comes from three things: learning to value themselves as worthwhile people, developing a sense of connectedness to their inner destinies or purposes, and having ways of expressing those destinies or purposes directly in their daily lives.

We can help in this quest from the very beginning. We can take an interest in what they value, notice their understanding of what they are doing and their reasons for doing it, and respect the meanings they give to things. We do this over the building blocks when they are babies, progress to what they are thinking about their friends and their school assignments in childhood, and expand in adolescence to sophisticated discussions of the meaning of life, our origins and where we go when we leave this life.

Real respect for them is very important. Children are affirmed by our valuing them and our actions at younger ages help to keep the door open on deeper spiritual developments later on. Look at the shift of emphasis as our children get older.

- *'Why did you put the block on that one?'* we ask curiously.
  'Want to,' our eighteen-month-old chortles.

'Oh, I *see*,' we say as if in response to a profound revelation. We thereby reinforce the importance of the baby's reason.

- 'You know the way you've got that picture in the middle of your essay. Why did you put it there?' we ask.
  'I think it looks best there,' our eight-year-old says. 'I tried it in a few places.'
  'Have you thought of the effect it has on the person reading it? I found it a bit hard to make sense of the words just under it, because the picture is about something on the next page,' we suggest respectfully.
  'No, I haven't,' our child says, and goes quiet for a while. 'I think I'll still leave it there. It just looks better to me.' Our child is resolved.
  'Well it's your project and your decision, and I like you thinking for yourself,' we say.

- 'Dad/Mum there is so much suffering in the world,' our upset eighteen-year-old says. 'It doesn't seem right that some people should be so well off and others have so little.'
  'Yes, we find it upsetting too. What's upsetting to you about it?' we enquire.
  'Well, I want to see everyone happy and living easily. When I see suffering I feel so upset. I've been thinking I want to do something to correct it. I just think it's wrong.'
  'What have you thought about doing?' we ask, avoiding the urge to volunteer all that we have thought over the years.
  'I want my work to change the world into a better place to live. I've also thought of giving some of the money I get from my part-time job to support one of those children we see advertised on the TV. What do you think?'
  'Basically, I think you need to figure out what is best for you. It's up to you. But I've thought a lot about this area over the years. My thoughts might give you some more ideas. Do you want to talk some more?'
  Discussion usually follows.

Sharing our own questions and answers is a very important part of this. When they are young, they may not appreciate the deeper meanings that we know underpin these discussions. Nonetheless, our training them to think about themselves creatively and to extend their thinking outside their own immediate concerns into broader understandings pays off. It generally evolves naturally into an appreciation of the spiritual dimensions of themselves and life's events as they get older.

Training them to live in the world

Most animals and birds teach their young how to cope in the world. It is a crucial job. And we human parents have the same job. From our children knowing next to nothing about the world at the beginning, we have about twenty-one years to prepare them for the world that awaits them in adulthood.

They learn most effectively when they learn directly from us. Parents teach hundreds of things to their children throughout the day. Every act is a lesson of some sort. By the time they are grown up, they will have learnt millions of things from us:

- putting their toys in the box or cupboard after they've finished
- using spoons, forks and knives, drinking from a cup
- how to talk, read and write
- going to the toilet, getting dressed
- telling the time, what time is and how it is important
- how to get along with others
- what is important and not important in life
- how to cook and clean and deal with laundry
- ways to earn, save, budget and spend money

The list is very, very large.

> Our goal with children is to prepare them while they are at home to live life easily after they leave home. Generally we see them leaving somewhere between the ages of eighteen and 21, provided all has gone well. When they depart, we want them to be able to cope alone, and be able to manage the routine demands of life. They, then, will not need to depend on other people to do these things for them.

Persevering for as long as it takes

Staying involved with our children throughout childhood is fundamental. Parents and children are genetically primed to live together until the young ones are fully grown. Conception sets these genetically driven programs in motion. They create imperatives in all involved – the mother, the father and the baby.

A significant interruption to these programs for any of us produces deep distress and often creates deep wounds. The significant absence of either biological parent usually produces a potent mix of intense uncertainty, rejection, rootlessness, detachment, or worse. These responses can go into the very foundations of our children's personalities, when the loss is deep enough. This is true, in our experience, no matter how good the substitute parents and other carers may be. Children need a fundamental confirmation that only comes from growing up with their biological mothers and fathers.

The profound loss carried by many children adopted as babies, the effects on the young of a parent or parents dying, and the intense grief experienced by both parents when a child dies, all attest to the power of our biological and emotional commitments to each other.

Our parental job is to make ourselves as consistently available to our children as we can. We are programmed to see it through to the end. Children of parents who have provided consistent support generally seem to do very much better as adults than the children of those who don't. Naturally, some events take us away from time to time, such as the arrival of other children, work commitments and illness.

Genetic links are special

Our genetic links seem to bond us in special ways that have significant implications for raising our children.

- We remain linked and interacting for life, even when we are not physically together.
- Biological parents have a primary effect that cannot be produced by others.
- Each biological parent has a unique contribution to make to each child that his or her co-parent cannot make.
- Other people can do a good job, even a great job, but they cannot substitute completely for the biological parents.

Nonbiological parents

Understandably, our emphasis on the foundational significance of the genetic bonds between biological parents and their children raises important questions. What about the effects of separation, divorce, and of having single parents, or gay or lesbian parents? What about creches, family daycare and childcare? What about boarding schools? What about adoptive parents, step-parents and foster parents?

Millions of nonbiological parents (step-parent, foster parent, adoptive parent, or relatives) are successfully raising children. We have observed them for many years and the commitment to, love for, involvement with, connection to, concern for and delight in the children in their care is awe-inspiring. We applaud the efforts of these wonderful men and women.

We know from our own direct experience what is involved in this. The children in their care are fortunate to have them doing what they do. They are, in our experience, often more perceptive about the children in their care than their biological parents. And the point still stands. They cannot do the impossible.

Nonbiological parents cannot provide whatever the biological parents alone can provide. Understanding and accepting this has been a relief to many – both parents and children. It helps to explain why many parents and children sharing a nonbiological bond often experience both the great beauty of the loving bonds between them *at the same time as* a quality of separation, detachment, distance, or lack of joining. These experiences are natural to this kind of relationships, not a sign of problems or lack of love or commitment on anyone's part. They are simply part of the reality that those involved need to deal with.

Planning around loss of parents

Because family circumstances change often these days, many of us need to make plans for our children that take us away from them. What can we do to ensure that their need for their biological parents is met as fully as possible in the plans we make? Whatever your actual living arrangements are now or become in the future, we suggest that you do whatever you can to enable your children to spend as much time as they can with both their biological parents. We base this suggestion on our thirty years of helping people deal with the effects of early and later childhood deprivation and trauma.

We realise that this issue is hotly debated at the moment. There are many important things to consider. As part of our contribution to that debate, we recommend the following:

- If separated or divorced, organise joint custody and make access for both of you as easy as possible. Also, your children's future wellbeing and balance, and their capacity to sustain their own future partnerships will benefit greatly from you developing at least a good working relationship with each other.
- As a step-parent or foster parent, encourage the children in your care to have contact with their biological parents. This may vary according to the situation, of course. Sometimes welfare and safety issues sensibly restrict or bar this.
- Whether a single parent, or gay or lesbian parents, do all you reasonably can to ensure that your children have contact with their biological mothers or fathers.
- Creches, childcare and boarding schools, each in their own way, deprive children of their parents and what they need through direct contact with

their parents. We advise using them as little as possible. We recommend that the average child not use creches and childcare at all, unless only for a few very occasional hours. Boarding schools have a similarly depriving effect, on children, even when first used as late as adolescence.

- When childcare is needed, using willing family members with blood ties to your children is often preferable to other people, because some genetic link is available. We think that family daycare is the next best option after this.
- If your family is intact and your job takes you away from home for long periods, do what you can to change this. Your children need you at home and available, not at the office, in the car, or occupied on work for long periods at home.

Balancing principles and daily realities

Principles are important. But practical realities need to dictate much of what we do at times.

Whatever our preferences, a mother or father who is unavailable (by choice or otherwise) is just that, unavailable. Parents who both need to work to make ends meet in their families, have to work. Parents who cannot support their families without using childcare of some sort are acting properly to use it.

We need to accept these realities and do our best with them. Being aware of the importance of ongoing, routine contact with their biological parents, however, may lead us to plan differently for our children than we might otherwise have done.

Caring for ourselves

We parents need to care for ourselves if we are to do a good job. The life each of us is living is precious and we need to nurture it well. We need to eat well, exercise, rest, have a variety of stimulation, and generally maintain ourselves in good shape. Failure to do this means that we will not be able to perform our other parental duties well. Just as significantly, we will not be able to enjoy our lives, both within and outside our families. Good health is basic to this. What this means in specific terms will depend on our particular health and situation. Whatever these are, we think it is important to take as good care of ourselves as we do of our children. So look after yourself.

Taking charge of our families

Two stories illustrate how important it is for us to be in charge at home.

Claire, the oldest of six children, was about five years old when she decided it was her job to run her family. She had already been doing much of the cooking and caretaking of her younger brothers and sisters. She felt older than her parents, who did not seem to cope well with many things. They were frequently in so much debt that summonses were brought to the door. She was expected to deal with these people. Her mother used her as a confidante about her parents' troubles, too. As a result, she would lie awake at night worrying about everyone. She thought about using her pocket money to help, how she could get work, how she would take the other children with her if something happened to her parents. It was far too much to expect of a little girl. Even in her fifties, Claire was still worrying about her parents and her brothers and sisters.

A very expensive family home was on the market. The timing was bad, because a slump in property prices meant that the family had no chance of getting what they paid for their home several years before in the middle of a boom. A very generous offer was made and the parents wanted to take it. But they refused it, 'because our children won't let us sell'. Their children were twelve and fifteen. When told this story, we were shocked that the children were allowed so much say, whatever their reasons were. The father was the manager of a large foodstore chain and was used to making sensible financial decisions. The market kept falling as predicted, and when they eventually sold, it was for several hundred thousand dollars less than the original offer. The parents were not wise to give their children such power in an adult decision. Clearly, the children did not understand as much as they thought they did.

Most people know families that are not well-managed. Either no-one is in charge, or whoever is is not doing the job well enough. Often people live from crisis to crisis, lose track of necessities like food and clothing, the children run riot or manipulate the adults to suit themselves, and foreseeable difficulties occur without preventive action being taken.

Well-run families are generally easy to recognise.

- One or more of the parents are in charge and do the job well.
- Money and other resources are used well.
- The parents involve their children in discussions while doing the final planning and making the final decisions themselves.
- The children usually seem secure and know where they stand.
- Children play a significant part in the servicing of themselves and the household.

- Everyone enjoys spending time with each other (most of the time!).
- A sense of purpose and direction is normally obvious in the family.
- The family operates well as a unit and is able to make the best out of things in a crisis.

The main areas to control or manage

Financial matters – budgeting, saving, paying bills.

Daily chores – beds made, rubbish out, cooking done, washing finished, rooms tidied, and gardening done.

General admin – taxation returns completed, school applications in, the house gutters fixed, the washing machine repaired.

Family balance – time is well shared, fun and work are balanced, all children and adults share in the rewards of family life.

Useful one-liners . . .

Dealing with the boss

Your primary school aged child returns from school saying, 'You can't tell me what to do. **I'm** the boss of me'.

Our response can be, '**Yes that's true. You're the boss of you, and I'm the boss of you being the boss of you, until you know enough to take over completely. Now do what I just told you to do**'.

Escaping the 'But I've already done ...' trap

You are dealing with nonperformance of something and your son or daughter says, 'But I've already done so and so', or 'But I did everything that I had to last week'.

We say, '**That was then; this is now**'. Then we add, '**You are supposed to do all your jobs, every week**'.

Chapter 2

Being a successful parent

How do we know if we are successful parents? Most of us want to know this. Our short answer is simple. Successful parents do their best to raise their children to live happily and effectively in the world, seek help from others if they need it, and keep learning throughout.

Of course, the results we get are also important in this assessment. Paradoxically, however, we are often better able to judge how well we have done at the end of the process, than while our children are growing up. At the end, we see the adults they have turned into. Whereas, in the short run – through a period of weeks or months – what they do and don't do, how happy or unhappy they are, and how easily or otherwise they are learning, are not good guides in themselves.

Completely normal children go through many changes as they learn to handle life. And they often behave in ways that require correction. This is actually very creative, because, by presenting us with their troubles, we know what we need to teach them. For example, they may act provocatively, unacceptably, disruptively, or even unlawfully. They might even do so for months or years.

All of this is normal. Some people judge that this kind of behaviour proves the parents are not doing well. However, it can often show that the parents are doing an exceptionally good job.

- A mother dealing firmly with a tantrum-throwing two-year-old in the supermarket, generally warrants smiles of support and approval, not censuring frowns.
- Parents in the midst of setting consequences in proportion to some misdemeanour are doing their job properly, not abusing their child.

Successful parents find ways to meet their children's needs and shape what they do. Misbehaviour is usually a sign of a normal child, not automatically of a bad or neglectful parent.

A lot goes into successful parenting, of course. In this chapter, we cover seven important ingredients:

1. You are not perfect.
2. Each child is unique.
3. Make time for your children.
4. Program your children.
5. Censor what they are exposed to.
6. Trust your instincts.
7. Keep learning.

You are not perfect

Part of being a successful parent is to understand that none of us is perfect. Many parents care so much and try so hard that they worry that they are not doing the right things and blame themselves if things don't go well. Accepting our limitations helps. Here are some simple truths:

- We won't anticipate everything, nor should we.
- Normal children have problems like catching colds, getting cuts and bruises, breaking limbs, getting into squabbles at school, making mistakes, and getting into trouble with teachers. We cannot shield them from these events.
- We will do things that upset our children at times, sometimes accidentally, sometimes deliberately. Life is about beauty and ease, *and* upsets and discomfort.
- They may have problems that we miss, even though after the event we can see the signals they were sending us. Doing our best is all that we can reasonably expect.
- We are likely to get upset, tired, angry, frightened, disturbed, irritated or something similar. We are completely normal human beings. These reactions prove it.
- Sometimes we discover later that we have created serious problems for our children without realising that we were doing so at the time. While regretting this, blame is not appropriate. We cannot be expected to use something we do not know.

So go easy on yourself. Just do your best. If your best falls short of handling things as needed, then learn how to do what is necessary and do it, or get someone else to help you.

Each child is unique

This book is largely about our parental side of child rearing. We cover areas such as what parents need to do, our feelings and goals, how to manage the challenges our children present to us, and the outcomes we are hoping to produce. It can seem 'parent heavy' at times, that we are only concerned with parental responses and issue. However, the balance we reach between our own and our children's needs and perceptions is very important. We need to know our children well. We need to know what is going on from their points of view. This is central in everything we do, crucial to our success as parents.

> Our success as parents depends on us responding to and connecting with what is actually going on for our children.

If you have more than one child, you will already know that each is unique. One of the wonders of the world is the way every child is completely different.

- 'My first was always placid and happy. My second would get upset at the drop of a hat.'
- 'Even in the womb, he was on the go – and he's never stopped. Then I had a special feeling about the third child. I knew we would get along really well, which we do.'
- 'Something seemed wrong with my daughter from the moment she arrived. She was different somehow. It's never been easy with her.'

Successful parents deal with this uniqueness in two ways. First, we shape what we do to fit the children we have.

One very frustrated mother came to see us. She said, 'I wish José would be like Carmen. Carmen is so good. She always does what she is told. I tell him, "You should be like your sister. But you're not. You're so naughty" '. We asked her what José was like. To her, he seemed angry most of the time. He was busy and into everything. She seemed to be chasing him from one end of the day to the other.

We encouraged her to see her two children as different, as unique, instead of through comparisons with each other. She began to understand that she was

*parenting them as if both of them were Carmen. Carmen was the good
Carmen, José was the bad Carmen. With only a little help, she was able to see
all sorts of things that were unique to José, many of which she liked. From
then on, she later told us, 'I had two children instead of one. All I needed to
do was to deal with them differently, instead of acting as if they were the same
and getting angry every time José proved he wasn't'.*

We also help our children both to connect with what is unique in them and
to express it in their lives. Each has his or her own interests, talents, skills
and dislikes. A child interested in dance may have no interest in football;
one interested in science and numbers may have no interest in history or
comparative religion; and one interested in cooking may have no interest in
drawing or painting. They do some things very easily and struggle with
others. All of this is natural.

Children thrive on our support for their creativity and what comes
naturally to them. They usually do less well when basic interests or talents are
blocked or thwarted.

*Renata drew and painted at every opportunity. She would do so for hours at a
time. Her parents were counsellors and for most of her adolescence she talked
of working in childcare. A year before leaving school, her father pointed out
how excited she was every time she talked about her art and how dutiful when
she talked about childcare. He wondered if she would be happier using her art
in her future work. She investigated, forgot the childcare and delightedly
pursued her natural artistic creativity from then on.*

*Mark came from a large family. Each of the children was 'given' a special area
by their parents. Mark's was science. Throughout his childhood they also
stopped him from following his interest in languages and history. For years he
tried, without success, to enjoy his job as a research physicist. In his early
forties he gave up, returned to university and graduated as a language and
history teacher. He was happy with his work for the first time in his life.*

*Angela's family had been 'full of doctors' for several generations. From very
early on, she was expected to follow the family pattern. She complied, but
secretly hankered for the chance to become an actor. Even in old age, she
regretted that she had not followed her own yearning.*

As we think about what we want for our children, we can value and appreciate
their uniqueness. With so many opportunities now available, it is more a
matter of ingenuity than opportunity for them to find something that suits
each of them.

Make time for your children

Parenting takes time. Successful parents make the necessary time available. We urge all parents to do this if they can. It is well worth it. Take the time to:

- soothe your children when they are troubled;
- encourage when they are uncertain;
- joke when they are too serious, or just for fun;
- celebrate when they succeed;
- commiserate when they falter;
- push when they want to give up;
- watch from a distance when they are managing.

Wonderful, capable people can grow in the fertile soil of our devoted and loving attention. Here is a reward worth years of effort. Even if it seems a long wait at times, our fulfilment as parents is wonderfully completed when we can look at our grown-up offspring with joyous pride.

The 21-year journey

Childhood lasts on average for 21 years. (We expand on this in Chapter 21, 'Phases of childhood'.) Neither we nor they have any choice about this. Some parents 'love every moment of it'. The creativity of helping to shape forming human beings – and the world of the future through them – is wonderful. The time with them often passes very quickly.

Others do not like it much at all. They can get more caught up in the demands and the toil of it. Knowing that it will take 21 years can help with this. It lets us know what to expect and what to accept. Our children are with us through our actions. Blaming them will do little to make the time pass faster. Also, standing over a tree and expecting it to grow more rapidly than it is, does little except to increase our impatience. Providing the nutrients our children need so they grow rapidly, easily and well seems like the best course.

Actual time and quality time

Given that success as parents requires that we put in the time, we see no way around it. Others, however, suggest that actual time is not as important as quality time. Many parents are organising themselves around this difference, particularly separated or divorced parents, and those who work long hours. 'Even if we don't spend much time with our children,' they say, 'the thing we do is to make the time we do spend really count. We have quality time.' And certainly making our time with our children as good as possible is helpful.

But our children need more than short bursts of special time. They also need to have time just for play and hanging around with us.

Much learning requires years of ongoing involvement from parents. When parents are not available to do this, this kind of learning does not get done. And others cannot substitute for a mother or father. For example, it takes years for a daughter to learn to be a woman from her mother and father, and the same for a son to learn to be a man from his father and mother: years of repeated exposure. Think, too, of the special learning about parental caring and persistence that we communicate through being there day after day. Both parents need to get involved as much as possible: getting children up and ready in the morning, taking them shopping, ferrying them to visit friends, helping with the homework at night, and much more.

The time spent just 'rubbing along together', whether it is lovely or not, whether we are happy or frustrated, also teaches children what it is like to live day by day with others. It also makes it possible for them to learn that life does involve times of stress and difficulty. People don't always function at top form. Not all contact will involve high stimulation and special efforts. Life can be mundane.

> The adults who seem to do best in life, generally have had parents who arranged time to love, guide, direct and support them day by day for most of their childhoods. Actual time is more important than quality time, even when the quality of the actual time is not ideal.

The challenge these days for many parents is: how can we do it? It will be much easier for some parents than others, of course. Think of separated or divorced couples, for example. We suggest that they make arrangements, if at all possible, for both of them to have ongoing, daily involvement with their children. Any challenges that this may create are worth facing for the sakes of the children.

And here are a few ideas: Telephone calls are great for some children, not so good for others. Drop-in visits, 'I'm just here for a minute', add a lot. Calling in to say, 'Good night', even if the children are already asleep, is well worthwhile. We do this when we live with them; we can arrange to do it if we are not. Rostering each other to take responsibility on certain nights of the week can help. Living as close as physically possible helps make all of this easier, of course. Living around the corner is much better than living a drive away. When they are old enough, too, the children can go back and forth between their parents much more easily. Think of the hours in the car this could save.

Program your children

A prime job for parents is programming. Everything we do is programming our children. Here are some pointers on how to do it deliberately and well.

Model what you want

The most powerful way of programming the young is to set a good example. 'Walk your talk' and 'practise what you preach'. Live in the way you want them to live. Our children are 'swallowing us whole', so we are becoming part of their personalities anyway. As wise parents, then, we will ensure that we act in ways that we would like them to adopt.

When we need to decide specifically how to act, a very simple approach works well.

1. We investigate what is going on in them.
2. We figure out how they need to manage themselves inside.
3. We then do the same things with them externally as they need to be doing internally.

   They will take this in from us and then be able to do it for themselves.

   - If a child is upset and we think he needs to learn to talk through what is going on with himself, then our talking it through with him is the thing to do. Our yelling punitively will prompt him to yell punitively at himself inside.
   - With a child who needs to persist 'rain, hail, or shine' with her daily tasks, we need to persist by reminding, stimulating, and following through, until she does all this herself. Our forgetting, not following through, not being bothered, leaving it for someone else, all trains the child to forget, not follow through, not bother, or leave it for someone else, too.

Even inactivity is recorded. Doing nothing is an action and is recorded by our children just as strongly as the things we do. Not responding when people invite struggle, when someone is upset, when we have things to do, are all examples. If doing nothing will take care of what is going on, then this is helpful. If, however, action is needed, our doing nothing will lay unhelpful foundations.

Get them to commit to specific changes

Most parents are familiar with the scene in which they do a lot of directing, suggesting, demanding, encouraging, or teaching, while their children listen either attentively or with glazed eyes. Little change may come from this kind of exchange. To get sustained change, we need them to decide to take control of their own actions.

The idea is to get them to **commit to do** what we are guiding them to do. And all it takes is a question from us before we end the discussions. We ask them, 'What are you going to do from now on?' We need to get a definite response that includes **what they will do**. It is often helpful, also, to get them to commit to **what they will not do** from then onwards.

Their answers need to be something like, 'I will do X from now onwards'.

- 'I will ask for the toy. I won't just snatch it.'
- 'I will turn off the TV when you tell me. I won't keep watching it.'

Or 'When so and so does such and such, I will do X'.

- 'When Cathy shouts at me, I will talk to her, I won't hit her.'
- 'When you don't give me what I want, I will ask you "Why?" I won't run off to my room.'
- 'I will come to you for help, if he won't listen to me. I won't just grab what I want.'

Or 'When I think (feel, do, want, expect, need) X, I will do Y from now onwards'.

- 'Even if I want to stay out longer, I will get home when I say I will.'
- 'I will wash the car and I understand that this is part of what I have to do, if I want to use it. If I don't wash the car, I don't drive it.'

Putting it into words for them can be a trap. For example, 'Will you act politely from now on?' may get 'Yeah', 'All right', or 'Okay'. But what does that mean? 'Yeah – up you', 'All right – while you're watching', or 'Okay – since you won't give it a rest until I say something'. Getting them to put it into their own words can by-pass a lot of this.

Selectively reinforce what you want

Praise the qualities and skills you want, discourage the qualities and skills you don't want. Do this every day. Actively shape the behaviour, thinking, feelings, expectations, or values of you're children. Remember as you do, we all have five senses, so give the input through all of them.

- 'Well done!' Make eye contact, smile, warmly squeeze an arm or give a hug, offer something sweet to eat, and sound excited and pleased.

- 'Don't do that. I don't like you doing that. Do such and such.' As you say this, make eye contact, frown, firmly squeeze an arm, and sound determined.
- 'I am glad you stopped yourself and decided to act differently just then.'
- 'You have changed a lot. Good on you.'
- 'You are learning very quickly. Keep going.'

Describe them as you would like them to be

The things we say and do repeatedly are very powerful. Repeat something often enough and our children start to live what we are repeating. Doing the same thing 'over their heads' to others is very powerful, too.

To the child:
- 'You are wonderful.'
- 'You have a fantastic memory.'
- 'You are very considerate (caring, loving, expressive, lively etc.).'

To someone else:
- 'John usually gets very good results at school.' (John listens.)
- 'Lee is very good with people.' (To a friend. Lee is playing within earshot.)
- 'Veronica is very persistent.' (To the teacher in front of Veronica.)

Describing their undesirable qualities works just as powerfully, so take care about what you say to them and to others. Give them the sorts of messages about themselves and their capacities that you want to come true. Avoid reinforcing ones you feel are not good for them. It is worth remembering that, if moved to say, 'You are just like uncle Fred,' it is best to make sure uncle Fred is who you want your child to be like. If you don't, then don't.

Use nicknames that program them as you want them to turn out

Nicknames really stick. Repeated often enough, they have a very powerful programming effect. So, be very selective about the names you call your children. To understand the implications of this from another point of view, read Chapter 13, 'Communicating Clearly', and look at the material on concrete understanding.

Call them names like 'Beautiful', 'Handsome', 'Champ', 'Sweety', 'Precious', 'Bright Eyes', 'Star', 'Brave One', 'Gem', 'Treasure', 'Princess/Prince', 'Sweetheart', or 'Happy'. Avoid names like 'Stupid', 'Clumsy', 'Jinx', 'No Hoper', 'Fatty', 'Skinny', 'Bean Pole', 'Reject', 'Baby', 'Slut', or 'Dopey'. Being affectionate when we use unhelpful names actually only compounds the problem. The affection encourages the children to live out the name even more strongly.

> Our children are gradually turning into what they experience. That is, into what they watch, listen to, touch, taste and smell.

Censor what they are exposed to

All experiences shape our children – the way they think, feel, act and define themselves. As successful parents, we will filter what our children are exposed to. The point of doing this is to use our understanding of life to help our children develop into well-balanced adults. Also, we will do our best to ensure that their inner lives are as peaceful, loving, tranquil, balanced, intense and life-affirming as we can.

Children actively engage in whatever they are witnessing. They are not passive observers. They learn through imitation, by internally enacting what they are exposed to. Repeated exposure to something, whether it is 'real life' or pretend, potently shapes their personalities. Think of the common violence of many cartoons on TV. You may also remember the way even very young children started to act out the violent antics of 'The Mutant Ninja Turtles' to such an extent that many schools had these games banned.

Stories in books, TV heroes and villains, cartoon characters, comic strip characters, fairy stories, other children's stories, or the 'stars' and 'dropouts' often referred to by us, can all become models for our children to follow. Whatever our ages, we are all open to this kind of influence. However, the younger we are, the more impressionable we are, so it pays to guard our young well.

The best way to influence the impressions your children are affected by is to find wholesome things for them to enjoy. In this way, we offer something that is different, instead of creating a gap by stopping something. We can get more acceptance and less fuss, if we say, 'You can watch ...', instead of, 'You can't watch that'. Even so, direct, strong prohibition of some things without offering alternatives may be necessary occasionally.

We can build up collections of 'good videos', 'wholesome children's stories' and 'okay songs'. We can ensure that the video games and computer games they use are life-supporting. Life-affirming experiences can be organised and encouraged: camps, sports, school plays. We can discuss school assignments and, if necessary, intervene with the school to insist that a particular assignment is unsuitable. We can monitor the people with whom they spend time and keep our eyes open for congenial companions. Certain types of content can be 'prohibited' in any form, except as an issue to be discussed. For example, we could adopt as a rule, 'No violent movies, nor acts or threats of violence in our home'.

Areas to monitor
- TV, music, the lyrics of songs, movies, radio
- yard games, and computer and video games
- wall posters and pin-ups
- Internet sites, chat room participation
- source material for school assignments, class discussions and school books
- friends, relatives, acquaintances, groups
- solitary and group activities
- caretakers, like child-minders and baby-sitters
- conversations – both content and style

Trust your instincts

Our instincts are a very important part of our parental repertoires. Parents usually know what their children need. Our systems are very finely tuned to our children and deeply aligned to their quests for life and fulfilment. At times, all parents can be wrong, of course, because we may be enmeshed in difficulties, or have insufficient information or experience in some areas. On balance, however, we parents do know what our children do and do not need.

Parents say:
- 'If only we could get him to do (think, feel ...), then everything would be okay.'
- 'I know something is going on (is wrong), I just don't know what it is.'
- 'I just have a feeling that ...'
- 'I see a picture (had a flash) that ...'
- 'I don't know where this is coming from, but I think (feel, etc) that ...'
- 'I have a really strong urge to ...'
- 'What she really needs is to ...'

Our persistent or unexpected insights, doubts, wonderings, or vague ideas may come from something much more important than overactive imaginations. Often, when encouraged to follow through in some way on their intuitions, parents have discovered that they were right.

In general, we recommend that you do something to express it when you have an intuition.

- Hold his/her hand, if you have the intuition to do so.
- Persist with your questions, if you experience an inner prompt to do it.
- Express your doubts, fears, uncertainties, worries and other reactions as you communicate.
- Laugh and make a joke, if you are inclined to it.

Intuition and experts

Experts can provide us with a lot of direct, needed help and information, and this is valuable. At the same time, our children are our responsibility, not theirs. It is very important that we evaluate the advice we are given. If possible, check the results others have got by following the advice and watch the results your children get when you do what an expert recommends. If you get the results you hope for, this is helpful. If not, then you are best to try something else.

Apparent confidence, strong assertiveness, or professional education in experts is no guarantee of balance, maturity, accuracy, perceptiveness, truth, knowledge, or understanding. Not all experts are parents, not all of those who are, are 'good parents'. Also, they don't share a biological connection or live with our children, as we do. Even just the exposure we have day after day gives us a head start in knowing what our children need.

> Always think about things and check their truth for yourself. Have you ever thought that the professional helper talking to you might have barely passed his or her exams?

We make this point, because many parents these days lack confidence about their perceptions and abilities. Parents are encouraged to consult trained professional people, who are supposed to know what is best. And many experts are available these days through a variety of avenues. Parents coming into contact with these experts may doubt themselves and so easily give way to their 'expert views'. We urge you to continue to include your own 'gut instinct', knowledge and experience in the plans that are made for your children.

Keep learning

Parents usually learn something new every day. Every new situation, issue and event confronts us with our need to learn. And we have to learn 'on the job', because we have to deal with things as they happen, without the time to go and find out what to do. Many parents, particularly first-time parents, want some guarantees they are doing a good job. However, life does not provide them. Even very well-prepared people have to deal with not knowing what to do at times. All we can do is to do our best on these occasions. We can all take heart, nonetheless, from noticing that the vast majority of children thrive on their childhoods.

Our experience is that our learning as parents is mostly exciting and, only at times, a little hair-raising. When we do well, we learn from 'the trial and the success'. When we don't do well, we learn from 'the trial and the error'. Whatever we do, we are best to notice the results we get. If things work out, remember to do them again. If things don't work out as well as we'd like, notice the parts that did work and repeat them, and try something different for the rest.

When we do have time, we can seek out the learning we need. And there are many places we can find it.

- Talk to other parents, friends and relatives. Find out what works for them. Include successful parents from the older generations.
- Talk to professional people when you have need. Always remember to test for yourself what they tell you.
- Read books, look at videos, listen to audiotapes. You can surf the net and join chat room discussions.
- You can join 'real' discussion groups, or parent groups, or attend courses.

In some ways, the challenge these days is not to get advice, but to work out which advice is 'the right advice'. Experts do not always agree. So we recommend that you take what makes sense to you and try it. Only then will you know its value for yourself.

YOUR FAMILY

Families are mini-communities or mini-societies. They form one of the most important building blocks of the wider world. They are the context in which much of our children's early learning takes place. Our roles as parents in our families are central in all of this.

Chapter 3

Your experience of families

Dan is about to go to school. It is his third day and his second was not a happy one. An older boy had picked on him at lunch time.

Seeking some sort of help, he goes to his father, trying to appear brave by sniffing away his tears. His father, reading the paper, looks up and takes this all in with a glance. His son acts a bit weak at times and, like his father before him, he knows just what to do.

Without waiting for his son to speak, he says, 'Listen boy. None of that.' He's trying to sound kind and firm, and feels a bit irritated. 'If that kid does anything today, you just tell him to go away and leave you alone.'

'But I can't, Dad. I'm scared.' Dan was pale at the prospect and began shaking.

Seeing this, a rising tension begins in his father's belly. By the time it reaches his throat it bursts out in an angry shout. 'No son of mine is scared. Get that clear. Men stand up for themselves. Just do what I tell you!' He goes back to his paper with a frown, only partly aware that Dan is still standing there, not knowing what to do. He is completely unaware that he has just re-enacted a scene that he and his father had repeated many times while he was growing up.

'Are you ready to go, Dan?' says his mother as she rushes in, wanting to leave quickly so she can get him to school on time. 'It's time to leave.'

Dan sniffs, but says nothing.

'What's wrong dear?' Her voice softens; her face is full of concern. She takes him by the hand as she crouches on her haunches next to him.

'Don't want to go. I'm scared of the boy.' He leans against her to soak up her support.

'That awful boy. He shouldn't be doing that sort of thing.' She scowls. 'When I get to school today, I'm going to tell the teacher to punish him. They shouldn't allow children to do that sort of thing to each other.' She is righteous in her indignation and pulls Dan tightly against her as she speaks. Her feelings mask fearful concern about what could happen to her child without her there to protect him. Sounding and looking just like her own worrying, overprotective mother from twenty-five years before, she says, 'Don't worry, Danny, Mummy won't let anything bad happen to you.'

Dan isn't so sure about this. He feels good for the cuddle, but, even with his inexperience, he is sure his mother's intentions could get him into even more trouble from the boy. The teacher mightn't like it either. He quakes internally at this double prospect, but follows his mother to the door as she heads out. 'Mum and Dad haven't been much help,' he thinks, and almost decides that he'll just have to be brave and not talk like this any more.

Dad, still reading, calls after him affectionately, 'Have a good day, Dan.' He is thinking, 'Angela will weaken him with all of that soft stuff.' 'Bye, Dad,' Dan calls back, trying to sound confident so his father won't worry. 'See you tonight, Rob,' calls his mother from along the passage. She is thinking, 'Rob is always so hard on him. He doesn't see that all he needs is a bit of love and understanding.'

Dan and his mother meet Julie Alexander, Dan's teacher, when they get to the classroom. She listens patiently as Angela, barely able to contain her maternal protectiveness, bursts out with the story. She reassures Angela that she will do what is necessary and thanks her for letting her know as she leaves. Fortunately for Dan, Julie takes care of everything with an experienced hand.

Probably everyone has done, or seen others doing, this kind of thing. Instead of our real needs and current realities determining what we do, we let old programs decide our actions. If the old programs enable us to do the job, then they are useful. When they do not, then our responses can be widely off target and unhelpful, like Rob's and Angela's.

What Julie did

1. She realised that there are always as many sides to a story as there are people involved.
2. She got the two children together. They took turns to tell her their versions of events. Nate was a year older than Dan.
   - Dan said that Nate picked on him without provocation.
   - Nate said that Dan had walked sand into his lunch as he passed.

What Julie did (continued)

3. Julie told each of them what they needed to change in the future.
   - 'Maybe you didn't realise you put sand in Nate's lunch, Dan. Watch what you do and you won't get into trouble. Do you understand?'
   - 'Nate, you're older and could have handled this better. Explain to other kids what you want. There's no need to bully them. And take it easier on the younger kids. They're still learning. Do you understand?'
4. She then got each to apologise to the other.
   - Dan for the sand: 'I'm sorry for putting sand in your lunch.'
   - Nate for being unpleasant: 'I'm sorry for shouting at you.'
5. Finally she got them both to make decisions about what to do in future and to tell each other their decisions.
   - Dan: 'I'll watch where I walk from now on and be careful of your lunch, and I'll listen carefully when you talk to me.'
   - Nate: 'I'll tell you what's wrong in future, so you know what you did. I won't shout at you just 'cos you did it.'

How we are programmed early

Our original families have profound effects on us. We are with them in our early years when our deepest foundations as people are laid. From then on, everything in our lives is either partly influenced or fully determined by our early experiences. This is not to say, by the way, that external influences are the only significant factors in how we turn out. More on this throughout the book.

As we grow up, we are recording everything. Later in life, events inside or outside us can stimulate replays. A smile, a smell, a frown, a tone of voice, particular situations, certain events, and many other things, can press the recorder button and produce a replay. We then think, feel, act, look and sound in the ways that we or others did when we made the recordings.

We seem to record two things most strongly: the things that are repeated often; and specific, high intensely events.

- While not aware of it at the time, you recorded the ways your parents usually talked to each other. When you became a parent, you probably noticed yourself talking similarly to your partner.
- Your mother smacked your legs and screamed at you when she got upset. You discover yourself doing the same with your children, although you swore you never would.

We also record the gaps or unfilled needs from childhood. The absence of what we needed is recorded by the presence of what we got that did not help.

- Donald's parents did not insist on him completing jobs, and in later life he now has difficulty completing things. He had nothing inside to prompt him.
- Julie was severely neglected as a child. Her mother would leave her alone for hours, even when she was a baby. As a mother, Julie wanted to love her children easily, but it was just not in her, until she organised to get help.

What do we bring to parenting?

Patterns pass down through the generations. Our parents passed themselves on to us, just as we pass on ourselves to our children. They will do the same with theirs. Little wonder that 'things run in families'. The results are generally obvious.

- 'Good parents' often produce children who are 'good parents'.
- Not so competent ones often produce not so competent ones.
- Inadequate or abusive parents often produce children who act inadequately or abusively when they become parents.

This is not a matter of blame. It is a matter of fact. The only internal programs available to us when we have our own children are those we recorded from the

> Our childhood gives us our first program for parenthood.

people who took care of us when we were growing up. So, of course, our first responses to our own children are very likely to be the same as we got from our parents.

This situation is great if we are happy with our programming and it is not so good for those who are not. There is some good news, however, if we want to change what we got. Whatever our original programming, we can change it. Two routes for doing this are readily available.

If information alone is enough, we can change our programming by expanding what we know.

> *One father said to us: 'My grandparents were great. And my parents were great too because they copied from them. So I suppose I could have done the same. But when I thought about it, I decided I wanted to do more than them. I wanted to get ideas from as many people as possible, so I could do an even better job for my children. And that's what I've done.'*

Some of us need more than information, however. When our past experiences have left big gaps emotionally, or when we were actively neglected or abused during childhood, we may need to do something to correct what we still carry with us. Spending time with good parents can help fill gaps very adequately. So be on the lookout, if you need this. For more serious problems, counselling, therapy, or some form of ongoing help can be very helpful. Techniques and therapies are available to help people deal with even the most extreme early experiences and their effects.

Challenging our attitudes

Updating our old recordings is important for everyone. Most parents are at least twenty years older than their children. So, even the best programs passed on from our parents can be more than twenty years out of date. Happily, just getting on with living changes some of them. And when we need to do something specific to change them, several guidelines are helpful.

Let go of blame

As adults, each of us is responsible for ourselves, whatever our origins may have been. Our lives are much easier if we take this responsibility without blaming. Blame cannot successfully shift our responsibility for ourselves to anyone else. It actually interferes with change by distracting us from ourselves, which is where we need to be concentrating our attention. We find little value in blaming parents or others for the lives we are living.

> Practise affirming: I am a good parent and I'm getting better every day.

Decisions from our past can limit us

As we grow up, we often make decisions about how we will act in the future. At the time, the decisions make sense. However, in the future they may be extremely limiting. It is better to decide, 'I will only do that if it is helpful or necessary', instead of 'I will always do this', or 'I will never do that'.

- Petra was always very soothing and calming with her children. She always smoothed things over, just as she decided she would when she was eight years old. All her children soon learnt that they should 'put on a happy face', even when they were uncomfortable. All sorts of things used to fester away under the surface, because no-one was allowed to deal with them directly. The family blew apart from its own unresolved problems when the children were in middle to late adolescence.

- In response to a beating from her father, Shula decided, 'I'll never lay a hand on my children; and I'll never shout at them either'. Sealed with the passion of that long-ago moment, she found herself having extreme difficulty even touching her children affectionately, or taking them firmly by the hands when they need restricting or protecting. She also felt the sound block in her throat, whenever she needed to raise her voice, even just to attract her children's attention.

Building on what we have is very powerful

Every quality has value. We can find this value and expand it. Instead of thinking about the downside of something, think about situations in which it is really useful.

- If you generally wait too long before you act, avoid thinking something like, 'I'm so passive, I never get things done'. Think instead, 'I'm very patient and tolerant with my kids; I will act quickly at times from now on when they need me to'.
- If you are generally unfriendly and aggressive, avoid thinking things like, 'I'm a pushy twit'. Think instead, 'I'm strong enough to get the kids to do things that they don't want to do; from now on I'm also going to make friends with them and love them openly'.

Keeping track of ourselves

We advise all parents to monitor themselves in gentle, accepting and active ways. When under pressure, we usually revert to what is most familiar as we seek to cope with the pressure. Past patterns are often the most familiar. By monitoring ourselves, we can keep track of how we are responding and do what is necessary to make sure that we act in ways that are up to date and relate to the needs and welfare of the people involved.

Chapter 4

Your own family patterns

Noticing patterns can help us lift our thinking out of the detail of everyday events. Doing this can help us make clear decisions about strengthening what we want to promote and changing what we wish to modify.

How it helps to notice patterns

Family patterns have to do with what we repeat. For example, we often see patterns in who generally washes the dishes, who works for income, in the way decisions are made, who does the homemaking work, in the feelings that family members express regularly and the ones they regularly don't express.

We think that two main benefits can come from deliberately noticing patterns. One is to do with family directions and styles. The other is to do with understanding the significance of specific events.

Family directions and styles

When couples get together, they often discuss what sorts of families they want to create – their ideal families. And these ideas guide much of what they do in their early time together.

- 'I want our kids all to be friends.'
- 'Parents should talk to each other and be consistent with their children.'
- 'Let's make sure everyone has as much fun as possible.'

Sharing our overall goals for our families helps us to keep a general appreciation of the way we do things at home. Families in which the parents actively relate to their ideal family images tend to do well. Life for all has a greater consistency, direction and meaning than in families where the parents don't do this. Also, their families seem to have strength and substance, as a unit, that other families do not have. Spending time developing our ideals is well worth it. Some of our ideas might help:

- Each member speaks and acts respectfully to the others.
- Everyone expresses love and affection.
- Saying 'Good morning', 'Good night', and 'Hello' are all important.
- Politeness is important.
- Threats or acts of violence are not acceptable.
- Expressing feelings directly and respectfully is encouraged.
- Thinking clearly, logically and drawing accurate conclusions are valued.

In our experience, it is easy enough to lose track of these ideals. The pressures of daily activities can easily overtake the images some parents have and they forget what they wanted. Eventually they settle for what they have, rather than what they want. And what they have may only be a pale reflection of what is actually possible for them.

Take a few moments to think about your own family. What patterns do you notice? You can add some fun by thinking of a motto that covers most things. Some common ones are:

- 'Share and share alike'
- 'Everyone for her/himself'
- 'United front against the world'
- 'First in; best dressed'
- 'Family knows best'
- 'Broken skin gets love'

Noticing the patterns in our daily lives gives us a base from which we can think clearly about what we want.

- The children seem to spend a lot of time fighting and squabbling. You stop each incident, but don't do anything to teach them how to play cooperatively and happily with each other. Realising this, you start to teach them to act differently.
- Most of everyone's time is taken up with household chores, work and sleep. Fun is forgotten and nothing enjoyable is planned, not even trivial things. The moment you notice this, you begin to plan small treats, like takeaways, and bigger events like a weekly family night and a holiday together.
- You notice yourselves as parents saying contradictory things to the children. You have been so busy, you are not taking time to discuss how to handle things. After becoming aware of this, you arrange with your partner to get together for a talk about a few 'hot issues' the children are provoking at the moment. You decide to get together for regular talks. (See Chapter 7, 'Working as a team', and Chapter 24, 'Family meetings' for more information.)

Good questions to ask about your family

1. Who generally decides things and how generally do you do it?
2. Do you generally manage the family alone or with help?
3. Who helps around the house and how much?
4. Who does little or no helping around the house?
5. How do you talk and act with each other?
6. How do the children generally talk and act with your partner?
7. Are there some times of the day that are more challenging than others?
8. Who gets the children up, dressed and off to school on most days?
9. What are your bedtime patterns with the children?
10. How do you and your partner decide what to save and what to buy?
11. Does one of you soothe and nurture the children more than the other?
12. Do girls get treated differently from boys?
13. How do you treat each child generally?
14. Do you have favourites?
15. What is the balance between play, chores, parenting, work, sleeping?
16. What are you generally happy with in your family?
17. What are you generally unhappy with in your family?
18. Who generally oversees and helps with the homework?
19. Do the children want anything changed?
20. Do you want anything different?

Think of your own questions too. After answering them, think about what you want and then plan how you will get more of what you want and less of what you don't want.

Background patterns

Consider the following situation. Notice the way its significance and what we need to do about it changes when we include contextual information.

Theresa rushes through a doorway, roughly pushing her little brother out of the way. He falls to the floor and cries.

- If this is a one-time event, a simple caution like, 'Take care of your little brother, Theresa. Don't push him like that', could be enough.
- If she often pushes her brother, you may need to use 'standing to decide' to get her to stop, to consider her actions and to make some decisions about future behaviour, like 'I'll be careful from now on and wait when Mario is in the way'. (See Chapter 11, 'Standing to decide'.)

- If she has already made this decision twice before, you may need to use 'standing to decide' and make greater demands on her as you do. You might also set more uncomfortable consequences to bring the point home more strongly, provided Theresa is old enough to benefit from this.
- If she was more gentle than previously, or you saw her waiting for longer, even just a little, before pushing through, you have something to applaud as well as correct. You might say, 'Theresa, you know to be gentle with Mario. I'm glad that you waited for as long as you did. But you have to wait even longer so he can get all the way through the door. You're older than he is, so you need to be patient sometimes'.

Out of context, specific events can have many different meanings. The moment we become aware of background patterns related to those specific events, however, we can understand them more fully. Also, by taking account both of what is generally true and of what we would like to be generally true, we can:

- act more consistently
- take more practical approaches in the ways we do what we do
- be more precise in deciding what our children and our families need.

Changing patterns

To change a pattern all we need to do is to change what everyone does to create the pattern.

- Three of the five children hassle each other a lot. Concentrate your efforts on getting those three learning to sort things out cooperatively. When they have, the pattern will be different.
- Mother does most of the housekeeping and father most of the bill paying. You want to share things out differently. Have a talk and redistribute your responsibilities. When you have, your patterns of responsibility will be different.

Some change is easiest to make when we get each of the relevant family members to change, some by engaging the whole family at once.

- You begin to notice that two of your children often argue. Making general comments at dinner, or to them when they are in the middle of an argument has made no difference. So you talk to them separately about what they are doing with each other. Find out what the trouble is for each of them and help them come up with practical solutions for resolving things. Then get them together to make agreements with each other about what they will do from then on. (See Chapter 17, 'Managing brothers and sisters', for more on this.)

- While everyone in the family has chores and they know they have to do them, you notice that it takes lots of effort to get everyone started on the dishes after the evening meal. When together at the next meal, you make general statements like, 'When we finish tonight, everyone is to clear the table at once. Everyone will stay until the whole job is done. Watch each other and make sure you all do your share'. When you get a change, make another general announcement like, 'Well done. You all did a great job last night. Let's do it that way again tonight and keep doing it that way'.

A little at a time

Changing things a bit at a time is often better than trying to change a whole lot at once. When we do things in little steps, everyone can generally adjust much more easily. Big steps are often more noticeable and more of a challenge. Be prepared to take whatever time it takes – years if necessary.

- One of your children is very uncomfortable with touch and physical affection. He squirms away from physical contact, except when very relaxed or tired. You make up an expanding program. You begin by touching him at every opportunity, just a light touch on an arm, on his head, and bumping into him lightly as you pass. As he gets used to this, you make your contact a little more intense and sustained, like squeezing his arm, giving him a kiss on the head, cheek or mouth, and briefly pulling him close to you. Then you move to even more intensity with things like holding his hand, holding him against you as you stand together, hugging him strongly and for longer, sitting together on the couch and holding hands, sitting with your arms around him, and sitting him on your lap (depending on age and size!).

> Remember: small achievable steps will usually get us further than attempting big leaps.

A word of warning

Where people are in danger, we often don't have time to do things gradually. We need to get immediate and complete change, or build in complete protections to ensure everyone's safety. It is far, far better to act strongly now than to regret not doing so later.

- Your toddler is found biting the baby very hard.

- Your older children are not closing the gate to the pool, so the youngsters can get in unsupervised.
- Your teenager is very depressed and talks to you or a friend about not wanting to keep living. (See 'Dealing with suicidal children' on p. 118.)

Time and repetition

Learning something new takes time and repetition. Some changes take years. So as you seek to change the patterns in your family, accept this. The whole process is likely to be much easier for you when you do. Examples of areas of long-term learning and change include learning sensitivity to others; to persist in doing daily chores; self-care and personal balance; politeness and other forms of respect for others; when to take a stand and when to cooperate; and how to express feelings and solve personal problems. This is perfectly normal and it is our job to do what is necessary.

Consistency and persistence pay off.

We simply keep on for as long as it takes, hopefully comforted by knowing that we need to persist. Knowing the qualities we wish to encourage in our children, we keep correcting, supporting, interrupting, praising and criticising with this end in view.

Benefits of involving the children

All of our children help produce family patterns from the day they arrive. Also, from relatively young ages, children have good ideas about what would work better at home. So we suggest that everyone get together for regular discussions about how things are going in the family. Using their good ideas, we can make decisions about family guidelines, rules, regulations, limits, rewards, consequences and shared activities.

The children can benefit in special ways from this process. These discussions provide wonderful opportunities for them to learn about many aspects of life. They also learn to make suggestions, discuss things, and both participate in and witness decision-making. This is all important learning for them. Their participation often makes them much more inclined to follow any decisions made than if we 'impose' rules without discussion. We think it is important for parents to remain in charge of these discussions and the final decisions. Parents know much more about the world and what is needed in life.

Playtime for kids

Children enjoy different things at different ages, so when we are thinking about what to do to have fun, we need to take account of this.

Infants love emotional warmth, physical affection and touch, and they love to move a lot. Hugging and cuddling, carefully throwing them up and catching them, swinging them around, holding on so they 'fight free', piggyback or horsey rides are all hits. Ball games and other activities that stretch physical coordination are great too. Word games, reading and counting can all be fun and help with later development.

Children play physical games involving running, jumping, ball throwing and catching, skipping, climbing frames, swings, and contortion games. Activities that are less physical include card games, spelling and scrabble, adding and subtracting, riddles, and joke book sessions. Skill games are great, too, particularly as they get older: skittles, team ball games, such as rounders, and team sports. Playing huts, playing house, playing doctors and nurses, all come into their own at different stages.

Adolescents thrive on both competitive and noncompetitive games and sports. They enjoy themselves and learn many important lessons. Outings and holidays with friends and family, going to movies, hanging out with peers are just right for many adolescents. Great enjoyment can come from sharing interests like football, cricket, and other sports, or reading and discussing social issues.

Useful one-liners . . .

Interfering for good

In adolescence, many young people try to wrong foot us by saying, 'Don't interfere. It's my life and I have to live it'. We are supposed simply to accept this and, sometimes, to feel guilty that we are thwarting what they want.

We can say, **'It's my job as your mother/father to interfere, whenever I think you're mistaken, or doing something that is unsafe, unhealthy or wrong. Right now I think what you are doing is ... [specify which] and you are not to do it'.**

Chapter 5

Family dynamics

When things go well in our families and our personal lives, we enjoy ourselves and get on with living. We celebrate how easily we live together, love and share life with each other, support one another, delight in each other's successes, resolve the difficulties that arise between us from time to time, and move from one situation to the next with ease and security. Ah, yes.

Well, as most of us know, life is not always so easy or kind to us. Most of us go through periods of difficulty and challenge in our families. At these times, it is helpful to have some guidance on what is going on so we can better deal with it.

In this chapter, we explore two areas of family dynamics and make some suggestions on how to change things for the better. The areas are family dramas, and manipulations.

Family dramas

Soap operas appeal to so many people because of their dramatic ups and downs. Many families live like this. We can see what is going on easily when we use a tool called the 'Drama Triangle'.

The Drama Triangle has three positions. Each one has its own style and quality. The positions are the *Persecutor*, the *Rescuer* and the *Victim*. The names themselves tell us a lot about the positions. For many people, the 'excitement', 'entertainment', and 'drama' in life comes from using these three positions and from switching them regularly.

Consider the following scene. The family is sitting watching TV. A dispute develops over the program to watch.

ANNE: I want to watch 'The Nature Program'. [*She is seven years of age.*]

FRED: I want to watch 'Freaky Stories'. [*He is nine and got his choice last week.*]

ANNE: It's not his turn. [*There is a rising whine in her voice as she moves into Victim.*]

FRED: [*Sensing that he could lose this to the sympathy vote, he decides to try and win the Victim position himself. He speaks with even more of a whine in his voice.*] You always get to watch what you want. I never watch what I want.

ANNE: [*Mother and Father look to her as if they might swing support to Fred, and with a well-practised flourish she starts to cry.*] Fred's older and always does things I can't do. [*She's now got the Victim position all sewn up.*] .

MOTHER: [*Looking concerned, Mother is about to say something when Fred interrupts. She is well into the Rescue position, looking straight at Anne.*]

FRED: [*He sneers, aiming a venomous look at Anne.*] Oh she's such a sook. [*He's shifted into the Persecutor position with her. But, realising he will earn his mother's anger by that, he quickly shifts again.*] It's not fair. [*The whine is back.*] It's my turn. [*But Mother continues looking softly at Anne, so Fred now resorts to generalised nastiness, easily moving back into Persecutor to do it.*] I suppose mothers and daughters will stick together yet again.

FATHER: Who do you think you are? How dare you talk to your mother like that! [*Not unsympathetic to the last thrust, nevertheless, Father has rules about how to speak properly that he enforces.*] You just watch your mouth or you'll feel the back of my hand. [*Father immediately wins the Persecutor position with this masterful display. Fred subsides with his head down and shoulders slumped.*] Apologise to your mother this instant. [*Father is now more neutral, but with the Persecutor still obvious.*]

FRED: Sorry. [*He mumbles, affecting the Victim position, but no-one is fooled. He is still boiling with anger and wanting to take his revenge.*]

MOTHER: [*Trying to salvage something nice.*] Now let's all settle down and have a pleasant evening. We don't want all of this fuss, do we? [*She is still firmly established in the Rescuer position, from which very few family discussions dislodge her.*]

KIDS: [*The two children start to shout at each other, trying to score points.*]

FATHER: [*Shouting more loudly than them.*] If you don't both behave yourselves, no-one will watch anything. Then we'll all miss out. [*He is Persecuting again, threatening everyone with the Victim position, including himself. This is very virtuous, particularly since he wants to watch '60 Minutes'. After the children exchange a few more barbs, he makes his decision and they all watch '60 Minutes'. Dad wins.*]

The outcome may seem to have happened by default. However, it was determined by the various positions. Looking at them in turn, should give you the general idea.

Persecutor

While in the Persecutor position, people generally behave to others in ways that are unpleasant, denigrating, abusive, or unreasonably controlling. Their basic position is 'I'm okay, You're not okay'. This means that they think there is something wrong, negative, or lacking about the other person.

They use name-calling, put-downs, belittling, violations, sneering, mocking, outrageous statements, coldness, vengefulness and other ways of trying to hold onto power. By shifting as much discomfort as possible to others, they keep the upper hand themselves. Not at all interested in other people's welfare, Persecutors remain insensitive and uncaring about them.

They get on very well with Victims and will generally try to persecute Rescuers, whom they perceive as soft, wimpish and not understanding what is really going on.

Rescuer

When in the Rescuer position, people generally do things that are supposed to be helpful, solicitous, caring, supportive, or kind. However, whatever is done has the effect of holding other people back, of reducing their power, and of making them more reliant on the Rescuer. Their basic position is usually 'I'm okay, You're not okay'. Most Rescuers think that there is something lacking or wrong with the people who need their help, support, or correction.

They may appear helpful, caring, tender, concerned, dedicated, or powerfully committed towards others. However, they are basically self-serving. They ignore people's actual capacities and needs in the service of making themselves indispensable to the people they are affecting to help. Their attempts to take care of the discomfort of others are actually attempts to take care of their own discomforts, something they often block from their own awareness.

Rescuers assume that those they are Rescuing are incapable of doing things that they are quite capable of doing. They get on very well with Victims, and don't like Persecutors, whom they try and Rescue from their inadequate or wrong perceptions about the Victims.

Victim

While in the Victim position, people generally present themselves to others as less adequate, capable, competent, powerful, or self-sufficient than they actually are. For example, they pretend, often to themselves as well, that they cannot do things that they can do; that they cannot think, or remember, that they don't understand what they can understand; or that they are unaware of things that they actually do know. Their basic position is either 'I'm not okay, You're okay', or 'I'm not okay, You're not okay'.

Victims take a dependent position and invite responses from others that reinforce the inadequacies they are presenting. They may have a preference for harshness or kindness, but either beats neither. They may whinge, whine or suffer, or act cutely, seductively and coyly; or they may be angry, provocative or unpleasant.

They get along well with both Persecutors and Rescuers, often having a preference for one or the other. Unconsciously at least, they usually realise that their position is far more powerful than either of the other two, since Persecutors and Rescuers depend on having a Victim. The essential aspect of the Victim position is the perception of and commitment to inadequacy by the Victim.

> The goal in all three positions is to stay in the Triangle.

All three positions are limiting

When we communicate within the Triangle, what we do is usually futile, repetitive and limiting. We may switch position frequently, or act mostly from our favourite ones. Whatever we do, problems rarely get solved. In fact, problems are often created. Whenever we are within the Triangle, we are diminishing ourselves or others in some way. And people usually end up enmeshed in a web of feelings that make life less easy to live and more uncomfortable than necessary.

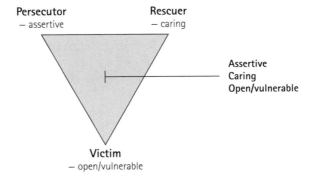

The way to change these unhelpful patterns is to act outside the Triangle. To do this, we can use a technique called 'straight communication'.

Straight communication

The best communication is straight and direct. It is clear of the behaviours that are characteristic of the Drama Triangle. Outcomes are determined by the facts of situations, and our actual capacities, needs, feelings, wants, and understandings. The position is 'I'm okay, You're okay'. Boring and dull to some people, this kind of living regularly opens us to enduring feelings like happiness, love, security and fulfilment.

Now, to stay in any position in the Triangle, we need to exclude the other two positions. This means that we will not allow ourselves to experience or act in ways that are outside the limits of the position we are occupying.

- Persecutors exclude softness or caring (which they associate with the Rescuer) and recognise no vulnerability in others (which they associate with the Victim).
- Rescuers exclude making demands on others (which they associate with the Persecutor) and don't recognise personal incapacities in themselves (which they associate with the Victim).
- Victims have little or no hope or adequacy (which they associate with their need for the Rescuer) and think they can't meet demands made on them by others (which they use to invite the Persecutor to act).

So, what if we discover we are in the Triangle? How can we act differently? The guidelines are very simple. To get out of the Triangle we act in ways that realistically and practically combine the helpful qualities of the three positions: assertiveness (from Persecutor), caring (from the Rescuer) and openness (from the Victim).

- Be assertive. Declare what is important to you and what you notice is going on with others.
- Be caring. Remain sensitive both to yourself and others.
- Be open. Express your own feelings openly and directly.

> Straight communication is out of the Triangle.

How would acting like this alter the situation at the family TV night? Let's take another look.

ANNE: I want to watch 'The Nature Program'. [*This is straight.*]

FRED: I want to watch 'Freaky Stories'. [*This is also straight.*]

ANNE: It's not his turn. [*Try the following.* **Assertive**: I really want to watch 'The Nature Program'. Fred watched what he wanted last time. **Caring**: I know you like 'Freaky Stories'. **Open**: But I like 'The Nature Program' and I'll be very disappointed if I don't see it this week.]

FRED: You always get to watch what you want. I never watch what I want. [*Most of this is already dealt with by Anne's previous statement. Both statements are clearly lies, which could be pointed out directly, if he did say this. Try the following.* **Assertive**: I'm not interested in 'The Nature Program' and want to watch my program. **Caring**: But I don't want you to miss out. **Open**: The only trouble is I don't want to miss out either.]

ANNE: [*This time there is no need for her tears at this point.*]

MOTHER: [*Instead of considering rescuing, she could stay out of it longer, or she could say something different. Try the following.* **Assertive**: Well, you both clearly cannot watch what you want at the same time. **Caring**: I like how direct and open you are with each other. **Open**: I always feel upset when you two argue. *Then guiding them to sort it out between them,* How can you sort this out?]

FRED: Oh she's such a sook [*This is now unnecessary. Try the following.* **Assertive**: I feel very angry about that. I don't like it when you cry to get your own way. **Caring**: I know you want to watch your program. **Open**: It's as I said before, I'm just not interested in it.]

FATHER: [*Assuming all of this has gone well, he could make a suggestion about some options they may not have thought of. Try the following.* Well I can think of three things you could do. You could each watch half your program; or you could decide on a completely different one; or you could do what we usually do and take turns. It's Anne's turn this week.]

Hopefully the discussion progresses smoothly and a mutual decision is made. Mother or Father may still need to make a final decision, if Anne and Fred do not reach agreement. With the new atmosphere, however, they are much more likely to base it on practicalities and reasonableness than before.

How to avoid being manipulated

We manipulate when we get others to do something they would not normally do by behaving or threatening to behave in ways that they don't like. Parents actually need to learn to do this for the benefit of their children because it is a natural part of setting consequences. Here, however, we are referring to manipulations that produce unwanted outcomes.

People can seem to have enormous control over others through unwarranted manipulation. Here are some examples:

- The youngest son 'is scared all of the time'. The family revolves around him. Whenever he has to do something he does not want to do, he gets scared. When they plan family outings, he has asthma attacks.
- One of the children 'hates pizza'. Initially it is only a temporary food fad, but it gradually develops into something affecting the whole family. Now, pizza is never on the menu, even for those who like it.
- When in conflict, children who go silent, or run away, are drawing attention towards themselves. They make it seem as though others should put more energy into sorting out what is going on than they should.
- Every time we expect some children to do things they don't like they throw tantrums, or set in motion a predictable sequence of uncomfortable exchanges with us. We notice that we are starting to avoid either raising certain issues or expecting certain things of them, because of the fuss it will 'cause'. They are in control in a way that is not good for them or us.

Several things rarely work to deal with these kinds of activities.
- Trying to make it all right; trying to please the children. ('What would you like, dear? What about such and such?')
- Appeasing so we avoid the upsets or other consequences. ('It's alright, you don't have to do it. Daddy will do it for you. You can have something else.')
- Doing nothing about what the children are doing. (Changing the subject, saying and doing nothing, looking the other way.)
- Venting our frustrations abusively instead of staying goal-directed. (Name-calling, not doing what is necessary to change the child's behaviour.)

What works is:
- Staying active and addressing the problems.
- Realising that illness or vulnerability is a powerful force in the hands of the manipulative. (We don't know if the person is sick or not.)
- Responding to the feelings that are under the behaviour and deal with them. (The scared, asthmatic boy above was furious most of the time, not scared.)
- Relating to outcomes and acting to produce the ones you want. Don't 'punish' others because of one person's behaviour. (Find ways to have the pizza.)
- Separating the real from the manipulation. (Some things start off as real, like illness or food fads, but end as manipulations when children learn to use them to try to control others.)

Ten guidelines for blended families

Respect

- Realise that everyone has their own feelings, thoughts and priorities.
- Each family member is a person, not part of 'them' or 'us'.

Accept

- Everyone is part of the family. There are no exceptions, nor is there any choice.
- Get everyone to express feelings and thoughts directly about this and each other.

Expect

- Proper behaviour is fundamental: courtesy, caring, cooperation, directness – no matter what the reason for misbehaviour.
- While hoping for love, only expect civility and that everyone keeps sorting out any difficulties.

Correct

- With standards and limits set for all in the family, all adults have a role to play in ensuring they are met. This is because they are adults and it is their job, not because they are or are not 'mother' or 'father'.
- The adults are free to draw attention to the need for correction both in each other and with any of the children.

Act

- Parents need to stay active, taking lots of initiative, so helpful patterns are reinforced and unhelpful ones are interrupted. This applies both to the children and to each other.
- Be prepared to allow time for everyone to adjust. Sometimes the best thing is to wait, but do not do this for too long.

Useful one-liners . . .

Making 'not fair!' work for you

Your child wants something and you've said, 'No'. Your child says, 'Aw, that's not fair', with the suffering whine that usually goes with it.

You reply, **'That's true. It's not fair and you're not going to have it anyway'**. An alternative, if you need a touch more confrontation is, **'True – it's not a fair world. Now accept what I've told you'**.

Chapter 6

Balancing work and family life

How can we spend enough time with our families and still make ends meet financially? This is a very important question for today's families. Somehow we need to deal with all the pressures and tensions that push and pull us in different directions.

In this chapter, we present some of the important issues as we see them. Each one could be debated at length.

Money pressures

Parents have the job of providing financially for families. These days many mothers and fathers share this responsibility. They both work. Prior to the 1970s, the common pattern was for fathers to work and mothers to stay at home. Naturally, this meant that the mother was at home to care for the children.

These days, lone parents continue to carry heavy burdens, as they presumably have throughout history. Unmarried mothers have opted in increasing numbers to keep their babies and raise them alone, if the fathers are not around. Fathers in increasing numbers are working as househusbands and taking primary responsibility for child rearing. And many couples have their children later than previously, opting to wait until their thirties and forties. The later start enables them to buy a home, to get themselves established financially and to pursue their own job interests before the children arrive.

These new patterns, evident in the 1980s and even more obvious in the 1990s, present parents and children with new challenges.

- Meeting the financial requirements of a family from one job, from government support, or other support, is usually a major strain. Lone parents often need to work to pay the bills.
- Parents working in many (one-parent or two-parent) families, means that children cannot count on a parent being at home. 'Latch-key kids' are numerous and childcare is in increasing demand.
- The price of housing and rental is now pitched at higher levels. It has been driven up since the 1980s partly by families and couples with two breadwinners. This is making life much more challenging for all families, particularly those with only one income.

> The financial pressures on families are real and demanding.

- Blended families face additional financial pressures. These families are created by the members of at least two other families coming together. So, for example, Ella and Tino marry; Ella brings two children from her previous marriage and Tino brings one. Extra pressures come from supplying the needs of the expanded family and from maintenance or child support payments to previous partners.
- Those who wait to have children until after they are materially established, often have expectations about maintaining a certain lifestyle. They develop a taste for abundant money, time, freedom and other comforts that family life tends to change. Then when they drop to one income with the birth of their babies, they have big adjustments to make.
- Then, too, there are the financial and other costs of childcare itself.

Family demands

Children need both their parents. Other adults can do a wonderful job. But children can only be nurtured in particular ways by their biological parents. Together, biological parents provide many fundamental ingredients for their children. Separately, they each provide something unique that only a mother or a father can provide.

A brief summary of our position includes the following:

- Throughout the 21 years of childhood, our children's needs change. (We outline these changes in Chapter 21, 'Phases of childhood'.)
- The younger the children, the more important we are to them.

- Mothers start off with a much greater direct significance than fathers. Children need more from their mothers than from their fathers in the first three to four years.
- Fathers only gradually become fully and directly significant with their children. It takes until the children are about three and five years of age to complete this process.
- The 'weight of the demand' of children for intense parenting changes. The first four to five years is very heavy. A somewhat lighter load follows until children reach about thirteen years of age.
- The 'weight' increases again substantially from about thirteen to seventeen years of age. It then tapers off again as they approach adulthood.

Matching a child's need for parents, is the parents' need to parent the child. We have a 'primal imperative' inside that prompts us continually to tend and care for our children. Most parents feel this keenly. We also see it in stark relief in both men and women who are denied access to their children through separation, divorce, death, or childcare. The following statements from parents express aspects of this imperative very eloquently.

- 'It breaks my heart to leave my baby every morning. It just feels wrong, but I feel I have to do it, so I pretend I'm okay.'
- 'I get home from work and try and cram in all that they need from me. It feels like a big hole that has to be filled and it's my job to fill it. But I know I can't and I always feel under pressure.'
- 'I really miss my kids. I'm gone before they're up in the morning and they're in bed when I get home at night. I know more about the tops of their heads in bed than anything else.'

> Our need to parent our children is as strong as their need for us.

Childcare

Childcare centres are definitely second best from our points of view. Wanting children to have the best, we would almost always choose the care of the parents over the care of others. All the same, there are necessary qualifications and guidelines, some of which follow.

If you need to choose childcare, we suggest that you think about the following observations:

- Some people have to work and don't have a choice.
- Some parents have such troubled relationships with their children that childcare is preferable.

- Standards of childcare vary; be selective.
- Childcare can be wonderful for the right child and the right parents.
- The older your children are before they start in childcare, the better they will handle things.
- The shorter the time in childcare each week, the less detrimental the likely, usual effects.
- Ration the time your baby is away from you, because significant breaks in the mother–child bond have devastating effects on babies.
- Introduce your children to childcare gradually.
- Choose blood relatives for childcare in preference to others, if someone suitable is available.
- Use good family daycare in preference to childcare, if it is available.
- Ensure that the childcare centre delivers good quality care and has a stable staff. Check that a particular caretaker will take primary responsibility for your child. Also check that this caretaker and the others are attentive, responsive, affectionate and stimulating.
- Keep the hours in childcare to a minimum.
- Preferably only use one childcare centre at a time.
- Make sure you spend lots of time with your children when they are not in care.
- Visit your child unexpectedly from time to time at the centre, both as a surprise for your child and to check on the care he or she is getting.

> Our children are exquisitely delicate and our most prized assets. When leaving them in the care of others, we should remember their value. We rightly put very much more time into assessing who will care for them, than we would into selecting a plumber or car mechanic.

We know children who love childcare and seem nourished by it. They have good strong loving relationships with their parents. The parents generally give primary importance to their children. Children who do less well are those who come second to other parental interests, such as jobs or leisure activities.

Job pressures

Much is expected of many workers these days. It is not unusual for people to work 9–12 hours a day. Many self-employed people and managers do this routinely. Dealing with these pressures and balancing them with the needs of our families is very challenging at times.

While a lot has changed in the last decade and the changes are encouraging, the workplace still has little awareness of people's general needs. And the needs of children, husbands and wives, and of the family generally, are rarely considered. Employees are often expected to put their jobs first and their families second. They are dealing with three very strong influences.

The seductiveness of the job

When work is stimulating and satisfying, people often enjoy the excitement, fulfilment and exhilaration. Real pleasures are available through working together with others, making deals, or succeeding in joint ventures. Workers can start to find work more enjoyable than home, if the time they spend at work cuts them off from the joys of family life.

Compulsion

Some companies state very clearly, 'Unless you are prepared to work these hours, you will not keep your job. Your employment here depends on you doing this'. Or, 'We expect you to work overtime, whenever we tell you we need you. Your previous arrangements don't count at these times'. When not stated directly, the expectations are clearly present in the way management acts. Only those courageous enough to risk their jobs are likely to stand out from the crowd in such circumstances.

Group pressure

Colleagues at work apply pressures, too. They say things like, 'If you don't do this you are letting your workmates down', 'Look how hard all of us are working and you leave at five o'clock', and 'You're a clock watcher'. Or they say these things about others in your hearing, so that you get the message. When someone asks to leave early or arrive later for family reasons, they get scowls, gruffness, disappointed looks.

Our children and partners suffer greatly from our absences. Health suffers greatly, too. We now know that a direct correlation exists between stress and ill health, accidents and early death. Long hours are an accumulating stress on everyone. The body and the human spirit need rest and a chance to do other things besides work.

Some important considerations

Good families take time and effort to create and maintain. They don't just happen. Just because people live in the same house does not mean they form a well-functioning family unit. We suggest that you structure life so what is important gets the energy and concentration from you that it needs. Don't let work take you away from your partner or children. Here are a few ideas:

- Give your children more of you, rather than deprive them. You are far more important to them than a TV set, a holiday, or some computer game, so do without or wait for a while.
- Work out how much time you need for handling family demands and doing the essentials. Then add on time for play, relationships and fun.
- As you plan your daily timing, take into account that the most significant action in families often occurs at breakfast, during school drop-off or school pick-up times, at home just after school, at dinner and at bedtime.
- Childhood is very short. Make the most of it. The years speed by and can disappear before you've even noticed they have gone.
- Make arrangements at work to allow you to leave in the event of an emergency with your children.
- Allocate enough time to be with your children. There is no substitute for good contact and shared experiences.
- Your family needs you with them. Ask yourself if the extras you get from working long hours compensate enough for your absence.
- If work currently dominates your family life, consider a variety of work options: one full-time job with one part-time, two part-time jobs, occasional work, job share arrangements, shift work, or home-based employment.

An effective test

Imagine that you are lying on your deathbed, reviewing your life. Think about your life so far. List the things you like and the things you regret.

A priest once told a friend of ours, 'I have been beside many people as they died. Not one of them said, 'I'm sorry I didn't work harder, or make more money', or things like that. They all said things like, 'I'm sorry my children grew up without me knowing them', 'I wish I'd told my husband (wife/son/daughter) how much I loved him (her)', or 'I now realise that I had my priorities wrong; it was far more important to spend time loving and sharing at home and with friends, than competing and winning at work'.

Too late for them, perhaps, but not for us. We still have time.

The family that plays together, stays together

Fun is a very important ingredient for us all. It lightens our hearts, loosens our bodies, relaxes our thinking and expands our beings. Unfortunately for many, the serious things can take over so that we get out of the habit of having fun, forget to do it, or have not ever known what a difference it can make.

Here are some ideas of things you can do as a family.

- Go to the park and play on the swings.
- Have a picnic – in the backyard, in the park, at the beach, at the local swimming pool, on the floor of the living room.
- Make pizzas together.
- Hire a video, or go to a movie.
- Get out on the town for a meal, shopping or family entertainment.
- Get takeaway food.
- Go for a 'getting to know the neighbourhood' walk.
- Go bushwalking, swimming or surfing.
- Go camping, or rent or borrow a holiday house.
- Play music together, or go busking as a family.
- Play board games such as Scrabble, Monopoly or chess.
- Dress up in your best clothes and have a dinner party with everyone's favourite foods.
- Go to the football or cricket.
- Kick a football, throw basketballs, or play cricket, volleyball, or badminton.
- Fly kites, or go rollerblading, or roller skating.
- Tell jokes.
- Organise family tickle times.
- Organise weekly family nights.
- Build cubby houses as a family.
- Go to art galleries or museums.

SOME IMPORTANT SKILLS

Before we become parents, all of us have learned something about raising children. We have learned from being children in our own families. However, sometimes this learning is not enough, or is out of date when we have to do the job ourselves. This section will help fill in gaps, highlight specific skills you already have and introduce you to areas that you may not have come across before.

Chapter 7

Working as a team

A mother and father who act as a team generally find parenting easier, more productive and more rewarding. They also share more of their lives than they would otherwise.

Francesca and Mario share a nightly goal. It is to have the children fed, bathed and asleep in bed by 8.00 pm. One of the children is a pre-schooler and one has just started primary school. The parents have mutually decided on who will do what. Francesca does the cooking, table setting, food preparation and serving, and deals with the dishes. Mario does the bathing, pyjama dressing, pre-meal playing and entertaining, and the pre-sleep storytelling. Francesca starts her jobs before Mario arrives home from work. They spend five minutes together upon his arrival before sitting down to eat. After the meal, they both aim to finish at about the same time, so they can get together for some couple time. Most of the week this coordination works well, but special arrangements had to be made for Wednesday evenings. Mario has to attend a weekly sales meeting that usually runs late. They decide that Francesca will cook earlier on Wednesdays, and will bathe, feed and put the children to bed. By the time this is finished, Mario will be home and will eat his meal, then do the dishes and tidying up. Couple time is still on the agenda.

What is teaming?

The primary thing in a team is to coordinate our efforts. We need to learn to act as a single unit, not as two separate individuals who pull in different directions. To do this, we need to talk lots to each other.

In parent teams, sharing is the order of the day. We recognise the shared responsibility of raising our children, and deliberately involve each other in every step of the process. Whether we act together or alone, we use our shared goals and commitments as an on-going reference for what we do. We will not just 'go it alone'.

> *Herman has the impulse to take the children to the movies after picking them up from their Saturday sport. Instead of just doing it, he contacts Pauline to make sure she had no plans for them that afternoon. During the call they coordinate the time for arriving home.*

A short list of ways to promote teamwork with your co-parent is:
- regularly discuss joint goals and priorities;
- work out each other's roles whenever it is necessary by specifying 'who will do what';
- make commitments to each other about the action each of you will take;
- keep your commitments to each other, unless situations change unexpectedly and you have to act before contacting each other;
- consult with your co-parent before doing something that is different from previous discussions and agreements;
- respect your shared interests and responsibilities as parents;
- respect your individual interests and responsibilities as parents;
- express your personal opinions, perceptions, desires, suggestions and proposals to each other;
- include your co-parent in planning and decision-making;
- back each other up with others, including your children;
- compliment and support each other directly every day;
- do whatever is necessary to resolve conflicts.

Getting the most out of each other

Each of us has our own contribution to make. Our contributions are important and unique. We need to listen to each other, talk directly to each other so there is something to listen to, and find the value in every point of view expressed.

> *Philippe is in trouble at school. After getting very angry about another child spoiling his game, Philippe swore at the child and pushed him over. The parents are arguing with each other. The mother says, 'It's quite okay for him to express his feelings. He shouldn't have to do anything'. The father says, 'He did something wrong and has to go and make it right. He should apologise and say he was wrong'. 'You're always so hard on him', she retorts. 'And you let him get away with everything', he snaps back.*

After they take a grounding break (See Chapter 8, 'Handling parental conflict') they feel much calmer and notice that both of them are right. They decide to encourage Philippe to express his feelings and to give him very clear rules on what is okay to do when he is angry. He can, for example, talk angrily, but not swear, push or hit. He will go to the school the next day with his mother, apologise to the other child and tell him what he will do if the situation arises again. He is also to talk to the teacher and deal with any unfinished business that she may have.

Parents have a combined contribution to make as well. Children learn a lot from their contacts with us when we are together. Handling these times as a team works very well. Talking to each other and acting consistently will save many confusions and fights, whether we act alone or together after our talks.

*David and Josie had twin sons. When they reached about five years of age, they became highly skilled at stimulating fights between their parents. David and Josie worked out a lovely way to deal with this. They would go to another room to talk, agree on their shared position, return to the child or children acting up and, standing hand in hand, they would say in duet, 'You are to do … This is **our** decision'.*

Team parenting offers us much more as parents than doing it alone. We can share the load, discuss things, support each other, check out and share our thoughts and feelings, encourage each other, monitor what we are doing in areas we have difficulty, interrupt the action to help clear difficulties, protect one another, add weight to our partner's positions, unite in joint action, back each other up, and disagree. All of these have advantages and strengthen us as parents.

> Always remember *the three*: *You, Me* and *We.*

Clarifying our roles. Discussion of who will do what helps us increasingly learn our strengths and gaps. We learn when each of us needs support and how to give that support. We also learn about coordination, both between ourselves and with our children. Consider this list of common family activities: getting the children to their sport commitments after school and on weekends, arranging music lessons and overseeing music practice, making opportunities for hobbies and other special interests available, taking responsibility for any remedial programs the children need, and picking up and delivering our children and their friends for visits to each other. Obviously, there are many more and coordination is important in each one.

How can you clarify roles? Several questions are helpful:

- How are we going to handle this together? Who will do what?
- What are we good at and how can we use our different skills well?
- What would be best for each of us to do?
- How can we support each other and learn from each other?
  Consider the following examples.
- One of your children starts to challenge his father, who finds him very difficult to manage. You mutually decide to deal with him together. When the problem arises again, mother backs up father by saying things like, 'Listen to your father', 'Respond to what your father just said to you'; or 'I don't like what you're doing either; do what your father says now'.
- A mother finds a teacher is particularly unresponsive to her, but the teacher seems very available to the father. You mutually decide that father will raise the important issues about your child with this teacher.
- A big cleanup is needed around the home. You arrange to do it together, with each parent taking responsibility for certain parts of the work. Also, you decide the various jobs each of the children will do and who will be responsible for overseeing those jobs.

Dealing with the nightly rush

Francesca and Mario share a nightly goal. It is to have the children fed, bathed and asleep in bed by 8.00 pm. One of the children is a pre-schooler and one has just started primary school. The parents have mutually decided on who will do what. Francesca does the cooking, table setting, food preparation and serving, and deals with the dishes. Mario does the bathing, pyjama dressing, pre-meal playing and entertaining, and the pre-sleep storytelling. Francesca starts her jobs before Mario arrives home from work. They spend five minutes together upon his arrival before sitting down to eat. After the meal, they both aim to finish at about the same time, so they can get together for some couple time. Most of the week this coordination works well, but special arrangements had to be made for Wednesday evenings. Mario has to attend a weekly sales meeting that usually runs late. They decide that Francesca will cook earlier on Wednesdays, and will bathe, feed and put the children to bed. By the time this is finished, Mario will be home and will eat his meal, then do the dishes and tidying up. Couple time is still on the agenda.

Team meetings

Get together regularly to chat about the family. Any issue is worth including. They may range from general issues like your overall family directions, to very specific planning of upcoming events. You also have the opportunity to discuss how you are handling things with each other and what improvements would help either or both of you.

Regular meetings are best in our experience. Some parents like having them at a set time each week. You could even make an appointment in your diaries. While some parents like spontaneity, we have seen many advantages in making these meetings at set times.

Family management generally becomes systematic and planned, rather than haphazard and reactive. Many parents value this approach. Comments include:
- 'It's great to know when I can discuss things.'
- 'Our family is much better organised now; it used to be chaotic.'
- 'We keep much better track of the jobs that need doing, like excursion forms, bills, holiday arrangements, dental appointments and shopping.'
- 'Before the team meetings, we always seemed to struggle to get time to talk about the problems the kids were having. Now we don't and we are working things out very much better.'
- 'Now we know when we are going to talk about these things, we no longer fill up recreation with family matters.'
- 'The kids know where they stand with us much more because we know where we stand with each other.'

Do regular reviews

We recommend that you notice the results you get. When things work out well, notice. When they don't work out well, notice this too. Then:
1. Deliberately repeat what works (if it works, don't fix it).
2. If it doesn't work, change what you are doing; seek advice, if you don't know what to do.
3. Keep reviewing and modifying what you do until you are satisfied.

Lone parents

We suggest that lone parents find others to join them in team parenting. Many parents would like to get together to talk about parenting. You might also find someone who wants to take a special interest in your children. This kind of contact can be just as valuable as co-parents getting together. You could get together to team parent. You would be able to support each other emotionally and practically to share the load of each other's children. Initially these may seem too much to organise. Still, these possibilities frequently only need a bit of persistence and a nudge from us to get things going.

Handy household messages

If you move it, put it back where you got it from.

If it belongs to someone else and you want to use it, get permission.

If you make a mess, clean it up.

If you borrow it, return it.

If you value it, care for it.

If you break it, declare it.

If you don't know how to operate it, ask someone, or leave it alone.

If it's none of your business, don't ask questions and don't read it.

If you empty it, refill it.

If you unlock it, lock it up again.

If you turn it on/off, turn it off/on.

If you open it, close it (properly).

Useful one-liners . . .

Standing 'alone'

Your child tries to force you to agree to something by saying, 'Aw, all my friends' parents let them do it'.

You say, **'Well I am your mother/father. It's my job to raise you in the best way I can. That's what your father/ mother and I are doing. You are to ..., and you're not to ...'**

Blackmailed by 'the other parents'

Our kids say, 'Aw, you're so rigid (restrictive, unfair, conservative, controlling, untrusting, unfair), all the other kids' parents let them do it'. We are supposed to feel uncomfortable and motivated to do likewise. After all, what would those other parents think of us.

We say, **'That's them. This is us. Whether you agree or not, it's my job to look after you and make sure that you are doing things that are good for you'.**

You might add, **'Your friends' parents are responsible for your friends. I disagree with what they are allowing them to do, if what you are saying they are allowed to do is right'.**

8

Handling parental conflict

Conflict provides creative opportunities for people to learn from and to share with each other. A normal part of living, it is worth learning how to respond creatively to it.

Many people think that something is wrong with conflict. They worry about the consequences and about the possible harmful effects. When conflict has previously been connected to rejection or distress, these concerns are understandable. However, this is more an unfortunate association than a necessary outcome.

Conflict is an opportunity for closeness and an exchange of views. It gives a chance for all involved to have their say and to be heard. In the process, people can bring to the surface and look at important areas of agreement or disagreement. A new and fruitful mutuality is often experienced through our deeper exposure to each other.

We discuss three areas in this chapter:
1. Valuing different parenting styles
2. Resolving specific conflicts
3. Helpful hints for handling conflict

Valuing different parenting styles

Parents often have different styles of doing things, differences that can add wonderful richness to the lives of our children. Every style has advantages that can contribute to a growing child.

- Passive parents with high energy partners can teach their children a useful balance between rest and activity.

- Spontaneous people and those who think things out carefully before acting, can teach children to use thought to obtain what spontaneously attracts them.
- Parents who are expressive combined with those who are repressive can train offspring to hold back when necessary and to go with the flow when free to do so.

We can practise taking advantage of our different skills so everyone benefits. This is common sense and well worth doing. Just because our styles differ, does not mean that one of us is wrong. We discussed some of this in the last chapter.

> Let's celebrate our different qualities as skills, rather than criticise each other about them.

Each of us can learn from the other. We simply imitate the way each other does things: copying tones of voice, ways of asking questions, postures, facial expressions, and ways of touching.

Dealing with specific conflicts

We suggest four steps to follow when conflicts arise. Thousands of people have found them helpful. The four steps are helpful in adult–adult, adult–child, and child–child conflicts, although we concentrate on parent–parent conflicts here.

When everyone completes these four steps, they will be satisfied, and will not have compromised themselves. The steps are:

1. Define goals.
2. Find areas of agreement.
3. Take grounding breaks.
4. Persist.

Define goals

We start the resolution process by clarifying what each other wants by the end. Our goals give direction and sense to what we do from then on.

To arrive at your goals, we suggest that you first ask yourselves several questions that help focus attention on the outcomes that each of you wants.

- What is currently happening?
- What do I want to change?

- What will solve my problem or resolve this issue for me?
- What will the situation be at the end, if I get what I want?

The next thing to do is to discuss your goals. The ideal outcome of this discussion is to reach agreement on common goals. The clearest way of doing this is to state your goals or write them down as descriptions of final outcomes. Some examples are:

- The children are in the school we think is the best choice for them.
- Our agreed division of labour has made leaving on the holiday easy and enjoyable.
- We are communicating well and continue to do so even when the children try to set up fights between us.
- We have agreed on the arrangements for our daughter to borrow the car and the time she is to get home, and we are acting cooperatively with each other.

We don't have to have the same goals. This is important and the situations to which it applies are common. Resolution comes from each of us achieving something different from the other. For example:

- *Mother's*: to have decided which school the children will attend
  Father's: to have discussed the school issue when he was alert during the day, rather than last thing at night when he was sleepy
- *Father's*: to have decided who is the best person to do the different chores
  Mother's: to have expressed her frustration about the mess around the house and to know that she has been heard

Concentrating on what we want, helps to bring us together, while concentrating on what we don't want, tends to separate us.

So during all these discussions:

- Concentrate on what you and your coparent want.
- Avoid overattention to what either of you doesn't want.

Using our goals

Clarifying our goals as parents helps us to stay focused and on track as we talk. At any point we can ask, 'How is what I/he/she is doing right now promoting what I/he/she set as the goal?' If it isn't, we can modify what we are doing. If it is, we can keep doing what we are doing with confidence.

For example, our shared goal is that we have decided who will drive to the shops. Some comments will probably slow down the resolution.

- 'You always snarl at me when we disagree.'
- 'I never get my own way.'
- 'I just knew last night that you were going to pick a fight about something.'
- 'I'm going to sit here and not budge until you let me drive.'
- 'You look just like your father when you talk like that and you know what I think of his driving.'

Some contributions are likely to promote the goal.
- 'I feel okay about you driving, but I'm concerned at how tired you are.'
- 'You know the way better than I do, so it makes sense for you to drive.'
- 'What about you drive there and I'll drive back.'

Sharing the same goal may streamline resolution, because we are working for one result. When our goals are not shared, we need to produce two outcomes. To do this easily, we can decide to take turns to work out what we will do. The process is not completed until we are each satisfied.

Find areas of agreement

People in conflict who begin by concentrating on areas of agreement usually resolve things much more quickly, easily and deeply. So we recommend that you do this as soon as you can. Many couples find it easier to write down or to say out loud where they agree. Both ways help to focus us productively on where we are in harmony and we can build from there.

If we keep concentrating on areas of disagreement, we are likely to build them and to expand them.

> Agreement encourages agreement. With areas of agreement clarified, we can expand agreement naturally.

Take grounding breaks

These breaks can make the difference between steady progress to complete resolution and complete failure. Grounding breaks are a special form of time out. When we are upset and tensions are high, grounding breaks free us to take care of our own unfinished business, so it doesn't keep intruding into our discussions. We deal with old recordings that are intruding on the present.

Grounding is a very simple thing. To become well grounded we concentrate on physical awareness. Perhaps while walking or running, perhaps while sitting, you concentrate on physical sensations in your body and on physical things and events around you. You notice what your sensations are, and you pay attention to what you can see, hear, feel, taste and smell around you. (You will find more discussion and simple instructions in Chapter 22, 'Grounding'.)

During a grounding break, you make a special effort to notice the physical things in your experience, setting aside as much as you can, whatever else you may be feeling, thinking or experiencing. It is not that you stop yourself having these. You don't. You do pay particular attention to the physical, however, in addition to whatever else you are experiencing. Sometimes it helps to go for a walk, to engage in brisk or strong physical exercise, or to do something enjoyable like going to a movie.

The changes that take place and the benefits derived are truly amazing at times. Grounding helps us to restore balance and to resolve internal difficulties. Many rewards await a little practice with this process, so we highly recommend it to you.

> Grounding breaks help you when you are repeating old unhelpful patterns, getting nowhere with your discussions, or feeling too upset or highly-charged to stay rational.

Steps to follow

A simple pattern for taking grounding breaks helps to make them easier to take and more likely to produce good results.

1. Make a general agreement that:
   a. If you get bogged down in a conflict, you will take a grounding break.
   b. Either of you can call these breaks at any time.
   c. The break is specifically for using grounding to release unfinished business stirred up by the conflict.
   d. Before breaking, you agree on a time to discuss when you will continue.
   e. If you are ready when that time arrives, then you continue; if not, then you set another time.
2. During the break you might engage in shared activities, or you might stay alone. If together, you avoid any discussions of your conflict. Choose whatever method will work best for each of you.
3. When you return to the discussions, if your discussions go well, keep going until you are finished. If they don't go well, then either of you can call another break as before.
4. Keep repeating the sequence: Discussion→Break→Discussion→Break, until you have completely resolved the relevant issues.

During a grounding break, you are ready to return to the discussions when you experience that whatever you were stuck with has shifted, even a little, and you have calmed down somewhat. This does not mean that you will be completely calm, however, as any thought of the conflict, until it is resolved, may stimulate discomfort.

After a grounding break, you are very likely to notice changes. The way you see things, how you feel about them, or the particular slant you had on things can change, sometimes substantially. We have found that there are always some differences. Notice the changes and, even if they are not big, acknowledge them to each other when you get back together. Then begin your discussions again.

Persist

Even if it takes years, keep going with the process. Only stop when you have both resolved all relevant issues. Never give up. Get it all done. Unresolved issues tend to build discomfort in our systems that can then leak or flood out at unexpected or unhelpful times.

When we were first married, we had very different standards of neatness. While each of us was comfortable with our own, Ken was not comfortable with Elizabeth's. He wanted things much 'neater' than she did. Similarly, we had different approaches to shopping. Elizabeth loved to browse and window shop, delighting in looking at what was available and thinking about the possibilities that would open up with what she could buy. Ken initially did not enjoy shopping one bit and would avoid it as much as possible. In both of these areas, we both persisted. We kept asserting what was important to each of us. 'I really want you to keep things neat and tidy', and 'Just because I look in the window at something doesn't mean I want to buy it'. We had cause to use the four-step process many times. It took us fifteen years to resolve these differences completely. And it has been worth every minute of the time. Nowadays, Elizabeth is 'neat' and Ken is delighted every day. Also, Ken 'loves shopping', which Elizabeth really enjoys, and he even goes out spontaneously to shop alone.

We know we have resolved our issues when each of us is content. Either we have each achieved our original goals, or we have shifted our original positions. If we have shifted, we fully accept what we now agree on, without compromising ourselves.

Resolution without compromise

To resolve conflict, we need to be willing to reach agreement. This involves a mutual willingness to shift positions, perspectives, or principles. We may need to let go of an existing position to make these shifts. 'Okay, I swore I would never let my children go to a school like that, but what you're saying does make sense, and times have changed.'

At the same time, we only have true resolution when we have actually made an inner shift. Shifts are not real if we compromise ourselves in making them.

So, avoid changing before you are clear that change is right for you, and avoid holding out for the sake of it. Neither keep going for the sake of winning, nor give up just to get it over or for the sake of peace.

You will know when this shift is real, because you will feel the rightness, see things differently, and hear a different significance in the situation. You will have no doubts, or tensions about the shift, although you might still have some discomfort about what you need to do as a result of making it.

All of this can take time. However, even if it does, everyone can get resolution without compromising themselves. And the results are worth it.

Hints for handling conflict

We have found the following help to streamline and to speed up conflict resolution.

Actively respect each other in the ways that you talk and behave. Honour each other, your opinions, your feelings, your intent. Acknowledge to your partner what you like about what he or she does. Avoid name calling: 'rotten bitch', 'stupid fool'. etc. Steer clear of overgeneralisations, such as 'You always', 'I never', 'Everyone', 'No-one'.

Use 'I-statements' and avoid 'You-statements'. Most people find it easier to respond to 'I-statements', because they are self-reports. Whereas 'You-statements' are usually accusations, assumptions, or definitions about others. Used in the middle of conflicts, 'You-statements' generally add fuel to the fire, rather than promoting calm, ease and cooperation.

Examples of 'I-statements' are:
- 'I feel ...', 'I think ...', or 'What I understand is ...'
- 'I like/don't like ...', 'I want/don't want ...'
- 'I agree/disagree with ...'

- 'I do/did ...'

Examples of 'You-statements' are:
- 'You feel ...', 'You think ...', 'You perceive ...'
- 'You like/don't like ...', 'You want/don't want ...'
- 'You agree/disagree with ...'
- 'You do/did/will do ...'

Develop signals to alert each other to regular problems. Most of us have things we do regularly that create difficulties for our partners and others. We can use special signals to interrupt us when we begin to act like this. The process is very effective and can be great fun.

The signals can be relevant, irrelevant, humorous, intelligent, simple. It does not matter what the signal is, as long as it will attract your attention and prompt you to act differently.

Note that ensuring the signal works is your responsibility, not your partner's. You need to choose a signal that you will notice and you need to resolve to use it to change what you are doing, if you are to make the system work. Some examples are:
- saying something like, 'I think you're doing it', 'Are you into it now?' or 'You're looking the way you wanted me to comment on';
- doing something noticeable like, putting on a top hat, licking his/her nose, tickling his/her side, clapping loudly three times, getting a cup of tea in a particular mug, or throwing chocolates into the room ahead of your arrival.

Support each other regularly. If you agree, agree openly. Give praise and recognition for jobs well done, for recovering poise, for keeping agreements, for making progress in challenging areas. Build up 'bank accounts' of appreciation and support. Then when things are challenging, you can draw on these to maintain good will.

If you disagree, disagree openly. It is normal to disagree with others. By disagreeing openly, we pave the way to working out what to do.

It is all right to disagree in front of the children. Our children know when we disagree. We see little point in pretending otherwise. Disagreeing in front of the children teaches them by example both how to do disagree and how to resolve disagreements. Children whose parents hide their disagreements, withhold this kind of learning from their children. We remember one family in which everyone was encouraged 'to be nice' to each other. The mother said, when asked how she and her husband resolved conflict, 'Oh, we go and hide behind our bedroom door and hiss at each other'.

Chapter 9

Parenting with love

Some people find it natural and easy to love, while others do not. And very commonly, most people find that their love ebbs and flows in the face of their children's behaviour and their own preoccupations.

In this chapter, we take a look at love, four ways express it, and how to practise each if we are not good at it. This is the most important chapter in the book.

Let's talk about love

Love is fundamental to everything we do as parents. It is the ground in which our children grow and the sun that shines on them as they do. Well-loved children thrive; love-starved children wither. This relationship is obvious to most caring people. Nevertheless, many people have not understood this, even in the recent past. Fortunately, we are living in more enlightened times than many others have.

Love draws people together and promotes growth. It nurtures, warms, soothes, teaches, heals, integrates, enhances, honours and respects. Love dissolves boundaries and separations between people. It draws people together in appreciation of each other. Very importantly, it makes our young capable of loving and being loved. It promotes sharing, mutual knowing, understanding, celebration of each other and complete union. This is really powerful stuff!

Unfortunately, many children are not loved as they need. Sometimes this is to do with the parents, sometimes to do with the children, sometimes both. Whatever the cause, the absence, or filtering of love is a great loss. It creates wounds and unmet needs, deprivation, and a sense of rejection or violation. It makes rifts between people. Unloved children usually grow into adults whose capacity to love themselves or others is stunted or distorted. Fortunately, we can do a lot to change all of this if we need to. More on this later.

The secret to 'making' love

Love is the most needed experience in the world. Of all experiences, it has a unique impact on us. It is perhaps, also, the most wanted and the most sought after. So wonderful when we share it, we usually want more and more. Apparently so out of reach when we don't have it, we can spend our lives in search of it.

The secret is simple. Every experience of love we have involves joining with another in some way. With the joining, we drop our separateness from one another and allow aspects of ourselves to blend. The more complete the oneness or union we have, the more intense the love is.

> Love and union always go together.

- You lie with your baby on your chest, just experiencing the moment, and feeling expanded by the intensity of the love you feel with your child.
- You sit cuddling your child, staying aware of each other as you do.
- Your child says, 'I love you, Mum', or 'I love you, Dad', and you feel your heart melt.

It is very much up to each of us. When we concentrate on what brings us together with others, what we like about them and love about them, what we enjoy, what we agree with, and what we share, we promote love. You can do this with anyone, although in this context we are discussing parents and children.

- 'I love the curl of the hair on your neck.'
- 'I really like the fun we have together.'
- 'You are so trusting and open with me. I love you doing that.'
- 'I delight in the way you tell me what is important to you.'
- 'Your laugh, your sense of humour, your ..., delight me.'
- 'I love *you*.'

By contrast, we only need to do the opposite, if we want to reduce love. To do this, we create separation. We probably all do it at times. With these thoughts or statements, love often dissolves.

- 'You don't tell me you love me.'
- 'I feel let down by you.'
- 'You should do what I tell you and you aren't.'
- 'You didn't do ... and I don't like it.'

- 'Whenever I express my love to you, you do something distracting, like talking about something else, or finding something to do that takes you away.'

> 'Making' love is simple. When you want love, then join with people. If you don't want it, then create and maintain separation.

What love is not

Love is love. Love is beautiful, obvious, varied and wonderful. However, some people confuse themselves about love; they quest for what it isn't. Love is not:

- the **desire for love**
- the feeling of **not wanting loneliness**
- the **yearning or emptiness we feel** when we do not feel love
- the **hope that we now have it**
- the **pretence** that we have it
- the **loss we feel** when it goes
- the **distress** at not having it

Four loves

Our children need us to love them in four different ways. Each makes a key contribution to the way they grow up and the sorts of people they become. They are:

- 'Body love'
- 'Feeling love'
- 'Person love'
- 'Being love'

Combined, these four ways of loving release powerful forces into everyone's lives.

'Body love'

Children need lots of physical contact every day. Most delight in touching, looking, listening, holding, caressing, smelling, and kissing. They love having physical nurturing from us. It is very clear that a special physical pleasure is shared with affectionate touch.

> 'Body love' comes from sharing physical pleasure.

To experience this love, arrange time so you have physical contact with your children, and notice the pleasure while you do. Feel the loving union produced by the sharing.

- Lie or sit in a warm bath cuddling your baby.
- Hold your children close when they lean against you.
- Take their hands and hold them for a while as you read a goodnight story.
- Have long hugs frequently.
- Sit on the couch cuddling up together.
- Look warmly at your children as they look at you.
- Sound warm, loving and nurturing as you talk to them.
- When they are excited, exclaim with them as you grab them into a quick, exultant embrace.

By contrast, touch disturbs some children. They may squirm, wriggle, resist, tense up or cry when touched. These children still need touch, and our job is to help them learn to accept it.

Practising 'body love'

If you or your child is uncomfortable with touch, we recommend that you practise until you are both used to it. You can put yourself or your child on a simple daily program.

Do physically loving, caring and affectionate things with your child and with others. Start with small steps. You could start with smiles, or a touch on the arm; saying something simple like 'Hello' or 'Hi there' makes it easier at times, too. Then gradually expand to longer contact, then to brief hugs, then to longer ones. Persist with the expansion, for years if necessary.

'Feeling love'

We nurture the emotional lives of our children by expressing 'feeling love'. For their sakes, we need to envelop them in this feeling. As often as possible we express our love to them, feeling it as we do. Sometimes strong, sometimes subtle, this love is very distinctive.

The feeling of love is centred in the heart. It flows from the heart into the rest of the body, saturating it with warm melting sensations. The body softens in response to this energy, a sense of mellowness develops in the sounds we hear and a soft fuzziness grows around the edges of what we see. Everything tastes sweeter and more fragrant to us. Acting impulsively as we feel it, we would reach out and gather our children into a loving embrace.

When we love our children like this, they melt into us. Our love automatically conveys understanding, acceptance, openness and sharing, just with the feeling and nothing else. It leads to a wonderful openness that enables children to open up to us and to share their

> 'Feeling love' comes from sharing feelings and emotions.

feelings about things. And, interestingly, it is the sharing of any feelings – even uncomfortable or challenging feelings – that stimulates this love.

All you need to do is make opportunities for emotional sharing. Open yourself emotionally to your children. Find out what they feel and share your feelings with them.

- Tell your children how much you love and enjoy them.
- Encourage your children to tell you that they love you.
- Talk to them about their feelings and accept what they tell you.
- Encourage them to tell you their feelings about you.

Do this during everything from a chat at the kitchen sink to a 'deep and meaningful' anywhere.

All feelings change from moment to moment – and love is no exception. Completely well-balanced people experience a whole range of feelings, only one of which is love. Other feelings like anger, happiness, sadness, security, and fear are all completely normal. So relax if you find yourself not feeling loving towards your children at times. It is normal for us not to feel loving towards them, for example, when they are acting up, or we are tired, or we or they are simply distracted by other things. This does not mean that we do not love our children. We always have two other forms of more enduring love that we can call on – 'person love' and 'being love'.

'Person love'

We nurture the individuality and wholeness of our children by expressing 'person love'. It is the loving delight we have in 'the people our children are in themselves'. By loving them as whole people throughout their childhoods, we encourage them to find, express and value their own individuality. 'Person love' goes with acceptance, appreciation and understanding of our children as separate people. They are not here for us, they are here to fulfil their own lives. If you have ever known this kind of love, you will know what we mean.

'Person love' has a constancy about it. Not bound to daily events in the same way as 'feeling love', it extends beyond the moment. To do with understanding and thought and perception, it is neither physical nor emotional, like the first two. It is, nevertheless, quite distinctive.

Practising 'feeling love'

If you need a bit of practice, we have some suggestions. We express 'feeling love' very much in what we say and how we say it. So using 'hearty words' as often as possible is wonderful. A short list is: 'caring', 'affection', 'tenderness', 'cherish', 'lovely', 'warm', 'love', 'friendly', 'admire', 'adore', 'considerate' and 'devoted'. Say, 'I love you' to your partner and your children often. If the word 'love' is too strong in the beginning, use other words such as 'care for', 'like', or 'enjoy'.

To make the way you talk loving, practise noticing your physical heart as you talk. Also, drop your voice into your chest, rather than speaking from the throat or the head. The extra depth and resonance from there has a very different effect from the more watery sound of the throat, or the higher pitch of the head. Learn to soften your face and smile a little as you talk.

Make yourself available to love and affection from others. When others 'reach out' to you, reach back, so you join with the people who are trying to join with you. You can do this physically by returning someone's touch. Or you can do it in other ways. When people acknowledge you, notice it. If they compliment you, accept the compliment and absorb the warmth behind it. Saying, 'Thank you' can be a good first step, as it interrupts the tendency of some people to push away gestures of affection with a quick comment or distancing act. Remember that love accompanies union.

To encourage 'person love', take opportunities to open up and share who you are with your children. Notice who they are and encourage them to reveal that to you. Also, get them to notice it themselves. Our children develop the capacity to do this surprisingly early.

- Ask your children what is important to them.
- As they grow up, find out what kind of person they want to be.
- Tell them what you, as a person, value in your life.
- Find out their opinions on things before giving your own.
- Show respect for their points of view, values and integrity.

'Person love' comes from appreciating someone as a whole person and sharing that with them.

Practising 'person love'

To love like this well, the first thing to do is to stand back from your children and take a distant look. You need to understand them from outside your own routine responses to them. Get out of the habit of them, and into their reality.

- Think about the children next door. Describe them briefly: 'nice boy', 'intelligent', 'happy', 'mature'. Then, using the same general stance, do the same with each of your children.
- Imagine you have just met your family. What sort of people are your children?
- Imagine what others would notice about your children.
- Get some friends to describe your children to you.

The next step is to accept your child as a person and celebrate who he or she is. We can say things to them like, 'I love who you are', 'You're great', 'I am here for you', 'Do what you need to do in your life', and 'You are important to me'.

Each day, hold each of your children in your awareness, then imagine them growing like beautiful plants. Appreciate that, while you nurture and tend the plants, the final beauty is already in them. Celebrate this, unite with it and love them.

Some parents see their children's 'personhood' clearly at all times and love it automatically and easily. Some only see it in glimpses, when a curtain seems to pull back and reveal the whole person inside the baby, the three-year-old, the adolescent. Whenever we do, our love affirms, 'Wow. That's you, is it? Well, great to meet you. I'm here for *you*. I'll do whatever it takes for you to grow up and *fulfil* who you are'.

This love prompts us to celebrate their expanding maturity. Every new milestone is a cause for joy, not for regret. Powerful and enduring, 'person love' is a force that we parents can use to endure through the years of childhood. It helps us to get up night after night to our children, to go to work for years to support them, and to forego our own pleasures repeatedly to ensure their wellbeing. It also helps us to do all the tough things that raising children involves.

'Being love'

There is much more to all of us than our bodies, feelings and personalities. Through 'being love' we embrace everything in our children. With this love, we open up to and embrace their destinies, their individual meanings and their purposes. In this love, we experience complete acceptance of our selves and the selves in them.

Transcendent, eternal and all-encompassing, this love is in everyone and everything. It comes with 'the touch of divinity' in us all. And as we join with our children through it, 'we touch their divinity with our own'. Doing this floods all our lives with transcendent grace at every level. We share a contact that is so profound, we aptly call it 'soul-to-soul contact'. And this contact transmits our 'soul appreciation' of them, to them.

> 'Being love' comes from sharing our beings.

We experience 'being love' either as we come into union with our own beings, or as we join with the beings of others. This process is very specific and not mysterious in the least, for those who have experienced it. We have a joyous, peaceful sense of oneness with everyone, including our children, when we experience this love. To experience it:

- Practise noticing the core of your children.
- Notice how the person in front of you is an outlet for, or surrounded by, something bigger.
- Regularly engage in some form of spiritual practice.
- Share your spiritual perceptions, understandings and experiences with your children.

Increasing numbers of people now knowingly love their children like this. They are fully aware of what they are doing. We think that this is a lot to do with the spread in recent decades of personal spiritual practices throughout the world. Even so, as with the other three types of love, many people have not been aware of experiencing this kind. So our description may not mean much to you at the moment.

If you are not aware of having experienced this kind of love, you may get some clues from reasonably common events in your life. We do go through times in our lives when 'being love' is very available. It is very strong in situations in which the life force is very powerful, or when it is powerfully challenged:

- at the birth of a baby;
- when we are in love;
- when someone is very ill and approaching death;
- during near death experiences;
- at the point someone physically dies; or
- when we are with evolved people such as spiritual masters.

Practising 'being love'

To become familiar with this love, we can cultivate total acceptance of ourselves and others. A very simple exercise or meditation helps us do this.

Sit comfortably and notice your heart for a few minutes. Put your hands over your heart and notice any warmth, mellowness, soft light or sweetness in there. While doing this, repeat, 'I am love'. Keep doing this for a short time. Then, allowing anything about yourself to occur to you, say 'I love you; I completely accept you'. This could be anything specific from the shape of your nose to much more general things.

After doing this for as long as you want, take each of your children in turn. Do the same thing with them. Start again with, 'I am love'. Then move to repeating, 'I love you (name); I completely accept everything about you'. After a short time, allow their various qualities to occur to you, affirming as they do, 'I love your (quality) and completely accept you'.

Spending two to five minutes a day doing this, increasingly produces a wonderful, loving connection with your own essence and the essences of your children.

Also, look for and seek opportunities to link 'being to being' with others. Find people who seem good at it and imitate them.

Combining the four

The four loves are always mixed in together. Enjoying the sensations of love, feeling the feeling itself, appreciating the understanding we have of the people involved, and celebrating their beings, all go together delightfully. Everyone we know does experience all of these, whether they know it or not, at least to some extent. We have never met anyone who has managed to suppress these four kinds of love completely. However, we have met many people who are better at some of the four than others.

The thing to realise is that our children need all four from us, if they are to thrive fully. So it is well worth practising those we are not good at, until we are. Both our children and ourselves will benefit.

But what if I don't feel love?

People don't automatically feel love for their children. Perhaps the children were premature, or the mother or child was sick and normal bonding did not occur at birth. Perhaps the children are not our physical children: maybe they are step-children, or adopted, or the result of artificial insemination by donor. Or maybe they are very difficult to live with. Some children are, for example, extremely needy, or competitive, argumentative, passive, or passionate in ways that we find difficult. And even if others would take such things in their stride, we don't. What then?

You have company. And with persistence, you can develop connections and flowing ease with your children. We suggest that you give yourself time, talk about your feelings and reactions to someone you trust, and persist in doing what your children need. Remember that 'being love' and 'person love' are powerful forces and may not be accompanied by much feeling. If you are troubled significantly by what you are or are not feeling and thinking, seek help from people who are competent to provide it.

Delighting in their beauty

You notice your children's beauty, prowess, developing maturity, creativity, openness, or whatever delights you about them.

Say, '**I love you**', or '**You're terrific**', or '**What a great person you are**', or '**I'm glad you're my son/daughter**', or '**I'm proud of you**', or '**I'm so glad I'm your mother/father**', or all of them.

Chapter 10

The discipline sequence

Discipline helps our children learn to manage their energies. All people need to learn this so they can live easily and well with others. In this chapter we discuss what discipline is, when to start disciplining our children, how to start, and the discipline sequence. This sequence is a simple way of handling specific disciplinary encounters.

Discipline is guided love

Discipline is an organised way of expressing love. We said in the last chapter that love is like the ground in which a plant grows and the sun that shines on them as they do. Discipline is what the gardener does to fertilise, water, prune, shape, stake and generally respond to a plant's growth to ensure it reaches maturity as beautifully as it can. Guiding what we do with our love, we act to produce desirable changes in our children's behaviour, when they need this from us.

Discipline is our means of 'house-training the kids'. Everyone benefits from this. Without training, they will rarely learn to live well in the world. They often become unruly, unreliable, discourteous, self-absorbed, messy, uncaring, impulse-driven people – or worse. At the same time, the advantages of discipline include more

> From discipline, children learn the power of making decisions and the freedom of acting on them.

than other people's convenience and comfort. Discipline is for the benefit of our children too. Well-disciplined people can command themselves and take the many opportunities life offers them.

Two parts to discipline

We generally do two things with discipline. We *set standards* and we *set limits*. The two things support each other in important ways.

Standards involve what children are to do. They are what children aim for, what we encourage them to achieve. If we list our standards, we have a set of rules, prescriptions, advice and guidelines that would enable our children to live life well.

- Brush your teeth after every meal.
- Tell the truth.
- Share with others.
- Do what you say you will do.

Limits involve what our children are not to do. They are supposed to avoid doing these things and we actively discourage them from doing them. If we remove the word 'don't' from a list of limits, we would have all the things to do to get into trouble in life.

- Don't act violently.
- Don't leave your room in a mess.
- Don't talk rudely.
- Don't be late.

Combining the two

When disciplining children, we find it works best if we set standards and limits together. One gives the things to do; the other gives the things not to do. When we do this, our children know more clearly where they stand. The result is a much more confident child. A friend once described this very well:

> 'When I grew up, I was mainly told not to do this and that. I don't ever remember being told what to do, except in very general terms like "be nice" and "do the right thing". And I wasn't ever told what these meant. So I got to adulthood and I was really uptight. I mainly knew what not to do, but I felt that I never knew when I was doing the right thing. It was like living in a box with lots of spikes pointing towards me and I didn't know where all the spikes were.'

We have found the following guideline very helpful when deciding how to combine the setting of standards and limits. *You set standards that automatically take care of the limits you are also setting.*

- 'You're to tell the truth to me (standard); you're not to lie (limit).'
- 'You're to touch your sister gently (standard); you're not to hit or hurt her (limit).'
- 'You're to listen to me when I talk to you (standard); you're not to keep watching TV (limit).

> To stop our children doing something, get them to do something else that makes the first thing impossible.

The age to start

The age to start disciplining children is at about eighteen months. Near that age, they begin to develop new levels of understanding and ability. They also start to do things that prompt us to shift gears and to start to expect them to adapt to the world. They will no longer be the centre of life. Gradually, they need to learn that everything does not come to them whenever they want it, that the world does not revolve around them. This is quite a contrast from what we have done up to this point. Before eighteen months, children still have baby consciousness and they need to be cared for as babies. (You will find more on the transition in Chapter 11, 'Standing to decide', Chapter 16, 'Developing self-esteem', Chapter 20, 'Four births, four bonds', and Chapter 21, 'Phases of childhood'.)

Babyhood is a time for our complete, continual and loving acceptance of our children – no matter what. This is definitely the time for 'being love' to be at the forefront of everything we do. (See Chapter 9, 'Parenting with love'.)

Babies are innocent, totally dependent, alive, questing, exploring, loving, trusting, vulnerable little creatures. Babies don't have self-control, nor have they developed any significant understanding. They depend totally on us for everything. It is our job to provide for them to the best of our abilities, without applying any discipline to them.

We wish to state this very clearly. *It is completely inappropriate to discipline babies.* They are incapable of controlling themselves and of understanding consequences related to what they do. Disciplining babies in any way is an abusive violation. We realise many people don't understand this. Parents all too often:

- punish their babies by shouting at, hitting, or shaking them;
- withdraw attention when they think their babies aren't good;
- think their babies are misbehaving;

- talk about crying as nastiness or an attempt to punish parents;
- think it is wrong for their babies to do something just for attention;
- describe their babies as naughty.

If you do any of these things, or anything similar, we urge you to stop for your child's sake. Learn to love your babies with complete acceptance. Whatever they do, continue accepting them and, with nurturing love, take care of whatever needs to be done.

If you cannot manage this, then get some help. Disciplining babies does untold damage, damage that can last for life. It tilts or distorts the foundations inside them, so that what they build on for the rest of their lives is tilted or distorted too. We have worked for many years with the consequences of this kind of thing, which is why we are presenting this to you so strongly.

> Always love, nurture, care for and protect your baby. Never discipline your baby.

Introducing your child to discipline

One of the wonderful things about young children is that they are so obvious. And the signal they give us that they are ready for discipline, is very obvious.

At about eighteen months they begin to struggle with those around them. They may switch into this quite suddenly, although more usually, they gradually increase the intensity and frequency. Distraction and soothing stop working to calm upsets. Our children become determined to get what they want and hold out for much longer than previously. They act angrily and persist in their little miseries, rather than allow themselves to be coaxed out of them. At the same time, parents often begin to feel increasingly impatient, where before they were likely to feel calm and inclined to soothe and console.

Whatever change we observe in our children at this time, we introduce children to discipline *gradually*. A sudden shift from complete acceptance to conditional responses is likely to create unnecessary upsets. However, we do need to make the shift and this can take determination. After all, we have had almost two years of finding out what our babies want and need, so we can soothingly supply it. At this stage, however, while we remain interested in what they want and need, we become increasingly inclined to expect them to adapt to us. This is a shift of gears for both our children and ourselves.

We begin by acting with increasing insistence over what we want our children to do. And even if they become upset as we do this, we persist.

- 'No. You have to wait for your milk. I'll get it in a minute.'
- 'It's time to eat. Come and help me clean up your toys now.'
- 'You are going to bed now, so calm down and do it easily.'
- 'No, mummy (daddy) can't play with you just now. But you can play here beside me.'
- 'You can have milk or juice, not ice cream. Which one will you have?'

Parents not used to persisting through their children's upsets can become very upset at this stage. For some parents, this can feel like reason enough to give up the whole idea very quickly. The loving strength to persist is inside us, however. We find it in 'person love', the love that gets us to think of the person we are raising, not just the baby who doesn't want her milk right now. (See Chapter 9, 'Parenting with love'.)

Persistence is far better than 'falling into the coaxing trap' of continuing to treat our children as babies. This is where we avoid confrontations by trying to find ways of soothing and coaxing our children to do things they don't want to do.

One family was caught like this with their first daughter. Because she made a fuss, they stopped telling her insistently to go to bed. Instead, her father used to 'entertain her' up the stairs. He would move backwards out of the living room, doing all sorts of things to try and engage her so that she would follow him. By the time she was three years old, he was having to dress in a full clown outfit to get her to bed. If he was a clown when she was three, what would he have to do by the time she was fifteen?! It would have been far simpler to train her differently from the beginning. We would have recommended saying, 'It's bed time', then setting off immediately hand in hand, or with her in his arms, so going to bed became an easy routine.

How to use discipline

We use what we call 'the discipline sequence'. Its five simple steps guide us through what we need to do so our children get what they need from us.

The steps of the sequence are:

1. **Expectations**   Say what you expect of them ***and*** what you limit them from.
2. **Reasons**   Outline why you are saying this.
3. **Consequences**   Set consequences for compliance and noncompliance.

4. *Agreements*   Get agreement(s) about the future.
5. *Follow-up*   Ensure that you get what you expect.

Here is an example.

> (Expectations) *'I expect you to come home at 10.30 pm. You are not to return later. (Reasons) You are still too young to decide how late to be and we have to make sure you are safe. (Consequences) If you keep returning at 10.30, we will quickly be convinced of your reliability and more likely to be relaxed about you getting home later. If you don't, then we will not allow you to go out. (Agreement) Do you agree to come home at 10.30 pm?' Then, of course, your child agrees immediately!*

Expectations

Expectations need to be clear to everyone involved. This means that they need to be understood and preferably unambiguous, otherwise confusion and avoidable difficulties can arise. Making them specific often takes care of all of this.

- 'If I can hear the TV through the door, it's too loud', rather than 'Keep that noise down to a reasonable level'.
- 'Keep your hands to yourself, or touch gently (showing young children what gentle touch is)', rather than 'Be gentle (nice, or loving)'.
- 'Come to dinner at 6.00 every night', rather than 'Be on time for dinner'.

Remember to set both your expectations and your limits. Telling children both what is expected and what is not acceptable is important. It is surprising what adults and children miss at times.

> *An adolescent boy called Alfredo was on the point of expulsion from high school. He was acting very violently every day.*
>
> *The teachers 'had tried everything for months, but to no avail'. When a consultant asked exactly what teachers had said to Alfredo, everything became clear to her. The list included, 'Get out, you know you're not supposed to do that', 'Go and see the principal', and 'We'll just ignore Alfredo, won't we, class? We don't like what he is doing'. Because they all thought it was obvious, no-one had told him explicitly what they were disciplining him for. But Alfredo actually had no idea what he was doing to get into trouble.*
>
> *A program was devised for him. From then on, every incident of violence, was followed by a clear statement about what he had done that was not acceptable, and what he was to do in future that was acceptable. For example, 'If you are frustrated, don't hit people or throw the desks around. Sit quietly,*

put your hand up, and I will come across to you and talk to you as soon as I can'. Within three weeks, he was behaving completely normally.

Expectations make clear what is to be done and not done.

Reasons

Children have their own reasons for doing things, just as we do. Finding out what their reasons are is important. For example

- 'I wanted to, so I did.'
- 'You told me to put everything in the bin; you didn't say not to put the plates in too.'
- 'I kicked him because I thought he was going to hit me. I didn't know he was going to pat my head.'

Whatever **we** think their reasons are, we need to connect with **their** reasons. What we do to change their behaviour will have much more impact, if we explain it so that they understand. Just the act of asking why they did what they did, also helps us to keep them engaged in the process.

Our reasons are important too. By telling them why we do what we do with them, we train them in all sorts of important ways. We teach them to think about themselves, so they take account of other people and situations. They can also learn that just because they have reasons, doesn't make them right.

Discussing reasons gets children to think about their actions.

We recommend that you talk so that your reasons are easily understood. Match them to the understanding of your children. (Notice the increasing sophistication of the examples.)

- 'Ouch, that hurts. Stop it.'
- 'Other kids don't want to play with kids who hit them.'
- 'Hitting hurts and people don't like it.'
- 'Acting kindly attracts people, acting nastily will probably drive them away.'
- 'If you want to be a caring person, you will take care of others. Hitting and screaming abuse at them is not consistent with this.'

Consequences

We use consequences to add weight to what we tell our children. We choose the consequences to encourage them to do what we want them to do and to discourage them from doing what we don't want. We have found several principles useful when we think about consequences. The first one is the main one.

Reward children for successfully meeting expectations, in preference to penalising them for nonperformance. What we concentrate on we get. So we are best to emphasise meeting our standards by rewarding our children for doing so. Our incentives can include anything from specific physical affection and verbal praise, to material rewards, to expansions of privileges, to special events or celebrations.

All the same, the reality is that children also need active discouragement at times, if they are to learn. We use the following principles to help formulate what discouragements to use.

Relate consequences to the interests and desires of the child. For example, being sent to his room might be just what Tom wants, because he loves spending time alone reading. So, if this were to be a reward, it would work well, but as a deterrent, it would not be so good. However, he places a lot of value on his weekly pocket money. Losing some of this makes him sit up and pay attention to his father.

Use minimum force to produce the effects we want. In other words, avoid using a baseball bat, when a feather will do. Missing out on tonight's episode of a favourite TV program may make the point with enough impact, where losing all TV privileges for a week might not make the point any better.

The younger children are, the more immediate consequences need to be. Very young children have no sense of time. So setting a consequence that will last for a week for a two-year-old is futile and oppressive. Whereas a consequence lasting for a week might be just what an eleven-year-old or a sixteen-year-old needs. Also, young children need consequences applied very much more quickly than older children. Young children might not even remember what they have done, if we wait too long.

Act respectfully while resolving problems or issues. Children get more from ending a disciplinary encounter with our respect. Resolution is the goal, not holding things against them. They need the chance to move forward free from the current incident. So leaving the issue behind is very important, once they have settled things well enough. Also, during the process of resolution, we need to remain open to the possibilities of change, even when we are sorely tested to commit to the opposite. So avoid statements such as, 'You'll never amount to anything', 'I'll never trust you again', or 'You never do what I tell you'.

All consequences (aimed at limiting) are selected to shift discomfort, so the child is motivated to act as expected. Our consequences need to 'bite'. The whole idea of consequences related to limits is that children both notice them and dislike them. When they bear little relationship to the acts, issues, or events involved that prompted us to act, it is best to clarify the connections.

Ensure that uncomfortable consequences stop as soon as the child changes the behaviour. 'Punishment for its own sake' rarely works. Children generally learn much more by getting relief as soon as they change what they are doing. So as soon as they change, we change.

Natural consequences make the whole process more educational. Natural consequences align with the way people in the wider world usually do things. They help to teach our children about the way the wider world works. So a child regularly late for school, may go to school dressed in pyjamas if he or she is not dressed when the car is due to leave; an adolescent asking for a note to excuse him from not finishing an assignment (due to watching TV) gets the option of no note or one telling the truth; or a child regularly not completing her household chores does not get paid her pocket money, because 'she did not turn up at work'.

> Consequences encourage children to act as expected.

Agreements

This step is very powerful. Getting clear agreements usually produces great rewards. It transforms good intentions into actual behaviour. The key ingredient in this transformation is *a decision to act*. And we get our children to decide to do what we want, by getting them to make definite, clearly stated agreements with us.

Without the decision to act, all the good intentions in the world made while the children are under pressure may not amount to anything. They can dissolve at any time.

- 'I *feel like* doing the dishes before going to bed.'
- 'I *want to* get my school assignment done tonight.'
- 'I *really must* get to my paper round on time.'

- 'I *ought to* go and see my teacher this morning.'
- 'I *must go* to sleep now, or I will be tired all day tomorrow.'

The reason these kinds of motivation often don't lead to action is that they are based on feelings. And the moment the feelings change, so does the intention. We may feel very strongly that we want to, should, need to, or feel like exercise tomorrow. But five minutes later, or when we wake up the next morning, we discover that we no longer want to, feel we should, or need to do what we were thinking.

> Agreements turn good intentions into decisions to act as expected.

A decision to act makes a great difference. Commitments endure through changes in our feelings. They 'draw a line in the sand' that shows us clearly what we are and are not going to do.

- 'I *will do* the dishes before going to bed.'
- 'I *will get* my school assignment done tonight.'
- 'I *will get* to my paper round on time.'
- 'I *will go* and see my teacher this morning.'
- 'I *am going* to sleep now.'

So, make sure that you get an agreement from your children about future behaviour. And make sure they put it into their own words, unless they are still too young to do it. The sophistication of the agreement will vary with age.

- 'Will you come to Mummy when she tells you from now on?'
  'Yes.'
  'Good. Now you say it.'
  'I come, Mummy.'
- 'So what will you do about school notices from now on?'
  'I'll put them in my school bag when I get them and give them to you when I get home.'
- 'How will you act with your brother/sister from now on?'
  'I'll talk to him/her about what I want, instead of fighting. And if I can't work it out I'll come and get you.'
- 'Now that you understand the safety issues involved in this, what will you do in future?'
  'I'll come home by taxi when it's after 8 o'clock and I'll ring you whenever I'm going to be home later than I told you.'

Follow-up

Follow-up is very important. We need to make sure our children do what we expect them to do. Children rarely learn things the first time, or even the second. They need the repetition. (See Chapter 15, 'Repeating ourselves'.) By following up, we ensure that they have understood and are acting as we agreed they would act. We also need to follow up to apply the rewards or penalties we arranged.

Following up shows that we mean business, too. Our children will take this in and be able to act similarly in their own lives. Follow-up helps us to avoid training our children that discipline is an empty ritual – a lot of words with no real impact. Many children learn 'to wait out their parents', knowing that 'the ordeal' will be over in a few minutes, hours, or days. Because their parents don't follow up, they learn that nothing really matters, because they never get held to account for what they do afterwards. This is not a good idea.

> Following up shows that parents are determined and care.

> Following up teaches children to persist, to keep their commitments and to succeed.

Struggle is useful

Children learn all sorts of things by struggling with us:
- handling conflict;
- managing their own strong feelings while relating appropriately to others;
- recognising their strengths and weaknesses;

- honing their personal capacities to stand assertively, while staying open to others;
- absorbing from us the strength they need to manage their inner struggles;
- taking in our values and expectations strongly enough to use in their lives.

Toilet training

We begin toilet training at about the time children begin to walk. Generally children are completely toilet trained sometime in their third year. The beginnings are very simple and gentle, with very few expectations. We treat it like a little game.

- Start by putting your child on a potty at regular intervals.
- Develop a pattern to this, for example, after every meal, before going out, after coming back home, before naps and bedtime, and after getting up in the morning. Making this routine helps them learn routinely.
- Relax your expectations; your children are likely to take time to develop control of their bladders and bowels completely, usually somewhere between two and three years of age.
- Demonstrate the process: boys go with dads and big brothers, girls go with mums and big sisters.
- Talk about how it is good to be dry and clean, and free of nappies.
- Celebrate when they use the potty or the toilet.

- Make sure that their last drink is a least an hour before bedtime.
- Wake them to take them to the toilet before you go to bed.
- Talk to them concretely about the sensations of needing a poo or a pee. Teach them that feeling these sensations mean that they need to use the potty or toilet.
- When they are almost trained, buy them underwear. The first time is often very exciting for kids.
- If they are not toilet trained as they approach three years of age, then get them checked by a doctor. If they are cleared physically, then use 'standing to decide' to get them to decide to stay dry and clean. (See Chapter 11, 'Standing to decide'.)
- It is normal for kids of four and five to have occasional 'accidents', when they are excited, anxious, or just very involved in something. Talk with them about what to do and avoid punishing them.

Chapter 11

Standing to decide

'Standing to decide' is a powerful tool for helping our children learn many important lessons. We can also use it to assist us when we discipline them. Children can learn how to claim their power creatively, rather than confusing this with resistance. Parents learn how to influence their children in effective, nonpunitive ways, and without using hitting or other forms of violence. Very simple to use, it helps us to produce wonderful results on many fronts. Here are some comments from 'satisfied customers'.

- 'It's fantastic. I used to feel desperate for something that would work. Now I've got it.'
- 'I feel I'm in control again. My kid doesn't run the show any more.'
- 'My children were out of control before I discovered "standing to decide".'
- 'I used to hit my kids and I don't any more. We all feel better.'
- 'The teachers have asked me what the miracle is. I said, "Standing to decide".'
- 'I couldn't get them to do things, even when I said it ten times. Now I only say it once.'
- '"Standing to decide" has given me back my life.'

Children whose parents have used 'standing to decide' or something similar are remarkably different from many other children. They are powerful, self-contained, sensitive, clear thinking, assertive, receptive and capable little and big people. They are living testaments to the value of having some way of helping children grow and develop internally.

Does this seem too good to be true? Well it isn't. Many people have used this approach to great effect with their children. In this chapter we will describe the process, discuss how to introduce it to children, list some of its benefits, and present some guidelines for using it. (Other relevant information is in Chapter 9, 'Parenting with love', and Chapter 10, 'The discipline sequence'.)

The steps

'Standing to decide' has five basic steps.
1. Instruction
2. Warning
3. Standing with a task
4. Decision
5. Resolution

Step 1: Instruction

The process starts when your children do something that you want them to change. You say, 'Do X. Don't do Y'. And you give your reasons. This is the instruction.

- If they obey immediately, you reinforce this in some way by acknowledging it. You might, for example, say, 'Good'.
- If they don't comply, you go to Step 2.

Step 2: Warning

When your children continue to act as before, or do not obey you, issue a warning. You say, for example, 'Do X; don't do Y, or you will 'stand to decide' until you decide that you will do it'.

- If your children comply then, you go no further. You might reinforce the obedience by saying something like, 'You are to do what I tell you the first time I tell you'. By following 'the discipline sequence', you then get your children to agree to act as required in future. To do this, you ask, 'What will you do from now on?' And when all goes swimmingly, they say, 'I'll do what you tell me straight away in future', or words like that.
- If your children still do not comply, you go to Step 3.

Step 3: Standing with a task

Immediately your children still do not comply at Step 2, you apply the consequence. You point to where the child is to stand and say, 'Go over there, face the wall and 'stand to decide', until you decide to do X'. For example, 'Until you:

- decide to stop stirring up your sister/brother;
- decide to remember to bring your drink bottle home from school;
- decide to go and make your bed immediately;
- make a plan about how you are going to do your assignment;
- have remembered what you decided to do last time;
- decide to stop talking to me rudely and talk respectfully and civilly'.

And you add, 'Let me know when you have decided'.

Your children then 'stand to decide' until they do as instructed. It is most important that they **are able** to do the task you set them at this point. Then you wait, usually with your child in sight.

Step 4: Decision

You wait for your children to say, 'All right, I have decided'. You then say, 'Okay. Turn around and talk to me about it'. If they seem to take a long time before saying this, or are still learning the process, check every now and then to make sure that they are doing what is necessary.

Emotional upsets during this step are common, particularly when the issues are highly charged. So you may need to stand near them or occupy yourself nearby. Your presence gives you the opportunity to repeat many parent messages about self-management and whatever else is relevant. Think about what your children need to do and put that into words, so it becomes a program they can take in from you.

- 'Calm down and think. Work out what you are there to work out.'
- 'No. You can't have a drink until you have finished.'
- 'You **can** work it out and you are going to stand there until you do.'
- 'I want you to be somewhere else having fun. I don't want you there. So get on with it and do what you have to do quickly.'

Step 5: Resolution

Check what your children have decided. Make sure they mean to do what they say. Get a specific agreement about how, when and where they will do it. In other words, follow 'the discipline sequence'.

- If all of this flows easily and you have a sense of completion, then release them from the process. You say, 'Okay. Come away from there. And make sure you do what you have said you will'. Follow up and ensure that they do act according to their agreements with you.
- If you are not satisfied with what your children say, then they continue to stand. You say, 'Turn around again until you decide to do X'. If you are not satisfied with the way they are acting, you say, 'Turn around again; stop doing such and such, and do so and so. I am not willing to talk to you while you are doing that'. For example: 'Stop whingeing and whining, and talk in a normal, strong, clear voice', 'Stop shouting at me and talk calmly', or 'Speak strongly and firmly, so I can hear you easily'.
- If you release them and they do not immediately do what was agreed, you go immediately back to Step 2. And you keep repeating the whole process until the child does what is expected.

‘Standing to decide’ replaces hitting and other violence in discipline.

How it can work

Sarah, a five-year-old, is engrossed in the TV, watching a late-afternoon children's program. Her mother, Jo, calls out, 'Sarah, turn off the TV and come here. It's time to set the table'. Sarah's evening job is to set the table for the family. *(Step 1 – Instruction)*

No response from Sarah.

Just to make sure she had heard, Jo says, 'Sarah, did you hear me?' If she hadn't, then Jo would repeat the instruction.

Sarah mumbles, 'Yes,' with a rising pitch that signals impatience.

Jo says clearly and firmly, 'Turn off the TV and come here. It's time to set the table. If you don't come straight away, you will "stand to decide" that you will.' *(Step 2 – Warning)*

No response and no move from Sarah to turn off the TV.

Jo goes in immediately, points to the place in the kitchen where she is to stand facing the wall. She says, 'Go over there right now'. Sarah does. Jo adds, 'Now you stand there until you decide to turn off the TV and start your job. Let me know when you have decided.' The TV is out of sight. *(Step 3 – Standing with a task)*

Sarah, her lower lip out in a pout, swings her hips and looks uncooperative. From the stove where she is cooking, Jo says, 'Doing that will only keep you there longer. Feel your feet on the ground, calm down and decide to do what I've told you. The sooner you do, the sooner you will be away from the wall.' (Jo is getting her more grounded. See Chapter 22, 'Grounding'.)

'But I want to watch the TV', Sarah whines at her mother.

'Well you are not going to watch any more just now, because it's time for you to set the table. And suffering about it will not make the job go away. So stand there quietly, and decide to do what I have said.' She pauses to let that sink in, then adds, 'And next time you talk to me, talk in a normal voice.' Jo hopes that Sarah will decide easily today. She's had a long day and doesn't want a long struggle with Sarah. But she steels herself for it, just in case. She knows from experience that trying to get around these things only drags the hassling out for hours.

On this occasion, Jo is pleasantly surprised to hear Sarah speaking in a perfectly normal voice. 'Okay, Mum. I've decided.' *(Step 4 – Decision)*

'Good, ' says Jo, 'what have you decided?' *(Step 5 – Resolution begins here)*

'I'll turn off the TV and set the table.'

'That's right', says Jo, adding, 'You are to do what I tell you the first time I tell you. Will you do that from now on?' Jo is taking the opportunity to reinforce a useful parent message.

'Yes, Mum.' And Sarah goes in, turns off the TV and returns to begin setting the table. Both of them feel very good about the process and chat happily as she does.

What it's good for

You can use 'standing to decide' in thousands of different ways. It is a magnificent teaching tool. Your imagination is the only limit. Here is a short list. Use it:

- to get obedience ('I'll do what you've told me.')
- to deal with resistance ('I'll stop fighting with you and do what I have to.')
- to get their attention ('I'll listen when you talk to me.')
- to stop the action and get them thinking ('I was getting angry and I wasn't thinking clearly about what I could do.')
- to change behaviour ('I'll look at you when you talk to me and I'll talk normally to you.')
- to focus attention ('I'll concentrate on what I'm doing so I don't knock things off the sink.')
- to get grounded ('I'll stay aware of my feelings and what's happening around me, so I stay steady and think.')
- to teach them to think about their feelings ('I just wanted to run away, I was so scared. Now I know what I can do next time.')
- to get a decision ('I'll make my bed first, then I'll sweep the floor.')
- to accept situations as they are ('I don't like it, and I accept that I can't go to Bill's.')
- as a timed consequence ('I don't like standing here for half an hour every time I forget, so I'll remember from now on.')
- to shift discomfort to them ('I want to be playing and don't want to be "standing to decide", so I'll do what you said.')
- to take responsibility ('I'll remember to take my washing to the laundry from now on without you reminding me.')
- to increase their strength and confidence ('I didn't want to do it, but now I've thought about it, I realise I can do lots, even when I'm scared. And you said you'd help, too.')

Introducing the technique

We prefer to start as early as possible. And we do it when children are about eighteen months old. Naturally at that age, we need to start very simply and increase the demands only very gradually. It is usually a very light and easy process at this age.

How to do it

Here are some guidelines for introducing eighteen-month- to two-year-olds to the process.

- We choose a wall in each room that we will use consistently.
- We take them through the process very simply at a time that they are calm and alert.
- From then on we take them to the selected wall whenever the need arises
- These are the places we go for 'little talks'.
- When they start to act in ways that we want them to change, we take them to the wall, with the statement, 'Come over here and talk to me'.
- Don't wait for them to come to you, because they are very young: take them by the hand and go with them immediately.
- Face them to the wall for about two to five seconds, then turn them around and talk to them, saying, for example, 'Right now you have to drink your milk. Are you going to drink it?' 'Yes.' 'All right, come away and do it.' And we walk them to the milk and hand it to them.

This approach puts them through the sequence easily and they generally adapt quickly to the routine. You might also say at times when you are introducing the process, 'From now on you will "stand to decide" like this when I want you to learn something or change something'. They will not understand fully what you are saying at this point, but saying it lays a foundation for future understanding.

With older children from the age of three to ten, we explain what we are going to do in simple terms that they will understand. Choose a time when they are calm or relatively calm. It is often helpful to take them through the process step by step, just as a trial. Then they know what to do because they have done it. This is easier than trying to get them used to it for the first time when they are upset about things.

With adolescents we would usually use other forms of consequence, like withdrawal of privileges or restricting freedom, rather than introduce them to 'standing to decide'. It is well worth noting, however, that if you have used 'standing to decide' when they were young, dealing with things in adolescence is generally much easier. They automatically use the process internally when they are older and become more amenable to all forms of guidance and discipline.

How easy is it to use?

Most children take to the process very easily. Most of them also resist and struggle at times. Their resistance is not a sign that we should stop, however. 'Standing to decide' is a means of dealing with resistance. And one thing to remember is that it makes them more self-sufficient. One mother said:

> *'I used to be worried that I would squash my kids' independence. But I was wrong. They have all become stronger and lovelier, not weaker.'*

The children themselves show us the value of the process. Even apart from how much more easily and quickly they learn, they do some surprising things. Quite often parents walk into a room to find their younger children standing docilely against the wall. When asked what they are doing there, the children say, 'Oh I just spilled some milk and I came here to decide to be careful', or 'I was upset because I broke dolly and wanted to calm down'. At other times, we find them putting their dolls and teddy bears against the wall, going through the instructions that we usually give to them.

These lovely signs show that they are learning, and that they are actively applying what they are learning, because they find it helpful. When a bit older, it is quite common for children to chat together as if they are members of a special 'stand to decide' club. If you listen, you will hear some wonderful stories. The best story we heard was from a seven-year-old whose mother stopped hitting him when he misbehaved and started using the process. He said with exultation, 'Oh this "standing to decide" stuff doesn't work with me at all. Whenever Mum tells me to do something or "stand to decide", I just do it!'

A natural life process

'Standing to decide' is a natural life process. Life itself repeatedly confronts us with things that we need to learn and to resolve, until we learn or resolve them. 'Standing to decide' trains children in the same way as life will. But unlike life, which does not filter consequences, we can control the consequences and interpret them so our children can manage them and learn from them. This protected version of learning some of life's harder lessons is preparation for the real thing.

Guidelines

The following guidelines have helped many parents get started. You may find it helpful to keep coming back to these as you learn the process.

Remember the goal. The goal of 'standing to decide' is for our children to learn to manage whatever stimulated us to use the process. As we manage them through to the resolution, they learn what to do. They also learn that resolution is possible. By contrast, if we walk out and leave them handling something that they cannot handle alone, then our actions become part of what they will do within themselves. Similarly, if we abuse, or rant, or rave at them, then that is what they will have inside.

Resolution and completion are obvious. Two definite events accompany a real end to the process. First, our children will do what they were expected to do. Second, both we and they will feel resolved and have a sense of delighted completion. Even if the process was very upsetting and disturbing at the time, we will feel like celebrating.

Incomplete resolution is also obvious. When children act up again very quickly after we have released them, we have stopped too quickly. Because they did not get enough the first time, we will need to repeat the process and complete it. They may need more passion from us during the process than we used the first time. Children frequently understand more from feelings than from words. So expressing what we feel is often helpful at any stage during the process. When telling our child to 'stand to decide' again, we could say, 'You just decided to do such and such and you haven't. Go over there, stand there and decide to do it right now. I feel ... (angry, frustrated, disappointed, scared, sad etc.) that you did not do what you said you would'. (Read Chapter 18, 'Natural transitions' for more on feelings and understanding.)

The task must be possible. The only way the process will work completely is if our children *have the ability* to do what we tell them to do. If the tasks we set them are beyond them, then we are violating or abusing them. Similarly, accepting proposals from our children that are beyond them is also abusive. ('I'll do all my homework in five minutes' – when we know it will take at least an hour.) We need to use common sense. Making the tasks we set simple and related to the issues at hand will usually ensure that we do this.

Keep track of time. Very young children should only 'stand to decide' for a few minutes. The attention span of young children is not long enough for them to benefit from longer periods. As they get older, however, children may spend half an hour, an hour, or more, before they resolve some issues.

As the time extends, stay alert. Children taking a long time may be caught in an unproductive inner loop. Changing the scene can help with this. We can tell them to do something different that will break the inner patterns and refresh their thinking: 'Go and wash your face', 'Walk around the garden and come straight back', or 'Run upstairs and get me such and such'. If you do this, it is most important that they go straight back to standing when they return, and that they complete the task as originally set.

Alternatives to standing sometimes work better. With some children, getting them to sit on hard-based chairs is better than standing. Children who go passive, or slump to the floor, often respond better to running or 'being run' (hand in hand with us while they are young). We can get them to run around the backyard, or up and down the stairs.

It is not supposed to be comfortable. Using an uncomfortable process helps to shift motivation to inside the children, rather than leaving it in us. The discomfort encourages them to complete the task. They say, 'I don't like it here (doing this)'. We reply, 'I'm glad. I don't want you to like it. I want you away from there, enjoying yourself. You can stop standing there as soon as you do what I've told you to do'. Also, choose a location where they cannot see very much, so that distractions are reduced to a minimum. The point is for them to concentrate on the tasks we set them.

'Time out' in a bedroom may not work well. Some children love going to their rooms, because they have plenty to entertain them there and they are away from our pressure on them to do what they have been told to do. Also, by sending them away, we teach them internally to send their own problems away until they somehow come up with a solution without help. Having them in the room with us deals with these outcomes.

If they get upset during the process, get them to concentrate on grounding to take care of the upset. This will help them manage their feelings and keep them thinking as well. (See Chapter 22, 'Grounding'.)

Keep going until the process is finished. When we persist until they are finished, we teach our children to persist until they finish things, too. If we don't persist, they can learn unhelpful things like: 'Nothing gets worked out in the end', or 'All I have to do is hold out for long enough and they will give up'. We want them to make more helpful decisions than these.

The way they act at the end is significant. During the *decision* and *resolution* steps, they need to talk in normal, adequate voices with matching postures. We also expect sustained eye contact, although not 100 percent of the time. Expressing their feelings about issues is fine, but doing it at or against anyone is not. Any suffering, petulance, seductiveness, cuteness, inadequacy, nastiness, or unpleasantness are signs that the issue is not resolved. Any tendency to act like a Rescuer, Persecutor or Victim (see Chapter 5, 'Family Dynamics') is something to confront. All behaviour like this signals incomplete acceptance and lack of resolution in our children. If we 'fall for it', we will know soon enough. Almost immediately, they will repeat what they did before, and we will have to repeat the whole sequence.

Take care if physical holding is necessary. Some children understandably don't want to stand against a blank wall, a fence or tree, or facing a corner. They want to get away and keep doing what they like. To deal with this, we need to hold them where we have told them to stay. We do this firmly, carefully and protectively, so we don't hurt them.

Some children need the physical struggle of being held in position, to learn what they need to learn. Children learn many things physically. (See Chapter 18, 'Natural transitions'.) Self-control is one of these. Many children learn to control themselves, through being controlled physically by others. They use the external control as a physical base from which to control ***themselves***. 'Standing to decide' gives us an opportunity to do this with them. If our children are already too big for one of us to manage at the point we begin using the process, we might need both of us there for a while.

Here is a very extreme example that highlights what some children will do and the power of persisting.

> *Harry was an unhappy five-year-old. His mother was a lone parent who could not control him. He would not do anything she told him. He was so violent and uncontrolled at school that he was under threat of expulsion. Elizabeth discussed 'standing to decide' in front of him with his mother. Immediately after she finished, he did something extremely provocative. Elizabeth turned and asked his mother if she would like to use 'standing to decide' to deal with it. She agreed. Harry was told to talk politely to his mother and would not. For the next three hours, this boy yelled and screamed in rage, struggled against their hold on him and tried to hurt them. They persisted until he calmed down, accepted what he had to do, spoke to his mother politely and agreed to do what he was told in future. The next day his mother rang in tears of relief to say that Harry was completely transformed. A week later, she rang again to say that the school were astonished at the transformation in him. He was calm, attentive, responsive and happy. His happiness was the most obvious change to everyone. By controlling him physically, he had learned to manage himself.*

Our strength helps them develop the strength to manage themselves. When our children struggle with us over discipline, the strength of the struggle shows us the strength of their need of us. They need us to join with them with the same strength. If they are dealing with a sledgehammer inside, using a feather outside will not help; if they are shouting inside, a whispered or quiet response from us will barely be heard.

Make appropriate allowances for tiredness or illness. It is appropriate to act with more leniency when the children are tired or ill. But making the allowance does not gives them permission to act in unpleasant or difficult ways when they are tired or sick.

Loving or not loving; that is the question

As you discipline a child, he or she might change the subject by saying, 'Do you still love me?' or 'You don't love me any more', or 'Why don't you love me?' You are supposed to feel guilty and get trapped into reassuring the child instead of pressing on.

You have an alternative. You say, 'I do love you, but that's not what we're talking about right now'.

Then you give him or her an instruction about what to do: 'Tell me why you didn't do the dishes', 'Answer my question', 'Go and do X right now', 'Decide that you are going to do Y from now on'.

Useful one-liners . . .

Interrupting the drama

You have a child who really makes a meal of inadequacy, or gets very worked up.

You say humorously – not nastily, **'Oh it must be worse than that'**, or **'I bet you could be even more convincing, if you shouted some more (produced more tears, spoke even more quietly so it's completely impossible to hear you)'**. When we do this well, they will often laugh with us and become more communicative. You need to choose your timing and do this only with children over about seven years of age.

Chapter 12

Knowing when and how to act

As parents, we are often in the position of wondering whether we should or should not do something. Also, not uncommonly, we simply don't know what to do.

- 'Should I leave them to themselves?'
- 'Maybe it will be all right.'
- 'It'll only create hassles.'
- 'I'm worried, but maybe I'm mistaken.'

This chapter is designed to help you to decide when to act and, to some extent, what to do.

We start the chapter by considering three general parenting styles that relate to initiative: *proactive*, *active* and *reactive* parenting. Then we present five useful guidelines for deciding when to act:

1. Safety first
2. Imagining the future
3. Meeting provocations
4. Choosing where to struggle
5. Direct observation

Who takes the initiative – you or your child?

Let's take a look at what we do with our children from the point of view of initiative. Knowing who is taking the initiative can help a lot when we need to decide what to do. It helps us answer questions such as:

- Do I need to take the initiative and act right now?
- Is it best just to get on with things as they are?
- Is it effective for me just to wait and react when the children do something?

What we do is to divide how we are parenting into three types:
1. In *proactive parenting* we take the initiative.
2. In *active parenting* initiative is evenly balanced between ourselves and our children.
3. In *reactive parenting* our children have the initiative.

Fairly obviously, good parenting involves all three types. With a balance of the three, we can more easily shape our children's talents and abilities at the same time as we support their uniqueness. So let's explore them so you can understand the way each contributes to our children.

Proactive parenting is most helpful when we need to set the agenda. Our images, feelings or senses of how we want our children to turn out, prompt us to guide them actively in those directions. We provide them with the opportunities they need, we make suggestions, we keep some level of pressure on them until they learn. We parent like this when our children would not learn what is important without us introducing and following through with the necessary lessons. For example, you want your child to be physically fit, so you organise involvement in sports and other physical activities; or you want your child to discuss things intelligently, so you talk at every opportunity and encourage wide-ranging reading.

Active parenting is most helpful when we simply need to get on with the job of dealing with day-to-day events. Much parenting involves this. We get on with paying bills, doing the washing, wiping away tears, buying school books, celebrating successes, discussing ways of doing things and having fun.

Reactive parenting is most helpful when we are responding to our children's initiatives. They do something and we get them to change what they are doing, because it needs rebalancing or correcting. During this kind of parenting, the children's actions set the agenda and we respond to them. For example, our children spend too much time watching TV, or don't spend enough time with friends, or argue a lot, or do not pay attention when others are talking to them, or hit others. At these times we will respond, deliberately shaping our responses so that they get the suggestions and corrections they need from us.

We can, however, parent too much in any of these ways. Overdoing any of them can create problems.

Act on the basis of what your children need. Their approval does not show us that we are right or wrong.

Too much **proactive parenting** can result in children who overemphasise the importance of other people's opinions and actions. They can lose a sense of what is important to themselves. At the same time, we can become dulled to their needs and desires, because we are so preoccupied with our own agendas. Too much **proactive parenting** can produce:

- children with other natural talents, who choose jobs that they think will please their parents;
- people who 'never' relax, because they 'always' had chores to do when growing up, rarely getting the chance to please and entertain themselves;
- grown-ups who 'stop knowing' what they hope for, think and feel while talking to others, because they were so overloaded as children by what their parents hoped, thought and felt.

With too much **active parenting**, we can get so preoccupied by the day-to-day events of our children's lives, that we don't pay enough attention to the important general issues affecting them. The bills get paid, many household chores get done, the squabbles and fights get dealt with, but overall outcomes are forgotten or not even noticed. In other words, everyday detail is noticed, while the general is forgotten or ignored. Too much **active parenting** can produce:

- a young person, who gets to the end of school and still cannot read, because she managed to 'become invisible' in class and won't talk about it at home;
- a child who has no friends and no-one has noticed, because parents spend most time correcting her 'faults';
- a primary school where no programs encourage physical exercise, because they are overbusy with classroom work.

Too much **reactive parenting** can mean that we unintentionally allow our children to determine what gets the attention. Attention is given to what they do, while other things are ignored. We wait for events to occur before taking action. Planning ahead is rare. We can easily forget important things. Too much **reactive parenting** can mean:

- you wait until you run out of food before doing the shopping;
- you miss the opportunity of a school camp by not sending in the application on time;

- you spend most time dealing with arguments and lose sight of the importance of sharing enjoyment;
- you prevent children from working easily and reliably as adults by not having trained them to contribute to the household every day when they were children.

Staying aware of the value of each of these three ways of acting can prompt us to do some important things and help us keep an overall balance in what we do.

> If in doubt about how to act, do something that you hope will help. Inactivity implies that we agree with what we are witnessing. Far better to repent after the event for having done too much, than to regret not having done enough.

Safety first

Safety is fundamentally important at all times. To ensure our children survive to become healthy, happy and fulfilled adults, we need to stay alert for and deal with real threats. In all situations, safety is the highest priority. We discussed some of the issues related to younger children in Chapter 1, 'Your job as a parent' and we suggest that you review this discussion. However, safety applies at all ages. You will find other relevant information in Chapter 18, 'Natural transitions'.)

All events that could cause death or significant harm have to be dealt with. They may be external threats, or threats posed by the children's own risk-taking behaviour. Be alert to:

- the traffic on the roads and in car parks
- underwater swimming hazards
- threatening-looking dogs or other animals
- depression in a child or young person
- dangerous driving
- train surfing

> Whenever a threat occurs, you need to do whatever is necessary to deal with it effectively.

We need to be on the alert always. Keeping our children safe requires that we move in and deal effectively with any potential or actual threats. Also, we need to make teaching our children to keep themselves safe a high priority.

Imagining the future

Casting our thinking forward into the future gives wonderful guidance about what to do now. When we understand this, either our goals or our children's behaviour can give us reasons to act.

Our goals

The moment we know how we want our children to turn out, many decisions about what to do with them become obvious. So, if you have not already done it, give some thought to the kinds of people you want your children to turn into. Parents can have lots of fun discussing this.

When we recommend thinking about children like this, we suggest you consider general ideas, not specific programs. For example, we want children to have happy, prosperous lives, in which they contribute to the world in some way that is fulfilling for themselves; we want them to be caring, intelligent, playful, assertive, powerful, sensitive and aware people.

Once you have even a general idea of how you want your children to turn out, do your best to fashion them accordingly. Use your ideas to measure them. This approach can easily guide you to when you need to act.

- If what they are doing is consistent with your ideas, then encourage them to do more of it.
- If what they do is inconsistent, then discourage them from doing it again.
- If what they do is not quite on track or inconsistent, you guide them to act differently.

Here are a few examples.

- Your young children remember names of visitors, or things you have said to them from several days before. Wanting them to develop good memories, you congratulate them.
- Primary school children are often unpleasant to each other. By actively encouraging them to care about each other, we can help them learn to live very differently with others.
- Babies often turn away and bury their heads in their parents' necks. You can say, 'Oh he's/she's shy', if you want a shy adult. For a confident adult, turn yourself around, or gently turn the child around for a full view.
- The pressure of school work mounts on your adolescent children. You want them to have the chance of tertiary education. Helping them cope with the pressure and insisting that they do the necessary work, will help them with this. Allowing them to give up, or doing it for them may well cut off the chance completely.

Clarify what kinds of adults you want your children to become. Then, every day, actively encourage them towards this outcome.

Our children's behaviour

Taking our children's behaviour as the reference is often equally powerful. A simple approach works with any incident.

We imagine that our children are twenty years older and are acting in the same way as they do now.

As we imagine this, we ask ourselves, 'How would I react to adults doing this?' If we like the prospect, then we encourage our children to keep doing it. If we don't like it, or could foresee problems with it, then we do something to change what our children are doing.

- A 40-year-old university lecturer was at a meeting. When thwarted during the meeting, she threw herself down, drummed her heels and her hands on the floor, and screamed in a full tantrum. It took little imagination to work out what she was allowed to do from about two years of age.

Our experience shows us repeatedly that adult patterns of feeling, thinking, behaving and understanding often come directly from the past.

- A boy pushes through people blocking access to a door, intent on his own goal of getting to the food first. Just imagine this behaviour when he is behind the wheel of a car.
- In response to people and events cutting across his plans, a boy dissolves into tears of frustration and acts helplessly in a manner that is out of proportion to the events. Can you foresee how he'll behave when he is grown up?
- When faced with challenging people, your children try to find out what is upsetting others, identify what is important to them and act in ways that help to calm things down and solve any problems. Do you want them doing this when they are older?

Remember they are still children

Obviously, our children are not adults. Just as obviously, they are not yet fully capable of doing things as adults do them. We need to stay aware of this as we act and ensure that we set reasonable expectations of our children that match their current ages. (See Section V, 'Ages and stages' for more information about this.) Consider the previous examples to illustrate this point.

- The boy can be stopped at the door, or brought back through it, expected to apologise for having pushed people and expected to wait until others have gone through first.
- The child prone to upsets can be encouraged to accept such inevitable events calmly. His parents may deliberately interfere in his plans at times, to help him learn. This gets him used to the process in protected places.
- Parents may encourage the clear-thinking, problem-solving children by complimenting them on their approaches. Further discussion may help to expand their already developing abilities.

A simple exercise

How on track are your kids at the moment? If you project forward twenty years, will you be happy for your children to act and live as they now are? Spend some time thinking about what you like about what they are doing, and what you don't like. Starting with one or two of each type of behaviour, decide what you can do to further encourage what you like, and what you can do to change what you don't like. Make a decision to do at least one thing a day in both areas.

Meeting provocations

Children often deliberately provoke us. *When they are provocative, usually our best response is to deal directly with the provocations.*

Three common ways our children provoke us to act

They put themselves or others at risk.
They break known rules inside or outside their homes.
They do things that create problems for themselves or others.

Reasons for acting

Their provocations are deliberate, though possibly unconscious, attempts to get the guidance that they need from us. When they have gaps in what they need to cope, they will often provoke us to help them fill the gaps. Also, when what they have got is not working well for them, they may provoke us to help them learn to manage themselves differently. They are provoking us to fill gaps and to help them better to learn to control and channel their feelings and other experiences.

When what they do is prompted by these needs, the only way of stopping them is to act decisively and effectively. If we don't, they will keep escalating the seriousness of what they do, until we do. This is very important to understand. They act more and more outrageously so that we will stop them, not so we will leave them to it. Once stopped, we can engage them in learning to act differently.

These kinds of escalations can occur over months or years, which can dull some parents' awareness of what is occurring.

- The boy, who at two would not do what his mother said, by three was hitting her, by four was kicking and biting her, and by fourteen knocked her unconscious and left her on the floor.
- The girl, who was quiet as a little girl, began running to her room to hide and cry when upset at seven, took an overdose at fifteen.
- The girl, who started lying to solve problems at seven and would not change, added stealing to her repertoire at about nine, played truant frequently at thirteen, stole cars at sixteen and robbed a bank at twenty-one.

When provoking us to act from a need for learning, they will only stop when they have learnt.

Trying to ignore or step around their provocations only leads to more serious and stimulating provocations.

They need us to stop them, using whatever vigour it takes to do so.

Children doing this kind of thing often have parents who have not given them enough limits in other areas. As the children escalate, they are trying to find something that will stir us enough to say, 'No. Stop doing that', or 'Not like that, like this'. Another ingredient is also important. They want us to enforce what we have said. They know in their bones that they need controlling by others, so they can learn to guide or control themselves. But they cannot do it for themselves. Fortunately, most children manage to find our sensitive spots eventually and so get us to set the limits they need. Tactics include:

- doing damage to a favourite possession;
- a maths teacher's daughter threatening to give up maths at school;
- the son of a probation officer of juveniles breaking the law and ends up in court in front of his father's friends;
- the daughter of an inflexible minister of religion getting pregnant at sixteen.

When parents don't act

Unfortunately, some children don't manage to stir their parents into action. This leaves it up to others to take care of the consequences. Teachers are very involved in this job. When parents, teachers and interested adults all fail to act, our children often get what they need from the police, ambulance, fire brigade, the prison system, psychiatric hospitals or armed forces.

Our shared view is that much social turmoil, and acting out in public, are attempts by people, who were not guided or limited enough at home, to get that guidance and those limits outside the home. We include much drug-taking, leaving home too early, fighting and demonstrating on the streets, crime and destruction of property. (See Chapter 20, 'Four births, four bonds' for more on this.) Many discussions with adults who did this kind of thing when young have told us remarkably similar stories.

- One side of it is: 'My parents never stopped me when I was a kid. I realise now that I needed them to stop me.'
- Another side is: 'I didn't like my parents limiting me, but in another way I knew they were right and I was relieved.'

What works

When questioned by her mother, one young woman explained why she had never even experimented with drugs. She said, 'I always knew you and Dad were there for me. You encouraged me when I needed it and I could feel your hands on the reins when I needed correction. Feeling secure in your presence, I did not need to provoke you by using drugs and doing other things, the way a lot of my friends did. I already knew you cared'.

Choosing where to struggle

Children need to struggle as part of growing up. We have already mentioned in several places the way this works. When our children struggle with us, they want us 'to win', not 'to lose'. It is our guiding strength that they are after, and they get it from the struggle. (You will see much more on this in Chapter 20, 'Four births, four bonds'.)

> Struggle is a normal and important part of raising children.

As you think about your children's struggles, you will almost certainly notice something very obvious about them. When struggle is part of their learning, it doesn't much matter what we do, they will keep struggling. There is no way around the struggle, if we want our children to learn. This understanding leads to a wonderfully simple guideline for us. *Since the struggle is what is important, not so much what they are struggling about, we can choose where to struggle with them.*

In other words, a little *proactive parenting* is the solution. Instead of waiting on our children 'to pick the next fight', we do some choosing about when it will be and what it will be over, too. We will generally feel much better if we exercise some level of choice over things.

All sorts of issues are available in our daily lives, including expecting them to do household jobs. And we can't go wrong. If they struggle over doing something reasonable and we struggle with them to ensure they do it, then we are on the right track. They get the struggle they need. If they don't struggle and do as requested or expected, they contribute to the household. And everyone benefits from their contributions. You can:

- expect them to put their clothes away, do the dishes properly, or make their beds daily;
- stop them swearing at you and each other;
- ensure brothers and sisters talk to each other respectfully;
- get them to go to bed at the right time;
- insist on truth and keeping commitments.

These are much easier issues to deal with than the more serious things they are likely to do if we don't give them the struggles they need. Also, remember a simple thing. Children and young people know that they need discipline. While they may fight our attempts to provide it, they are not fighting 'to win'. They are fighting so we will 'win', because with our 'victory' they learn what they need. In the end, of course, they realise that it never was a fight over who was going to win or lose. (Please understand that we assume that your parenting is appropriate and not abusive or violating. See Chapter 9, 'Parenting with love', Chapter 10, 'The discipline sequence', and Chapter 11, 'Standing to decide' for more information on how we approach this.)

Direct observation

Support your children's natural inclinations and expressiveness as much as is reasonable. Notice what they like doing and where their talents are. Then do what you can to provide opportunities for them to develop in these areas. Examples are:

- one little girl played with many different things and obviously loved drawing and painting;
- from when he could walk, a boy showed great prowess with bats and balls of all kinds;
- another child began counting, measuring, numbering and keeping track of physical things from the moment he could talk.

If you are unclear what is important to your children, ask them. They can tell you directly. Parents can often make the mistake of trying to work things out themselves. But this wastes much time and can lead to significant mistakes when we are wrong. Once they can talk, talk to them. Ask questions and listen intently to their answers.

- What do you want to do?
- What do you need?
- How would you go about doing this?
- Why did you do that?
- What did you think would happen when you did that?
- If you could have anything you needed, what would it be?

Go to the horse's mouth

Children can surprise us with their maturity, perceptiveness, insight and understanding. They can also startle us with their levels of confusion, misunderstanding and ignorance. In either event, we are better off knowing, and they can be better off for the discussions we have with them as we find out.

Dealing with suicidal children

Children can become very dejected at times and may become suicidal. Our actions at these times need to be direct, clear, effective and sustained. Suicidal or potentially suicidal children and young people are at risk and need immediate and effective adult help. We do not need special training to recognise the problem and act effectively.

Children as young as five or six may consider killing themselves and it is important to take these threats seriously.

Warning signs

Things to watch for include actual suicide attempts, threats to do it, talking about dying or not wanting to live, extreme acting out or withdrawal, depression, sustained isolation, stopping eating. We need to be particularly alert after a significant loss (of a parent, sibling, friend, pet), parental divorce, family breakdown, or during intense personal emotional crises. Most of these signs and situations do not automatically mean a child will be suicidal; however, they are definitely signs to us that we need to do something.

Things to do

We can all do a great deal to help. And what we do could save a life. Things to do when you think children are at risk:

- reach out and express your concern
- discuss their issues and feelings openly and directly
- avoid avoiding the issue
- ensure their safety by having someone with them until help arrives

- attempt to get a life contract and/or no-suicide contract
- remove all likely instruments: pills, knives, razor blades, guns, poisons etc.
- block access to any dangerous places: cliffs, high windows, roads, kitchen drawers etc.
- contact emergency services – police, ambulance – if necessary
- link them to professional help and follow up until the link is made
- follow up again after a while to make sure everything is working out

Agreements to live

Once physically safe, we can ask the children or young people to make special agreements with us. These help us both to assess how at risk they are and to secure their safety. The ease with which they make the agreements is the measure: the easier it is, the safer they are.

Life contract

I am living (will live) a happy and full life, and promote the same in others.

No-suicide contract

I will not kill myself nor harm myself in any way, either accidentally or on purpose, nor will I allow anyone else to do it for me.

How to make the agreements

These are simple statements that commit children and young people to staying alive. They can be made with or without a time-limit. The way to do it is to keep on getting the children or young people to repeat the words until they say them with real conviction.

We also ask that they make the contracts forever. If they are reluctant to do this, we ask them what the longest time is that they are sure they will keep them. This might be five minutes, an hour, a day, several days, a week, a month, several months, a year or more.

Any time limit is specified as part of the agreements. We also get them to agree to contact us again before the specified time limit expires. 'I will keep this agreement for ... And I will contact you at ...' To add extra security, we get them to agree to contact us at any other time that they think they are becoming unsure about keeping the agreements. Then we **must** make sure that we get the child to remake the contracts again **before** the time expires.

We also need to make sure we are available for contact, should they need to call on us. If we don't think we have the capacity to do this, or we are unwilling or unavailable to be contacted, then it is most important that we get someone else to take over this part of the process. (See Chapter 16, 'Developing self-esteem' for more on what we can do to help children and young people in this fix.)

Useful one-liners . . .

Entertaining themselves

Your children come in and say with a whinge in their voices, 'Mum/Dad, I'm bored', or 'I haven't got anything to do'. The invitation is to get us to come up with things to entertain them. It is our job after all!

Reply, '**So what could you do to have fun?**'

Then you can discuss their ideas. For example, you can respond to, '**There's nothing to do**' by surprising them with, '**Well that's great. Sit and do nothing. It's wonderful to sit and explore what's going on inside us**'.

This is true of course, but you might get howls of outrage.

You could also suggest, '**What about going into your room, (or wherever the toys and other entertainments are kept) and look at all the things you haven't got to do. Then come back and tell me what isn't there**'.

This usually gets a laugh, however, it is best only done with children older than seven, who are developing an ironic sense of humour.

Chapter 13

Communicating clearly

A child had his fingers on the moving surface of an airport luggage carousel. His mother, obviously concerned about the safety of his fingers, said, 'Can you be careful of your fingers?' The child moved his fingers about two millimetres, so showing that he had heard the question. She repeated her question and got the same slight twitch of a response. The child's eyes were still down, looking attentively at the moving surface. Then she repeated it twice more. By this time over a minute had passed. Finally, she said with irritation, as if the child had not done what he was told, 'Get your hand off!' And she slapped him, not hurtfully, on the shoulder. The child, looking confused, immediately moved his hand away from danger.

We witnessed this sequence and noticed several things.

- The mother was concerned and was trying to get her son to take proper care. We knew this because we shared her concern and were old enough to know what she intended, whereas the boy may not have understood.
- The literal meaning of her repeated question was, 'Are you able to be careful of your fingers?' This did not require much of a response from her son. 'Yes', meaning that he could be careful, or 'No', meaning that he could not.
- The child's slight physical response indicated that he had heard, but did not feel the need to respond further.
- The mother was obviously used to telling this boy to do things more than once, too, even things to do with his safety. It took four repetitions of the same question for her to act decisively. All the while, her son was trailing his fingers across the moving surface of the carousel.
- You might wonder if the boy was rebellious and just not wanting to cooperate; however, our impression was that he was absorbed in what he was doing, not rebellious.

- The moment she said clearly, 'Get your hand off!' and slapped him on the shoulder, he acted. The slap got his attention and the words said *exactly* what she wanted him to do.
- Her irritation seemed due to his unresponsiveness. However, it was only her last statement that communicated clearly what she wanted.

Our impression was that she would have been better to start where she ended: 'Get your hand off'. The boy would probably have acted immediately and the slap to get his attention may not have been necessary. This would have kept his fingers much safer, avoided the mother becoming irritated and prevented the boy feeling somewhat confused.

How many times a day does the average parent get into this kind of situation? This chapter is about what children really hear when we speak to them, and what we can do to ensure that they get the messages we want them to get.

What children really hear

As adults, we usually know what we and others mean. Life experience has taught us the significance of what they say and do. Children, particularly the younger ones, do not have our experience, however. What they make out of what we are trying to get across to them is often very different from what we intend. Take three examples.

- After playing with friends, seven-year-old Vito came inside at dusk. His mother caught sight of him with mud from head to foot. She said, 'Go straight to the laundry and put everything you are wearing in the washing machine'. And this is what he did. Everything went into the machine: shirt, pants, underclothes, socks, boots and watch. He did precisely what he was told to do.
- Anne's mother wanted her to prepare for the evening meal. Anne was four years old. Her mother said, 'I want you to pick up your toys.' Anne nodded as she said this and then did nothing about her toys. When she was reprimanded for not picking up her toys, she looked very confused and got upset. Anne did not know that, by '*I want you* to pick up your toys', her mother meant, '*Pick up* your toys'. To Anne, her mother had simply said something interesting.
- Wendy was having a great struggle with Sam, her nine-month-old boy. A large, strong child for his age, whenever she changed his nappy, he kept rolling over and trying to crawl away from her. Wendy was very frustrated and worried that he would become uncontrollable as he got older. Ken

suggested that she change Sam in front of him, so he could witness the process. As she put Sam on his back and took off his nappy, Sam quickly rolled over and tried to crawl away. Wendy said, 'Don't move'. He tried to get away even more strongly. She repeated herself, loudly, 'Don't **move**!' As before, he did his best to get away. At this point Ken said, 'Wendy, try saying, "Keep still".' Wendy immediately said, 'Keep still'. Sam stopped immediately. 'Now,' said Ken, 'put him on his back, and as you do, say, "Lie still while I change your nappy".' Wendy followed the suggestion and Sam did exactly what he was told.

Vito, Anne and Sam all did what they thought they were told to do. They did not do what their mothers intended them to do, but they did do quite literally what their mothers had said. There is a lesson in this.

> To get your children to do as you want, choose your words carefully and tell them *exactly* what you want them to do.

How this works

Young children are 'body minded'. This means that they understand the meaning of words and events physically. *The meanings of words and events are the actions and objects that go with them.* Children cannot understand in any other way, at least when they are young.

To understand anything, our children go through the motions internally. They live through it inside. Children up to the age of about four or five do this very obviously by acting out what they say as they say it. As children get older they seem to stop. However, even though they may look as though they have stopped, they still do it internally. So, in fact, do we.

Getting our messages across clearly

The first tip we have relates to body-mindedness. It is to put into words, pictures and action exactly what you want your children to do. All the suggestions that follow involve doing this. They can make all sorts of situations with our children very much easier, including the challenging job of getting them to do what we want quickly and easily.

Choose your words carefully

This could be the one piece of advice that makes most difference in your home. You can powerfully influence the lightness, happiness, ease and harmony there and in your life generally. Many parents have confirmed this. So look, listen and follow through!

Choose your words according to their literal and concrete meaning. You will almost certainly notice all sorts of things become much easier if you do. We can influence the moods and orientations of our children directly and we can get them to do the things that are important much more easily and cooperatively. Let's look at each in turn.

Influencing moods

Remembering that children act out the literal meaning of the words we use, we can program them with our words. When we want our children to experience and think about love, success, happiness, enjoying themselves, calming down, thinking clearly, solving problems, cooperating, cheering up and many other things, we simply use those exact words. Experiment. Next time your children are with you, decide how you would like them to feel. Then as you talk, start to use the words that go with those feelings. Every time you do, you will stimulate your children and yourself to have those precise experiences. After very little time you are likely to notice a shift towards what you are saying.

This has general and specific value. Take our families. We can monitor the words we usually use as we talk to each other. Knowing that we are all acting out the meanings of them, we can assess the influence these words are having. We can use this influence, simply by changing the words we use. We have seen families shift their overall atmospheres within hours of starting this process. Each member can become a monitor of everyone else to help make the changes. It can be a lot of fun. For example, imagine the difference between acting out, 'I'm sick and tired of telling you ...', and 'I want you to do this right now'.

Specific value lies in our responses to each other's needs. Selecting our words can make us much more sensitive, effective and creative.

- Andrea walks in crying. 'I'm very upset', she says. (This intensifies her upset, which could be a good thing at this stage.)

  Mother says, 'Oh you poor thing, you look as though your world is about to end. Come over here and tell me about it'. (Notice the 'poor thing' and 'your world is about to end'. Is this what we want Andrea acting out?)

Andrea cries some more and struggles to say, 'I'm just so hopeless, everyone hates me. I'll never have any friends'. (All of this is probably a real expression of her feelings, but not true in fact, or at least not destined to stay true.)

Mother caresses her and says, 'You're not hopeless, everyone doesn't hate you. I'm sure you have lots of friends'. (The first two statements are not helpful, although intended to show sympathy. Andrea acts out 'so hopeless', and 'hate you'. Mother's last statement is better. Acting out 'have lots of friends' will be good for her, although Andrea may not be quite ready to hear this, yet.)

Now let's look at a different set of responses.

- Andrea walks in crying. 'I'm very upset,' she says.

  Mother says, 'Oh dear, come over here and talk to me about it. I'm sure we can work something out. What's going on? You certainly don't look happy.' (She plants a seed about working things out and requests more information. Then she gives her an internal nudge in the direction of feeling better by using the word 'happy'.)

  Andrea, still upset, walks across to her mother and says, 'I'm just so hopeless, everyone hates me. I'll never have any friends'.

  Mother, holding her hands, says, 'Sometimes when we don't feel happy, we imagine things are not nearly as good as they actually are. Usually, when we feel better, we realise that things are better than we thought'. (Note the selection of words and phrases like 'feel happy', 'nearly as good as', 'feel better', and 'better than we thought'. All of these, when acted out will help Andrea start to appreciate things differently.)

  'Oh it's all right for *you*, *you've* got plenty of friends.' Andrea is now both angry and sad. (This is actually a step forward. She is more assertive and is using words like 'plenty of friends'.)

  'That's not the point, Andrea. The main point is that you don't feel as if *you* have friends. You don't like yourself much at the moment and we need to work out what to do about it. Let's talk about it. There are solutions to all problems.' (Mother is still programming her and leading her both to face herself and to think practically about what to do.)

Changing behaviour with clear instructions

Many parents find their children are much more responsive to doing what they are told, when they are told what to do, rather than what not to do. Why they are, is very obvious, when we remember that children act out literally what we say to them. Think about the literal meaning of the following examples in the table. Imagine your children acting out the actual words used and decide if your selection would be the same as ours. Note that when we give someone a negative message (don't, can't, never, not etc.) we act out the message first and only then get to not doing it. In other words, 'Don't cry', means that the person has to cry internally before not doing it.

Expressions to use	Expressions to avoid
act gently	don't hit
talk quietly	don't shout
come away, hands off	don't touch
relax	don't be scared
act intelligently	don't be stupid
tell the truth	don't lie
get out of bed	don't lie there
remember	don't forget
think clearly	don't be confused
go well	'break a leg'
move carefully	don't be clumsy
act pleasantly	don't be nasty
walk slowly	don't run
obey the law	don't break the law

You will see that acting out the statements on the left will get your children to do what you intend. Many parents find that their children become much easier to manage, the moment they talk in this way. While the approach doesn't get one hundred percent success, it makes even those times when children struggle strongly against us much easier to resolve.

Use requests and instructions selectively

Requests and instructions are different. Using the differences well makes dealing with our children and helping them understand what we want them to do very much easier. Let's consider the differences.

A *request* is the act of asking someone to do something. Requests usually carry a tone of politeness with them. They also include the assumption that the person is free to choose. He or she can say, 'Yes', 'No', or 'Maybe'.

An *instruction*, by contrast, is a direction or command to do something. They are usually not thought of as polite. When we give an instruction, we expect to be obeyed. People given and instruction, can still say, 'Yes', 'No', or 'Maybe', but this would require that they go against usual expectations.

We have found that children are much more confident in many ways when their parents are clear on this difference. Mixing up requests and instructions can create all sorts of unnecessary difficulties. Look at the following example. As you do, remember that children understand things literally, so a request will get them internally acting out the question, while an instruction gets them internally actually doing what we expect.

A warder asked a prisoner, 'Will you go to your cell now please?' The prisoner replied, 'Do I have a choice?' The warder repeated himself, 'Will you go to your cell now please?' The prisoner repeated himself, too, 'Do I have a choice?' After two more repetitions, the warder became angry and put the prisoner on report.

Obviously, the question and seeming politeness were covering an instruction that had to be obeyed. The prisoner's question was appropriate under the circumstances, although perhaps not wise.

Make your requests as requests and give your instructions as instructions.

Take a quick look at the clear difference in the examples given in the table.

Requests	Instructions
Will you go to bed now?	Go to bed now.
Will you eat your meal?	Eat your meal.
Will you come home by midnight?	Come home by midnight.
Will you clean up your room before tea?	Clean up your room before tea.

Advantages of being clear

Several compelling reasons support making clear the difference between requests and orders.

- Our children will always know when we are offering them a choice and when we are not.
- Parents who ask their children to do things, when they are not actually offering a choice, imply a shift of power to their children. This is unreal and not good for either parents or children in many situations.

- Because our children record what we do with them and use the recordings to help manage themselves, they can take in two important things from us. The first is the power to command themselves to do things. The second is the freedom to choose for themselves. If we confuse the two, so might they. If we act clearly, so might they.
- When we act assertively enough to get our children to do quickly and cleanly what we direct, we can save hours of wheedling, pleading, coaxing and hoping that our children will do what we want them to do.

Reluctance to give orders

Even given the advantages, however, you may have qualms about instructing, ordering or telling your children what to do. Many parents react to this as harsh or bossy, or even nasty and abusive. And, while any of us can act in harsh, bossy, nasty or abusive ways, this is not an automatic part of giving an instruction. We can give instructions very mildly, even lovingly and humorously. Probably most situations allow us to do this, too.

- Said in a normal speaking voice, 'Eat your vegetables, John'.
- In a soft, mild, or even loving voice, 'Come on now. It's time for bed. Get going'. This could be said with a smile, or done with a kiss on the top of the head, or with other forms of affection.
- Loudly enough to be heard over the traffic, but still evenly and clearly, 'Come over here away from the road, Angela. It's not safe there. Come on, come here quickly'.
- Said with a laugh, 'Okay, the time has come for you to do your homework. Did you think I had forgotten? Your father isn't that forgetful yet! Go on, go and get started'.

> It is all right to tell your children what to do.

Sometimes we need to shout

When talking to our children, we do not usually need to shout, sound hard, or threaten with posture, gestures, or voice tones. Sometimes we do, however, so it is worth being prepared. This is particularly important when our children are not taking notice of us and we need something extra to get them to do so. Our intensity and noise are what we use.

- After a lot of repeated appearances at the door, we say in a firm voice, louder than usual, with perhaps a frown or two for good effect, 'I will not discuss it with you any more. Go to bed, now. Lie down and stay there. Go on – now'.

- 'You have not remembered your school notices all this week. You are to remember to give them to me every time notices are given to you. You are to give them to me the moment you get home.' All this is said very clearly, firmly (possibly loudly) and each point is made one at a time. Then you say, 'Now what are you going to do?' (See Chapter 10, 'The discipline sequence')

> Shouting, table-thumping and other displays of parental displeasure are valuable ways of getting attention, keeping attention and giving emotional significance to what we are saying. When we have their attention and they have got the message, we can behave normally again. Phew!

One of the wonderful things about using 'standing to decide' with children is that it removes the necessity for a lot of shouting and soothes much parental frustration. (See Chapter 11, 'Standing to decide'.)

The power of requests

Requests are just as powerful in their own way. They offer choices to our children very clearly.

- 'Will you help me with the dishes?' gives them the freedom to say, 'Yes' or 'No'. This encourages them to think for themselves and act cooperatively or independently. And in asking the question, we are implying that we are prepared to do the dishes without their help.
- 'Will you come and see me about that tomorrow?' implies that they can, and could also come at another time, or not at all.
- 'Will you ask your mother to make the carrots I like tonight?' also implies that they don't have to do it. We are asking it as a favour.

Politeness can be a trap

In an effort to emphasise politeness and to encourage respect, many parents add the words 'please' or 'okay' to the end of their questions.

- 'Will you drink your milk now, please?'
- 'Will you go over there and play on the carpet, please?'
- 'Will you finish your homework now, so you can get to bed early, okay?'

The words 'please' and 'okay' are supposed to act as some sort of verbal punctuation that turns the request into an instruction. The level of compulsion attached to these 'requests' varies according to the intensity in how they are said. When our children don't do what we have 'told' them to do like this, we generally become increasingly irritated and impatient. At these times, it usually becomes clear that our questions are shams. And the more forceful the emphasis that is put on the 'please' or 'okay', the more clearly the request is revealed as an instruction:

- 'Will you go to bed now, ***please!?***'
- 'Will you children ***please*** be quiet?'

Instructions that we pretend are requests, such as these, transmit very mixed messages to our children. Here are some of the possibilities:

- 'I am telling you to do this, but I don't feel confident enough to tell you directly.'
- 'I am in charge of you, but I ask your permission before taking control of you.'
- 'I hope you will take care of me by doing what I want you to do, without me having to assert myself directly and tell you to do it.'

Remember that every one of these messages is taken in by our children and used by them to get themselves to do what they need to do in their lives. Is this the inner heritage you wish to pass on to your children? We don't, although we know people who are quite happy to do it. We can call this 'parenting from the Victim position'. (See Chapter 5, 'Family dynamics' for information on the Victim position.)

We think the best thing to do is simply to give a clear instruction as outlined above and follow through so they do as they are told. This saves lots of time and parental wear and tear.

- 'Go to bed now.'
- 'Be quiet, children.'

When you expect your children to do things and they have no choice, give them instructions. When they have a choice, as they often will, make requests of them.

Useful one-liners . . .

From reason to action

A child repeatedly avoids action by seeking reasons why.

After they say 'Why?' you say, **'Because I am telling you to. Do it now'**.

Cooling it

'Oh, you're so uncool!' our children say in an attempt to sway us to their way of thinking.

We can reply casually, **'It's okay to be hot at times'**.

Chapter 14

Paying active attention

This chapter is about truly knowing what is going on with our children. To do this, we need both to pay attention to them and to get them to tell us what is going on.

Five ways of noticing our children

To pay attention to our children, we have to notice them. The simplest thing to remember about attention is that we have five senses. This gives us five ways of knowing what is going on with them: looking, listening, touching, tasting or smelling them. We can get significantly different information and impressions from each of our senses, so we are well advised to become proficient in using all of them. Let's go through them in turn.

> Use all five senses to notice your children. Get them to do the same as they pay attention to you.

Watch what they look like, how healthy they look, how calm or upset, how energetic or tired, how animated or depressed, and how they interact with others. Look at the state that their rooms are in, how clean their clothes are, how tidy their school work is, and how personally clean they are. Many clues come to us through really watching out children, many delights, too. Watching life is exquisite and children are so full of life.

We need to listen attentively to our children. What are they saying? What do they **mean** by what they are saying? Are they saying something important or trivial? Notice if they are telling us more by what they are **not** saying than what they **are** saying. How are they saying what they are saying? Words alone don't carry the full message. Do they sound calm, anxious, depressed, excited, loving, scared, sad, happy, hopeful, uncertain, or angry? Also, listen to what they say to friends and family. Listen to how they sound through the walls! You will hear them. Listen for changes in this.

Touch them and allow them to touch you. How do they feel to you? What do you feel about them as you touch them? Do they feel confident with touch? Do they respond well to being touched by you? Do they feel secure, needy, distant, repulsing, attractive, available, open, or closed to you as you touch each other. Many clues come through a hand on an arm, or leaning against someone for a moment, or through a quick hug. Notice their styles of moving around. Do they bump into things, are they sure-footed, graceful and coordinated?

Also, notice the taste and smell of them. Some people find this an unusual suggestion, while others know they rely on this as a primary measure of what is going on with their children. It is probably their smells that we will notice most easily of the two, although taste and smell seem to trigger each other. Their aromas are very present and relate to much more than hygiene. Most children and adults have consistent aromas, any changes to which can act as useful signals. Marked changes in aroma often indicate important emotional changes. So, be alert: do they smell sweet, sour, bitter, salty, foul or poisonous? Noticing how their rooms smell is another good indication of what is going on with them.

Active listening

To make strong links with our children as we talk, it is best to use all five senses. We mean this literally. We need to keep looking at them, listening to them, touching them from time to time and, for some, staying aware of their taste/smell. Expecting and encouraging them to do the same is also important. These exchanges through our senses are what keep us linked to each other. Here are some things you can say to do this.

- While looking at them, we say, 'Look at me as you're talking to me', or 'Look at me while I'm talking to you'.

- As we listen attentively, we say, 'I'm listening to what you're saying. Listen to me, too'.
- During our talks, we reach out and touch them occasionally; we encourage them to do the same with us.

The mothers or fathers who pay full attention will know much more about their children than those who don't. Think of the fathers and mothers who always have their attention elsewhere when their children talk to them. For example, they watch the TV, listen to the radio, keep cooking, or read a newspaper at the same time. Parents who pay full attention to their children, will stop doing distracting things, face their children and truly engage. Naturally, it works both ways and we are usually best to insist on similar attentiveness from our children to us.

How to listen actively

Two simple approaches help us ensure we are actively paying attention.

We pay attention to what is said, and we respond to it. That is, we stay on the same subject as our children. We do not change the subject.

- 'I'm feeling angry, Dad', says the son. 'Oh, you'll be all right. Pass the wrench, son.' This is a complete change of subject and is not effective listening.
- 'I'm feeling angry, Dad', says the son. 'Oh are you? Pass me the wrench, son, and tell me about it.' This is the same subject, but the listening is diluted by the task. Sometimes this is very helpful when a shared activity makes the talking easier. (An alternative is, 'Oh are you? What about waiting five minutes until I'm finished here, then I can give you my full attention'.)
- 'I'm feeling angry, Dad', says the son. 'Oh are you? I often used to feel angry when I was your age.' (There follows a long story about the father's youth.) This is not helpful as it shifts the focus away from the boy and completely onto the father.

We also pay attention to the way things are said.

- 'I'm feeling sad, Dad', says the son. 'Yes you're sounding sad to me. Tell me some more.' This is attentive and relating to the feelings generally.
- 'I'm feeling sad, Dad', says the son. 'You're feeling sad.' This often encourages the child to say more about the sadness specifically.
- 'I'm feeling sad, Dad', says the son. 'You sound sad to me and you also sound a bit angry.' The statement can get the son to explore what else is going on and to express more about either feeling.

How to encourage expressiveness in our children

Four simple guidelines can help us encourage our children to express themselves. Each of them involves paying slightly different attention to what they are saying and how they are saying it.

1. When you want a thoughtful response ask a question.
- 'What do you think about that?
- 'What are you feeling?'
- 'What did you do next?'
- 'How much did that cost?'

2. When you want to go with the flow and encourage self-expression, make statements.
- 'Say more.'
- 'Go on.'
- 'You look upset and sound it too.'
- 'You're telling me that you ...'

3. When you want to encourage expressiveness without influencing the content of what they say, repeat all or some of what they have just said.
- 'You think you will go now.'
- 'You don't like what he said to you.'
- 'You felt very angry and then started to think about getting even.'
- 'You felt excited and want to go out and play.'

4. Stay silent to show respect and to become strongly present with people.
- Keep looking at the person, making your look attentive and receptive.
- Possibly nod your head a little.
- Stay relaxed and wait for the next move to occur naturally, in either of you.
- Say with your posture, 'I am here and with you'.

Two examples of paying attention actively

Let's put this together in a couple of examples.

Graham and the pups

In bounces Graham, all smiles and obviously very excited.

'Mum!'

'Hi! Well you look excited about something!' She makes her statements to encourage a flow-on effect from his high spirits and to get him talking.

'You know that bitch up the street. Well, she's had her pups and Mrs Grant says I can have one.' He stops and looks expectantly, but a cloud appears in his eyes as he seems to remember conversations about puppy care and who will have to do it all.

Mother chooses to go with the excitement for a while though. She is enjoying sharing the pleasure with Graham. 'So you really want one of these puppies.'

'Oh yes. They're so beautiful. You should see them and feel how soft they are. It won't be any trouble and I'll do everything, I promise.' He uses his eyes, sparkling with excitement and hope, to good effect.

'You really want one of these puppies.' Mother is still wanting to go with the flow and to tap off some of this lovely energy. She and Graham's father have already decided that now is the time. But before talking about their terms and conditions, she wants Graham to be a little less highly charged.

'I really, really, really want one. You should see the one I want. He already knows me. He was crawling all over me and he came when I called him.'

Mother stays attentively silent, open to her son and sharing his excitement with him. Then she says, 'Tell me what else he did'.

Graham talks excitedly with little encouragement for three minutes more.

When he seems to have discharged some of his energy, his mother says, 'So have you thought about where he could go?' She asks the question to get him thinking about things. This would have the effect of toning him down a little more, so she can move the discussion onto practicalities.

'Well, I thought he could sleep in the laundry to begin with. Then, when he's old enough, we could get a kennel and he can sleep out in the yard. I'll do everything, Mum. I promise I will. You won't have to do a thing.'

This mother doesn't fall for that, but she knows Graham will do his share. 'And who's going to bath him, and get up in the middle of the night for the first few months to take him into the yard for a pee?'

'Oh, I'll do that,' he said before she'd finished, although he had spoken before 'getting up in the middle of the night' was mentioned. This changed his expression considerably.

Mother draws him out on this a little. 'You don't look very enthusiastic about getting up.'

'Well, I don't know if I'll wake up, and you know if I don't get enough sleep, then I fall asleep all the next day.' He was looking sheepish and a little pleadingly at his mother.

In fact, he was right and he was only seven, so she said, 'I'm sure your father and I can work something out with you so we all share things. Now what about training? You will both have to go to obedience school.' She rather enjoyed the thought of Graham going to obedience school.

From his response, so, apparently, did he.

Eight weeks later the puppy arrived.

Eliza's night off

Eliza, a fifteen-year-old, is making hard work of her homework. She wants to watch TV, but has to finish an essay. After a few exchanges with her father, she very reluctantly goes off to her room to do it. Appearing ten minutes later, she is obviously angry and sulky.

'It's just not fair. I've always got too much homework. Why can't I have a night off?'

Father thinks that any of these three statements might be fertile ground for close questioning. He realises, however, that trying to have a factual, practical discussion at this point is futile. Also, because she is so angry, sending her back to her room to get on with the job is unlikely to work. So he decides to draw her out, to tap off some of the energy. 'You don't think it's fair.'

'No I don't. Mrs Bryson does this deliberately. She gives us something every night.' Eliza sounds sour and petulant. 'She doesn't care how much we work in class. She always gives us more to do at home.'

Father gets the idea and puts it into words, 'She just likes to make your life miserable.' He pauses, noting his daughter's nodding head and thinking she is now calm enough to start to see sense. 'I guess that she spent weeks planning how to interfere with you watching this TV program tonight.' Warming lovingly to this theme, he says, 'In fact I think I'd better check with your mother just to make sure that she did ring us to be certain she had the right night.'

Eliza began to look puzzled when her father was part of the way through this and by the end was smiling and giggling a bit. 'Oh Dad, you know I don't mean that. You're just being silly.'

'Then tell me what it is that is really going on.' This is like a question, but is put in a way that will keep her flow going. He wondered about asking, 'Okay, so what is really going on?' but decided this would block her from the lightness that the fun had stimulated.

'I do want to watch the TV, but really the trouble is that I don't have any ideas about the assignment. It's just a stupid assignment.'

'You're saying the assignment is stupid because you can't do it,' Father says, arching an eyebrow. 'Could it be the other way around and that's what is provoking you?'

'Yes, I guess you're right,' she concedes with a little good grace. 'The trouble is I don't know where to start.'

'Is there some way I can help. Maybe if you go and get the book and show me what it's about, I can help you get started. Do you want to do that?'

'Yes, Dad. Thanks.' And off she goes. By this time, she is considerably calmer and probably ready to do her essay.

Chapter 15

Repeating ourselves

Repeating ourselves is a very simple and important part of parenting, yet it causes more upsets than many other issues.

- 'I don't want to be a nag.'
- 'I always seem to be after them to do the same things.'
- 'They accuse me of nagging and I know they're right.'
- 'When I was a kid, I didn't like my mum and dad doing it, so I don't want to myself.'
- 'Why can't they just do what they are supposed to without me having to remind them?'

Read on if you want 'good reasons' to nag, harp and make a fuss.

Learning relies on repetition

Take particular notice of the next two sentences. ***Children learn through repetition. They cannot learn well without it.*** This is the reason that they get us to repeat things many times. This is also the justification for nagging, if you need one.

Just notice what babies do. They repeat everything hundreds and thousands of times. The hand goes into the mouth and out again – over and over. The toy is shaken, the toes are examined, the head is turned. Everything is repeated. Doing these things repeatedly actually lays down and strengthens neural pathways in the body. Good coordination and effective body control rely on these pathways and, therefore, on these activities. Without the repetitive physical activity, the pathways do not develop as needed.

Because our children have to repeat things so they can learn, we have to repeat things, too, so they can learn from us.

Our experience is that all learning follows a similar pattern. It all relies on repetition. Some important areas in which repetition is crucial to help children learn are:

- patterns of behaviour
- physical skills
- how to relate to others
- remembering certain types of things
- talking, reading, writing, drawing, doing arithmetic
- relating in different ways with different people
- household duties
- making decisions
- following through on commitments
- school work
- ways of thinking about things
- ways of expressing themselves.

The more often children do something, the more strongly they are learning to do it. Our parental job includes doing our best to get them to repeat what is important for them to learn. Our guidance, encouragement and corrections all contribute to them learning well.

- When they spontaneously do something we want them to do, we encourage them so as to get them to do it, again and again and again. (For example, they are friendly and welcoming with visitors.)
- When they spontaneously do something that we don't want them to do, we discourage them from doing it, and encourage them to do what we want instead, again and again and again. (For example, they ignore visitors and go off to their rooms. So we encourage them to stay and say, 'Hello', to entertain other children of their ages, and only to go off to their rooms if released to do so.)
- When they spontaneously don't do something that we want them to do, we keep encouraging them to do it. (For example, they don't spontaneously go in and say 'Hello' and shake hands with visitors the way we want them to. So we teach them how to do it and then remind them to do it with everyone who visits.)

(See Chapter 9, 'Parenting with love', Chapter 10, 'The discipline sequence', and Chapter 11, 'Standing to decide' for guidance on how to do this.)

Things to repeat

It is both normal and important for us repeatedly to show them how to do up buttons, tell them what to say and how to say it, get them to look where they are going, remind them to do their household jobs and a myriad of other things.

> Repeating ourselves is not a sign that we are inadequate, nor that our children have nothing active between the ears.

It is also normal and important to repeat all the messages we want them to use for inner guidance. Here is a sample:

- Be on time.
- Put it back where you got it from.
- Go and have fun.
- Have you fed the dog (cat, bird)?
- Go and do your homework.
- Talk in a normal voice
- Remember to give me your school notices.
- Speak clearly.
- Have you washed your hands?
- Look for how you can make the situation better.
- Avoid making situations worse.
- If you're unkind to people, they probably won't want to play with you.
- Do what I tell you immediately.
- Wait your turn.
- Drive carefully.
- Come home on time.
- Think before you act and work out the likely consequences.
- Share and cooperate.
- Think of other people too.

As a timely reminder, we know that most children do learn easily and well in some areas. All learn more easily in some areas than others. We recommend that you notice where they do learn easily, or more easily – and celebrate.

Take heart

Persistence is well worthwhile, even in the midst of repetitious exchanges, when we get the impression that the process will go on forever. These impressions may explain why so many parents find this part of the job so challenging. However, as we persist, our children are affected.

- ***When we are repeating, they are learning.*** After a few years (let's say, 30!) you will be able to notice progress. Just remember what you were repeating a few years ago. You are likely to notice that you are only repeating some of this now. The rest is no longer necessary, because they are doing routinely what they are supposed to do.

- Also, when they repeat, so that we will repeat, it is as if *they are asking for more of their favourite desserts*. Don't let the fuss they make fool you. It might be an odd way of saying, 'More please'. But this is what they are saying. And the intensity of what they do, shows us the intensity of their desire for their 'just desserts'.

- *As we persist, they also learn to persist in their own lives.* The learning comes directly from us. Many a child has benefited from this. Unfortunately, also, many children have lacked follow-through as adults, because their parents gave up before they had learnt what they needed to learn.

A handy answer

When our children tell us to 'Stop nagging', knowing what you now know, you have a wonderful answer. Give it with confidence and flair, pausing for effect between each point.

> 'Yes I am nagging.
> It's my job to nag.
> And I will keep on nagging
> until you do what I'm telling you to do.
> So do it now.'

You may still get to the point of thinking, as our parents often did, 'If I've told you once, I've told you a thousand times, ...' However, this is a good sign if you do. Congratulate, rather than berate yourself. At a thousand times, you are probably getting closer to the required number. If not, another thousand or so should just about do it!

Eventually it's up to them

In the end, our children need to take over responsibility for reminding themselves and keeping themselves in line. Unless we are looking for lifelong jobs at their sides, we need to disengage eventually.

Many children make the transition naturally. This makes it easy for them and us. However, some children need a nudge to get them using what they have already got from us without our reminding them. And note that at times we may need to act strongly and decisively to achieve the desired results.

Chapter 16

Developing self-esteem

Most of us want our children to have good self-esteem. We want them to honour and value themselves realistically. Good self-esteem can form the foundation of many wonderful qualities, both during childhood and later in life.

This chapter contains a brief description of some things we can do to help our children develop self-esteem. The chapter is divided into two sections. In the first we discuss ways to help children develop it. In the second, we discuss things to do to help deal with low self-esteem.

At the outset, we point out that self-esteem is not a cure-all for problems, nor is its absence the cause of all problems. To solve some problems, children may need to develop other qualities, too. In fact, as we will see later in the chapter, sometimes having 'good self-esteem' even creates problems.

How to build self-esteem

A variety of things contributes to our children developing self-esteem. Each of them makes a significant contribution, so it is a good idea to do some or all of them.

Give complete acceptance

The foundations of good self-esteem are laid from the beginning of life. Babies who are loved with complete, loving acceptance are well on the way to developing it. Children loved like this are able to withstand all sorts of trials and tribulations. The love we bathe them in saturates the bedrock of their personalities. (See Chapter 9, 'Parenting with love' and Chapter 21, 'Phases of childhood' for more on this.)

Loving our babies with complete acceptance encourages the primary self-esteem of self-love.

We love everything about our babies when we love with complete acceptance. We don't need reasons. We just do. We love our children just because they are there, and for who they are. What they do, does not influence this love. We will love them forever in this way, regardless of what they do. This does not mean that we like everything about them, however. Nevertheless, our responses to what they do only begins to become conditional at about eighteen months of age. (See Chapter 10, 'The discipline sequence'.)

Provide active guidance and conditional acceptance

The next aspect of self-esteem comes from guiding our children to behave well with others. When they act according to the 'rules of living', we praise them. When they don't, we do things to discourage them from acting in those ways again. (See Chapter 10, 'The discipline sequence', Chapter 11, 'Standing to decide', and Chapter 12, 'Knowing when and how to act'.) In other words, we are selective about our responses.

In the process of becoming selective, however, we make sure of one very important distinction. We become selective about **what they do**, while we continue to accept fully **who they are**. Various themes are repeated with conditional acceptance.

- 'I love you and I don't like you behaving like this.'
- 'I like you doing that.'
- 'Well done', or 'You have done well.'
- 'Stop doing that. I don't like you doing that. Do such and such.'

Children who are well guided, who get clear messages about what is acceptable and what is not, usually feel confident with others. They feel secure in this, because they know where they stand with people. They know how to behave and how not to behave. They know what others like and dislike.

- Roy was a well-loved child, who nevertheless was very unsure of himself with children the same age. He used to go out of his way to avoid contact with them by playing alone in the schoolyard and staying on the edges of things in the classroom. Whatever he did at home was accepted, but at school he found most of what he did created trouble. As soon as his parents and teachers started an active program of teaching him how to relate to the other children, he became much more confident and more accomplished socially.
- Thea was also loved at home and as unsure of herself as Roy. The way she dealt with this was through boldness. She pretended everything was all

right and used to boss the other children around, bullying any of them who did not do what she wanted them to do. When her parents became systematic in challenging her bullying and tantrum-throwing behaviour at home, she became much more settled on the inside. Her confidence rose, because she was getting the guidance she needed about what to do and what not to do with others.

> Active guidance and conditional acceptance of our children's behaviour encourages the self-esteem that comes from relating well to others.

Expect self-control

People have self-control when they can make decisions and can follow through on them. Their decisions lead to the necessary actions. The sense of mastery this produces results in great self-esteem. It is the self-esteem of knowing that they can rely on themselves to perform well.

Think of the children you currently know who do what they do very easily. They don't seem to have any difficulties. They seem able to do whatever they set out to do. Compare these children to those who don't have the necessary abilities, who struggle to perform. Usually the differences in self-esteem between these two groups are very marked.

All of this comes naturally to some children. However, most need to learn it. They learn it directly from us, through our setting standards and limits, and our following through to ensure that our children act accordingly. By contrast, children with ineffective parents are much less likely to develop personal mastery and the self-esteem that goes with it. (See Chapter 10, 'The discipline sequence', for more on this.)

> Loving discipline encourages the self-esteem that comes from making decisions and following through on them.

Promote confidence in ability

Mastering skills can produce great confidence in children. Much self-esteem can arise from acting skilfully. We can support our children's abilities by applauding each new achievement and also by providing opportunities to challenge and extend them. Putting lots of effort into this usually pays off.

Nevertheless, we are wise to maintain a balance in this. If we push them to learn things that are beyond their current abilities, we can undermine their confidence. At the same time, if we hold them back, they will not have the opportunity to learn to meet and overcome new challenges.

- Even when only in primary school, Renata was expected to study maths every weekend under her father's guidance. In itself, this might have worked out well. Unfortunately, her father had no idea of what young children can learn. He set work that was far beyond her capacities. He compounded the problems for her by criticising and punishing her for not performing well. By the time she was an adult, her confidence in her ability to do things was seriously damaged.

- Oscar took ages to learn how to tie his shoelaces. His parents decided that while velcro would be easier, it was an important skill for him to learn, so they persisted. They got him to do as much as he could each time, and then one of them would finish the rest for him. Eventually, when they decided that it was time for him to do it all on his own, he resisted. 'I can't do it, Mum,' he said tearfully. But they persisted. His joy and sense of achievement when he succeeded was a great reward for all of them.

> Teaching children skills promotes the self-esteem that comes from personal mastery.

Insist on a contribution

Something happens inside us all when we can contribute to the people and systems that support us. Our contributions set up a circuit in which a flow develops in both directions, rather than just one. Many people are aware of the dissatisfaction that mounts when they give perpetually to others; many people are also aware of a dissatisfaction that mounts when they take too much from others.

The mutuality of sharing and exchanging of service has a wonderful effect on children. Instead of being dependent and having to rely on others, they can develop a sense of making worthwhile contributions to their families. As they get older, they can expand this to making valuable contributions to their schools, local neighbourhoods, their countries and then to the world.

The way we help children initially develop the self-esteem that comes from giving valued service to others, is through getting them to do chores at home.

We have already mentioned in several places, the importance of using chores as a way of preparing children for living in the world as adults. (See Chapter 1, 'Your job as a parent'.) The contribution to self-esteem that our children experience is another good reason for doing this. Those who don't know this from experience miss a great deal.

> *Maria had not been used to contributing. Her parents used to think that, 'Children are only young once, so we'll leave her to herself to enjoy it while she can'. After speaking to us, they decided to change what they had been doing, for Maria's benefit. They all sat down together and, much to her dismay, worked out a set of jobs for her to do. She was angry for a week or so and not very pleasant. After several weeks, they were all much happier. The sharing was mutually enjoyable and satisfying. Maria said to her mother at the sink one day, 'I didn't realised how much you and Dad did. I feel quite upset that I used to go and listen to music in my room or watch TV. And I enjoy doing all this now, too.'*

Doing chores helps our children develop the self-esteem that comes from making a valued contribution to others.

Encourage belonging

A sense of belonging is fundamentally important in self-esteem. Most children with good self-esteem have this. Many with low self-esteem do not. Belonging is experienced as 'I am important to (name)'.

What gives children this sense of belonging? The first element is having someone who is actively involved with them, who cares about them. The second is that this someone is accessible. The children can get to their special people to talk or do whatever else they need to do.

Interestingly, the belonging comes as much from the struggles children have with caring people, as it does from the good times. This makes sense, however, if you think about it. When we care enough to struggle with our children, to get them to do things that they may not want to do, we are very obviously saying, 'You belong with us and so you will do such and such'. Parents who avoid the tougher things like this do not convey this kind of belonging with the same strength.

Parents who are accessible and care enough to do both the tough and the soft things help their children develop the self-esteem that comes from belonging with someone.

Support realistic self-assessment

To have good self-esteem, children need a realistic impression of themselves. They need a grounded evaluation of their qualities and talents, and their attitudes and values in relation to others. With a realistic understanding of themselves, they are likely to be sensitive and aware of others, and to have a humble view of themselves. This is different from the arrogance, conceit, self-importance, selfishness and insensitivity that children can develop if their self-esteem becomes distorted.

The dependability of self-esteem is promoted by teaching our children to assess themselves and their talents realistically.

They are encouraged to be realistic by us being realistic with them. We need to give them practical, realistic and honest assessments of how they are acting, of the skills and talents they have, and of the effects on others of the things that they do. It is most important that we do this.

- 'No. You didn't do that well. You need to pay more attention here.'
- 'I realise that you feel you are right. But you are not. I will tell you what is true.'
- 'You did that wonderfully well.'
- 'Liking yourself is great. But condemning others is very unpleasant for them and they will react to you doing that.'
- 'There are some things that you cannot do yet. This is one of them. It is important that you not pretend that you can do things that you can't do.'

Summary

We help to make sure that children have good self-esteem by:

- loving them with complete acceptance
- giving them loving guidance on how to relate to others

- setting standards and limits to promote self-control
- teaching them the skills they need
- giving them real jobs to do at home
- spending lots of time with them and including them in our lives
- providing realistic assessments of their actual abilities.

Dealing with low self-esteem

What can we do to help turn things around with children who see themselves in a bad light? We have five general suggestions.

Acceptance

Use complete, loving acceptance at all appropriate times. While they may not accept us doing this openly at the time, it does make a difference. The idea is to persist through the days, weeks, months and, for some children, years that it takes.

- Say things like, 'I love you', 'You are a beautiful person', ' I like being with you'.
- Give them plenty of hugs and physical affection.
- Talk from the heart.
- Look lovingly at them.

Praise

Give true praise by acknowledging talents. Avoid exaggeration and false reassurance.

- 'You are sensitive, intelligent, capable, sporty.'
- 'You look great, dress well, do creative things.'
- 'You are dedicated, flexible, reliable, quick-witted.'

Guidance

Program the things that you want to become true. The idea of this is to think of things they are already doing and tell them that they do them. This will help build strength from strength. Avoid doing this to soothe or pretend. Also, give true examples of what you say.

- 'You remember well.'
- 'You like people and get along well with them.'
- 'You understand things easily.'
- 'You persist in the face of challenges.'

Sensitivity and realism

Deal with dejection and self-doubt directly by using sensitivity and realism.

- *Encourage the expression of feelings.* Do this by concentrating on the feelings for a while, not moving directly to problem-solving. (See Chapter 14, 'Paying active attention'.)
- *Give realistic feedback.* Our children know the truth. They know when we are making things up, or just saying something so they will feel better. Two examples are, 'You are capable and likeable', or 'No, you don't have many friends yet, that's true'. You might also add other thoughts, when they are ready for them, such as, 'Well you do act provocatively', or 'If you don't go and play with her, she won't know that you like her'.
- *Make practical suggestions about how to deal with things.* The more concrete and helpful these are the better. For example, 'If you want to make friends with her, say "Hello" every day when you see her. And smile and act in a friendly way'.
- *Follow up.* We do this to check that they are trying the suggestions we have made. As we follow up, three simple steps help:
  1. Talk to them to find out how they got on. Don't assume you know.
  2. Pinpoint and celebrate successes, even minor ones. Separate what they actually did from what they feel they did.
  3. Identify difficulties and deal with them as above.

The other side

Self-esteem is not a cure-all for problems, nor is its absence the cause of all problems. To solve some problems, children may need to develop other qualities, too. Sometimes having 'good self-esteem' even creates problems when children start to overrate their abilities.

Chapter 17

Managing brothers and sisters

Having more than one child can add great richness to everyone in a family. All sorts of pleasures and opportunities automatically arise that are not there with an 'only child'. Children learn through the repeated, intense exposure to each other that living together produces. This is extremely important in later life. So much so, that we recommend that families with one child do whatever they can to help their children have the contacts with other children that will help them do this kind of learning.

Living together with other children helps them:
- play together and entertain each other
- learn from each other through copying, teaching and competing
- learn to share and make space for others in their lives
- cooperate and do things in teams
- manage getting what they want when others miss out
- cope with missing out themselves
- love and support each other
- experience the inequalities of life and learn how to deal with them

While they get along well with each other, we can celebrate, encourage them to keep on with what they are doing and relax. At the same time, we advise you to remember to reinforce what they do at these times. By encouraging them actively, they will in all likelihood produce more of what we like. If, however, we mainly concentrate on them not getting along, then they are likely to keep not getting along, because that is when we seem to notice them. (See Chapter 10, 'The discipline sequence' and Chapter 13, 'Communicating clearly' for more on how to do this.)

While we think that this approach is crucial with children, we also need to act effectively when they have difficulties with each other. This chapter is primarily to do with handling the rivalries, competitions, jealousies, squabbles and other challenges that come under the broad heading of 'sibling rivalry'. This is a big issue in many families.

Well managed, sibling rivalry can be the basis of learning all sorts of helpful lessons for later life. Poorly managed, it can set people on a path of acting and reacting with others in adulthood in the same unhelpful ways as they did with their siblings as they grew up

Basic positions

Resolution between children is promoted by understanding three basic positions. These positions apply equally to adults. (See Chapter 8, 'Handling parental conflict' for more on this.)

Each of our children is different

Complete satisfaction in their lives, or resolution of any difficulties between them, relies on each of them understanding what we do from their own points of view. Whenever we get involved in situations with our children, it is most important that we find out what is going on for each of them. Their versions of events, motivations, understandings, feelings and goals might all be different. We need to check these, if we are to make what we do relevant to each of them.

- For the fourteen-year-old, keeping the seven-year-old out of his room might be what he wants, while the seven-year-old wants some time to play with his older brother.
- 'I didn't mean to knock over his Lego tower,' says the five-year-old, 'I was in a hurry to get past.' The two-and-a-half-year-old just keeps crying, clearly experiencing the event as an added insult during a day of working very hard at suffering. She is clearly beyond reasons making a difference at this point.
- 'She did it,' shouts one child. 'What a lie,' says the other, 'he did.' We wonder who did and, if we can, it's our job to find out who. Maybe both did, or someone else entirely.

'Where to from here?' is a shared issue

Whenever more than one child is involved, they always have a collective issue to sort out. They need to work out 'where to from here?'. How they will relate to each other from then onwards so they get along well is always important. We get the children to consider how both to promote ease and to manage likely conflicts in the future. A great way to do this is to get them to make agreements with each other. (See Chapter 10, 'The discipline sequence' and Chapter 11, 'Standing to decide' for more on this.) Whatever agreements they each make, need to deal with the issues from the points of view of each child making them. The agreements will help to guide future exchanges.

- One says, 'I'll knock before I come into your room in future. I won't just barge in'. The other says, 'I won't just yell at you to go away, if I don't want you to come in. I'll tell you "I'm busy" and give you a time when I'll be free'.
- One agrees, 'I'll talk politely to you from now on. Even when I'm angry, I won't call you names'. The other says, 'Good. I feel upset when you yell. But I'll talk to you first, even if you're angry. I won't just run to Mummy or Daddy.'

Sibling rivalry is normal

Children learn many important lessons as they learn to handle each other. That they squabble, compete and struggle with each other is not a sign that anything is wrong. Any two children are likely to do this at times. The important thing for us to do as parents is to teach them how to move through these kinds of situations to resolution. When all children involved have made clear what their points of view are and have made specific agreements with each other, then the process is finished.

Sorting things out

When encouraging changed behaviour between children, or when sorting out problems between them, we follow four basic steps. Sometimes the order of the steps is different from the one here; however, each step has a unique contribution to make.

1. Stop the action.
2. Get each child's story.
3. Parent each child.
4. Get them to talk to each other, to apologise and to make agreements.

Stop the action

This is most important, particularly if disagreements, or serious squabbles or fights are involved. Many parents have been told or have decided that it is best to leave children to work things out for themselves. Until all the children involved are experienced in sorting out their problems with each other, however, our experience is that this is not a good idea. Once they are experienced, on the other hand, we find that a time comes when we leave them to it. Possible things to do:

- Say, 'Stop what you're doing and come over here'.
- Move over to them and tell them to stop.
- Move over to them, get between them, if necessary, and insist they stop and pay attention to you.

Get each child's story

Asking each child his or her point of view is important. Useful questions include:

- What have you been doing?
- What do you think is going on?
- How did you both start? Then what did you (he/she) do? Then what?
- What did you do? Why did you do it?
- What do you want to happen now?
- What do you want (name) to do from now on?

A word to the wise: Our experience is that there are no innocent Victims (See Chapter 5, 'Family dynamics' for more on Rescuers, Persecutors and Victims in family dramas), so we parents are well advised to avoid taking sides. Our experience is that the apparent Victim always does something to provoke what occurs. A story illustrates this well.

> *A small boy called Colin came home from school one day, still outraged that a fellow student had punched him in the stomach. He was looking for sympathy from his father. Colin was surprised when his father's response was not sympathy, but a question: 'What did you do to get punched in the stomach?' After very little talk, Colin revealed that he had elbowed the other boy in the ribs just before getting punched. This somewhat changed the impression Colin was trying to create!*

Parent each child

Once we know what each child intended to do and actually did, we can give guidance, suggest other ways of handling things, make simple rules on what to do from now on, and set incentives and consequences if these will help. We may do quite a lot of this while getting the information, too. When, for example, they try to interrupt each other, we can say things like, 'No you wait your turn. I will talk to you next', or 'If you keep interrupting while we're talking, you'll go over there and "stand to decide" that you will wait patiently. You've already had your say'. This trains them in cooperative problem-solving.

For the best effect, the parenting and advice we give needs to be put so that each of the children understands it. The older the child, the more grown-up we can make our explanations and expectations.

Think about Colin again. The exchange may go like this. His father says, 'If you hurt people, you are very likely to get hurt yourself. So you keep your elbows to yourself from now on Colin.' Colin looks thoughtful. His father guesses what he might be thinking and adds, 'The other boy should not have hit you either. Neither of you should have done what you did'. Colin relaxes. Father continues, 'Now come over here so I can have a look at your tummy. While I do, you tell me what you will do from now on'. As his father checks for damage, he offers some appropriate sympathy. The instruction about future behaviour moves him to the next step of the process.

Talk, apologise and make agreements

Talking to each other

Throughout the sorting-out process it is very helpful to get the children to talk directly to each other. Whenever they say something to us that they have not said to the other one(s), we can get them to say it directly. Also, when they have said it, but have not been listened to, we can get them to say it directly again and ensure that they are heard and responded to. It doesn't matter that they have witnessed the whole conversation with us. It still makes a difference for them to do it with each other. Two examples are:

- 'Tell Jim what you just told me. And Jim, as Shelly does, I want you to think about how you feel and tell her after she has finished.'
- 'What about saying that to Kath now. Kath, I want you to keep quiet as David tells you and listen carefully to what he is saying about how he felt. His feelings matter, too.'

Apologies

Getting them to apologise to each other for any insensitivities, broken agreements, or for causing unwanted consequences is important. The act of apologising gets children to take responsibility for what they have done. It also helps to reveal any resistance in our children to them accepting their parts in the events. Examples are:

- 'I'm sorry for hitting you.'
- 'I apologise for standing in front of the TV so you couldn't see.'
- 'I didn't mean to stop you going to the movies. I didn't realise what I did would stop you and I'm sorry.'

Agreements

Once they are clear with each other on what they were doing and have apologised, we get them to make agreements with each other about the future. These help to pull together all the discussions and lead to change from then on. It would be a pity to spend all this time 'for nothing'!

As we have already discussed in several places, keeping the concentration on what they want with each other is worthwhile. This applies in the agreements they make as much as with anything else. So get them to tell each other what they like about each other as part of making the agreement. It helps children break through the 'oh yuck' barrier that some of them build up about the expression of love and affection.

The conversation may go like this. 'I like playing with you and want to have fun. I'll share my toys with you from now on if they are in the family room. I'll keep all my toys that I don't want you to play with in my room,' says the first child. 'I like that, because I like playing with you, too. I'll enjoy sharing my toys with you. I'll keep my hands off your toys, when they are in your room,' says the second child.

Take the time

As you have probably guessed, the process can be time-consuming. However, the benefits are well worth the time it takes. Think of two things: First, if you don't teach them how to do it, then they are likely to keep having difficulties that you will need to deal with. So you will end up having to get involved anyway. Deliberately following the four-steps process will teach them how to manage increasingly for themselves. Second, the children who have this kind of training grow up with highly developed capacities to act assertively on behalf of themselves, to remain sensitive to others, to negotiate for what they want and to handle themselves well when they are experiencing conflict with others. What a wonderful legacy from a few hours of structured talk when they are young.

What if their stories disagree?

As we all know, this is very unlikely to occur! However, when it does, how can we best handle things. We suggest the following, again not necessarily in the order given.

- Get reports from independent witnesses if possible. If you witnessed what occurred, you don't need other witnesses.
- Decide if both stories are likely to be true. Also, remember that sometimes both are right.

- If they can't both be true, tell them that what they are saying is not possible, that one or both of them is distorting the truth. Find out if this leads to a change of story.
- If so, then carry on from there.
- If not, then consider what is usually true with the children involved. This does not make it correct, but it may lead to progress. You can say, 'Well Jenny, you have often done such and such in the past, why should I not think that you have done it again this time. I've only got what you and (name) are telling me, so how can I know?' Find out if her answer gives you any more clues.
- We can also make guesses and tell them what our guesses are. We do this to test their reactions. As we do, we parent them on what we think they should have done and should do in future. Even if we guess wrong, they get more good parenting.
- We could tell them to 'stand to decide' to make sure that what they are saying is complete and true. The trouble with this is that the 'innocent' suffer along with the 'guilty'. Under some circumstances this might still be justified, however.
- If they continue to disagree, then we need to stay alert in the future so we witness what they do and don't need to rely on their stories. In the meantime, we parent them and set consequences and expect agreements that relate to their respective stories. We point out to them that we have to do this because we do not know the truth from them.

The following story shows how the fullness of time tends to correct unrecognised patterns. It also shows that it is best to find what our children have actually done with each other.

> We were visiting friends. We were all having breakfast. The son, Maurice, kicked his older sister, Helena, under the table. He made sure that his parents could not see what he had done. Helena yelped with pain and accused Maurice loudly. He, all injured innocence, suffered tearfully for the benefit of his parents and denied his guilt. Both parents said almost in unison, 'Helena, stop making things up'. Helena was outraged, but was clearly used to not being believed, because she immediately slumped in dejected submission. We also spoke in duet to Maurice, just after his parents, saying, 'That's a lie. I saw you kick Helena'. Her face was a picture of relief and amazement that she was believed. His was of incredulous rancour that we did not go along with his lie. We had broken 'the social rule' that guests should stay quiet at times like this. Maurice was counting on our silence to add weight to his position. Our response, however, exposed his guilt in an on-going persecution. Our friends

were also surprised, particularly at how long they had accepted Maurice's version of events. Their eyes were open from then on.

Other important guidelines

Here is a brief list of other guidelines that might help you in various situations.

- Set standards of behaviour between children and enforce them. For example, expect real sensitivity and respect between them. Also, remember to get real apologies and commitments to change, whenever they are necessary.
- Repeated patterns of difficulty between children frequently reflect conflicts within or between parents. We need to get our own acts together under these circumstances.
- Get the children to act kindly, lovingly, sensitively and with caring as a general way of living. With this as a background, many minor difficulties are much easier to deal with.
- Get them to do things regularly that involve sharing, even the older ones with the younger ones.
- Encourage individuality as well as cooperation.
- Help them learn to solve their problems together without your intervention.
- Tell them that it is all right for them to have different privileges. Underline that they are different people and different ages.
- Inequality is a fact of life. Deal with them according to their actual needs and the facts of situations, not only according to what they want or think they are missing. Practise acting in a matter-of-fact way about this. Your acceptance of this will help them accept it too.

Stay grounded in and open to reality. If they say, 'He's always allowed to do more than me', we say, 'Yes that's right. He's older than you. And that's okay. Your turn will come'.

- Use 'standing to decide' whenever you need to focus attention, encourage thinking, get acceptance, deal with entrenched resistance, shift children from nastiness, or stop the action. You can have all the children involved in an incident 'standing to decide' at the same time. We remember one time when we did not have any more space around the walls! About ten kids all got involved in something together and kept producing uproar until 'standing to decide' calmed them all down.

- When children feel jealous, get them to concentrate on what they want and on how to get it. Emphasise sharing. Jealous children often concentrate on what they are missing. They usually feel a mixture of anger, fear and sadness about what they are missing; and they feel blocked from feeling the love, or happiness they perceive someone else having with a third person. Getting them saying things like, 'Can I go next?' or 'Will you give me a cuddle too?' or 'I'd like to sit next to you, too. When can I?' often helps.
- Avoid trying to make things right for everyone. This can put us on a treadmill. All children need to learn to miss out at times and to accept this with good grace.
- Have a rule, 'Family membership carries with it the duty of giving proper respect to everyone. It is not a licence for abuse'. Some families' members behave very well with people outside the family, but not with the family members themselves.

When a child invokes the name of 'the Great God Fair' with the cry, 'It's not fair!', we reply simply and dispassionately, 'That's true. But it is just'. (We may need to explain what justice is, of course.)

PATTERNS IN CHILDHOOD

We shift gears a little in this section. So far we have mainly concentrated on fairly specific issues and specific things we can do about them. Now we turn to some overall patterns and some general orientations we have found valuable for making the most of those patterns.

Chapter 18

Natural transitions

Children make many transitions as they grow to adulthood. We deal with four of these in this chapter. Each is important for promoting the growth and development of our children. They are to do with:
1. Acceptance of behaviour
2. Understanding and learning
3. Freedom and control
4. Contributions to the family

Acceptance of behaviour

The way we accept our children's behaviour needs to vary according to their ages and abilities. We need to flow back and forth between *complete acceptance* and *conditional acceptance* as they get older. The following general guidelines can help you determine which to use when.

The early years

When they are babies we give them complete acceptance. Up to about eighteen months, this key ingredient helps to produce happy, fulfilled and capable adults. (We have discussed this more extensively in Chapter 10, 'The discipline sequence'.)

Increasingly from eighteen months, we move to conditional acceptance of what our children do. Through conditional acceptance, we train them how to live in the world. We do this by setting standards and limits that are appropriate to their ages and capacities. We praise and encourage what we want from them and do things to interrupt and discourage what we don't want. Then as the years pass, we continue to expand what we expect, until they are approaching thirteen years of age.

Thirteen and up

At about thirteen, we usually need to shift gears again, because young people often regress emotionally at about this age. (See Chapter 19, 'A second chance' for more on this.) This change signals the need to return to complete acceptance of their behaviour. Continuing to set standards and limits, and to use consequences in relation to them, is usually unhelpful at this age.

The ones who have become emotional babies will be unable to respond as we may want. It is beyond their capacities to make the connections. In fact, setting uncomfortable consequences usually only aggravates any difficulties. Thirteen-year-olds have a genuine vulnerability and dependency that we need to respond to with lots of nurturing. Only as they start to act with the wilful certainty of the fourteen-year-old, do we begin to get back to conditional acceptance. We then expand our expectations gradually as they become older, just as we did when they were younger.

Accept the person, shape the behaviour

As we set limits and standards, we are clear on the difference between the person and what the person is doing. We remain completely accepting of the person and conditionally accepting of behaviour.

- 'I don't like you doing that and you are to stop', is very different from 'I don't like you'.
- 'I love you and don't like what you are doing', is a helpful way to make the distinction at times.

(In Chapter 9, 'Parenting with love' you will find much more on this.)

Understanding and learning

Our children's learning involves four different streams. Knowing a little about these can help us to make it easier to teach and care for our children. Essentially, what we need to do is to adopt approaches that they can relate to and understand within whatever stream or streams predominate at the time.

The four streams are the body, feeling, thinking and being. Our children's learning relates to physical activity in the body stream, to expressing and sharing feelings in the feeling stream, to reasoning and discussion of issues in the thinking stream, and to general rules of conduct, morality and ethics in the being stream.

We discuss specific things we can do in each stream shortly. For now we want to introduce you to the general patterns. The following graph shows the ages at which the different streams are primary in our children's learning. As you look at it, notice the overlaps. Also, it is important to realise that children and young people are learning in all streams, regardless of the ones that are predominant.

Streams of learning

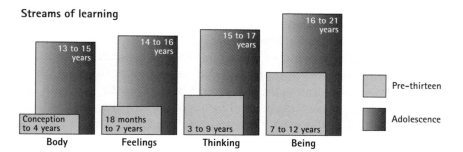

Gradual changes

Babies start off with a very physical focus (at conception). Then, as their physical growth and development continues to unfold, they begin to learn more about feelings and emotions (from about eighteen months). With both physical and emotional development progressing, learning how to think and reason moves onto centre stage (from about three years). At this point all three streams of learning are flowing at the same time. The final stream to appear is to do with 'Who I am' and with rules for living (from about seven years). They learn about what is 'right and wrong' and 'good and bad' and the basic rules we like to give them that govern how people relate.

At the beginning of adolescence, they start to go through the whole sequence again. So we find thirteen-year-olds needing much more physical emphasis in the way they learn. The rest of the sequence unfolds from there in the same order. At about fourteen, the emotional stream comes on line even more strongly than before; at about fifteen, thinking comes to the fore again; and at about sixteen 'Who am I?' surfaces along with developing values and ethics to guide behaviour.

To engage our children, we need to do so through the streams that are active. For them, too, to learn what they need in relation to each one, we need to match the way we teach them with what they are needing to learn. We will take each in turn.

The body stream

When children are physically centred, we are best to use physical methods of contacting, influencing, guiding and directing them. We may pick them up, take them by the hands, or put them physically through the motions of learning things. When they are adolescents, of course, we may not pick them up, but we may take them firmly by a hand or an arm to make a point. We can make sure we are in physical contact with them while we talk to them, as well. An occasional squeeze or nudge can keep their attention and help to fix the things we are saying to them.

The feeling stream

When feeling-centred, it is the expression of feeling that has the impact. The overlap with physical centredness may make physical intervention effective during this time as well. However, the physical aspects of what we do are likely to have little impact on the feeling dimensions.

- 'I like/don't like what you're doing', said as passionately as it is felt.
- 'I feel (name of feeling, e.g. happy) about this', said while showing the feeling mentioned.
- 'I want you to do (say what you want)', said showing your desire as you say it.

During the feeling phases, children connect significance and intensity. High intensity usually means something is highly significant, low intensity means something is not very significant. So we are best to allow our feelings to hang out or show. Here we can take permission to act emotionally with our children. They can thrive on it.

To some this is a great relief! Show them when you feel happy, sad, loving, angry, secure, or fearful. Those who generally think that reason and detached discussion are the best options, however, often find this difficult because of their discomfort with feelings. However, their 'natural' preferences rarely work as well as direct feeling expression, when we are dealing with the feeling stream.

- Compare: 'I love you', said very lovingly to a young child, with
    'Well now, love is an interesting phenomenon and something I often experience when in your proximity' said neutrally.
- Compare: 'I feel very angry with you for doing that', said very angrily, with
    'What you did is likely to provoke me at the best of times. Indeed, I suspect it would provoke most people', said abstractly.

The thinking stream

When thinking-centred, it is discussion of situations, causes, effects, reasons, consequences, implications and understanding that has the most impact. During these moments or periods, our children can respond well to expressing their thoughts and to exchanging ideas with us. We can valuably tell them what we understand and encourage them to think about this. We can also expect them to think for themselves, and to make decisions based on an integration of thinking, feeling and action.

- 'I think that I would only make things worse if I hit Jo when I'm angry. He would only hit me back. So I'll control myself and talk to him about what I don't like when I feel angry with him.'
- 'I like her and want her to like me. She thinks it's very uncool to show feelings, though. So I'll act cool myself and play down what I'm feeling, so I can make a date. After we get to know each other more, I can maybe tell her what I feel.'

The being stream

Being-centred learning starts off very concretely prior to adolescence. It becomes progressively more developed and based on principles as our children approach adulthood. When pre-adolescent, their appreciation of people and of how to relate is rule-based. So, we teach them what is 'right and wrong' and 'good and bad'. Particularly during the time between seven and twelve years of age, children think very concretely and literally. They usually do their best to live according to the rules they have been given in concrete and literal ways. They often also expect others to conform similarly.

- 'That's wrong. You shouldn't do that.'
- 'It's not fair that you always go first.'

Through the adolescent years, particularly from about sixteen to 21 years of age, young people begin to realise that rules have only limited value. There is not a rule for everything. This prompts them to generate more general ways of guiding their lives. They develop their own values, principles of living and ethics.

- Honesty is a good thing.
- It is best to talk openly and directly with people.
- Other people matter and we need to care for and about them.

During the adolescent being stream, we encourage them to learn by helping them to apply values, principles and ethics to different situations. Intense debates are common and useful. Here are some questions that often help the discussions.

- Is that the kind of thing you want others to do to you?
- What kind of person do you want to be?
- Is this the kind of thing that the person you want to be would do?
- What would be the just thing to do?
- Why do you think you/he/she/they should have preferential treatment?

Combinations

When children occupy more than one stream, we simply combine the streams in our activities.

- Reaching out to touch our child (physical stream), we say very emotionally, 'I feel very scared when you act like that (feeling stream). I think you know better than to put yourself at risk by running onto the road without looking. You could have been seriously injured or killed (thinking stream). I've told you that you have to look after yourself and not put yourself at risk (being stream)'.

Freedom and control

Striking the right balance between freedom and control is an ongoing challenge for parents. We have already mentioned the way we see this. It is our job to nurture, protect and guide our children through their developing years.

In the beginning they are totally dependent on the adults around them to care for and protect them. So in the beginning we exercise a very high level of control. We need to ensure that they are safe, both through guarding them actively and by making the places where they are free to roam safe for them. (See Chapter 1, 'Your job as a parent' and Chapter 12, 'Knowing when and how to act'.)

- We 'baby proof' the house when they become mobile, moving sharp or heavy objects away, so they cannot harm themselves. We don't leave babies unattended in rooms with unguarded objects, such as heaters, or stoves with pots on them.
- Swimming pools are fenced, garages are closed and locked, poisons are securely stored out of reach, so young children cannot get into trouble with them. If a present danger cannot be dealt with, then children are restricted, so they cannot get into trouble with or be harmed by it.
- They are accompanied to places until they are old enough to cross streets safely and to negotiate all the various hazards that going from one place to another involves.

- Children are always supervised by adults, closely when they are young and more loosely as they get older. Adult supervision of some form is necessary until they have reached middle to late adolescence.

To make the necessary decisions about how much freedom to allow our children, we need to know what they can handle and what they cannot. Direct observation is the best way to do this. And while we may listen to what our children claim, we don't uncritically accept their claims.

Children and young people often overrate their abilities, when fuelled by the desire to do what they want to do. We do well to remember that, even if all their friends do it, or that we are the most reactionary, limiting and unfair parents on the face of the planet, it is our job to make a sensible decision. The only realistic basis for these decisions is our answers to the questions: 'Can they actually handle this situation?' and 'Will they be safe?'

In adolescence, when they start to look so adult and develop the typical 'nothing can go wrong' assurance, many parents are tempted to allow more than is actually good for their children. We need to remember that thirteen-year-olds become emotionally very young again. It takes several years for them to grow emotionally to the level of maturity that allows us sensibly to let them decide most things for themselves. If anything, our children need us to tighten our hold on the reins in their early adolescence, not loosen it. (See Chapter 19, 'A second chance'.)

Contributions to the family

We imagine that children will properly leave home as adulthood approaches, provided all has gone well. When they leave, the ones that usually do best have learned to do all the practical, self-maintaining things that living by themselves requires. We can help to ensure they do know all of this by expecting them to contribute to the running and maintenance of the household. The list of all that they will need to know is the curriculum they need to complete before leaving home.

Our principle is to have children doing as much as they reasonably can at every age. When they are young, we start with small things. As they get older and more capable, we expand what they do.

- Starting as soon as they can toddle around and carry something, we get them involved. They can help to clean up their toys and mess at the end of play. As they get older and more competent, we get them to carry plates or utensils to the sink after meals.

- Young children can have daily jobs like opening curtains, clearing wastepaper baskets, putting toys away, tidying rooms with help, and washing and drying dishes under supervision. They can also begin to learn to cook simple things, by mixing ingredients together, and peeling fruit and vegetables with safe knives. They can help to take their own washing to the laundry, and help with bed-making and other jobs in their rooms. Much of this needs to be supervised and much can be done as a game. Kids love playing house.

- As they get even older, we may expect them to do all their own washing, help on regular, specified days with meal preparation, put rubbish bins out, clean driveways, do vacuum cleaning, clean bathrooms, deal with dishes daily and many other things. They can also, for example, gradually take over responsibility for one evening meal a week, where they plan and cook the whole meal.

- As they become aware of money, we introduce pocket money. The money is paid to them regularly with the statement that it is related to the performance of their weekly tasks. We use this as a vehicle to learn about saving and budgeting, and payment for work. When they are ready, we move to expecting them to use some of their money to make regular, basic purchases, like soap and toothpaste. Naturally the amount we give them is geared so they can do this. With greater age and sophistication, we move to them taking over purchasing some, then all of their personal hygiene items and clothing. By this stage, they would also be expected to be budgeting and planning ahead. If they have work, we would expect some of the income to be paid into the household as board. This helps them to learn to contribute to the upkeep of the system that is supporting them.

- By the time they are in middle to late adolescence, they are expected to contribute to the household at the same level as an adult member of the family. They would be doing all the usual self-maintenance jobs plus sharing the family maintenance jobs.

Through introducing these jobs gradually as they get older, most children and young people manage the process very easily. They also thrive on the chance to contribute. Where contention and challenges arise, they can be dealt with as part of the normal routine of family life.

Naturally, we parents need to monitor the overall demands we make on our children and balance these with other demands, such as the load of homework from school. However, our repeated experience warns us of the dangers of parents doing too much. Parents who do household jobs for their children are doing them a very great disservice. They are training them into dependency on others. Often, too, they inadvertently train them to use others, rather than to live in contributing ways with them.

We need to think long and hard before we consistently do for our children, either what they are capable of learning to do, or what they are already capable of doing for themselves. The young people who most easily move out into the world and take advantage of the many opportunities available to them, are the ones who have learned how to do the many ordinary things in life. We think parents have a responsibility to prepare their children to do this and to have the potential to act as good citizens.

The right balance

Many fads come and go in parenting. Each one may have something important to contribute; however, it is important not to overstate the value of any one of them. Consider your own parenting style in relation to these:

- 'All that children need is understanding.'
- 'Be permissive, don't set limits. Our job is to encourage creativity.'
- 'Discipline is what they need. Set limits and enforce them.'
- 'Talk to them, find out what motivates them, then engage them through what they want.'
- 'All they need is plenty of opportunity for physical exercise.'
- 'Children should be allowed to play until nine years of age, not have to attend school.'
- 'Parents are the key, and all we need are good parent education programs.'
- 'Children have to be well fed.'
- 'Whatever they do, just love them.'

Your child's different needs

At different times children need understanding, permissiveness, discipline, discussion, physical exercise, play, good parenting, good nutrition and love. If we provide only a limited number of these and act as if this is all they need, we are very mistaken. Different children need different experiences so that they grow in balanced ways.

- Teach very emotional children to think as well.
- Get the thinking ones to express their feelings too.
- Regularly encourage the overactive ones to stay physically still.
- Prompt the underactive ones to get busy at times.
- Help the overcooperative ones to stand their ground.
- Motivate the rebellious or reactive ones to cooperate.
- Insist that the careless ones take care.

Parents who balance their parenting like this usually have a much easier and more rewarding time.

Chapter 19

A second chance

This chapter is a lot to do with adolescence, both what occurs during adolescence and how to prepare for it, so we can to make it as easy as possible. We urge you to read it, even if your children are yet to arrive there. Acting before they get there is the best idea, then when your second chance comes you will have done as much as you can beforehand.

The whole process we consider in this chapter starts with the beginning of adolescence. At this time, parents often notice several significant changes. The changes are so marked in some young people, that we can easily wonder what is going on. Some parents even become quite alarmed, usually unnecessarily, we are glad to say. The changes can be that:

- previously mature and self-sufficient children become childlike and dependent again;
- we have to repeat old lessons, after thinking they were already well-learnt;
- they seem just as demanding as the babies they once were and remain very demanding for several years;
- passions and dramas become much more frequent again.

Two general phases

We can understand what is happening at this time, when we notice how childhood divides into two clear phases. With this understanding, we can deal with everything much more easily. The phases are different and, at the same time, similar.

Through the whole of childhood, from conception to 21 years of age, children go through a predictable developmental sequence. In each stage of this sequence, we need to parent them so their changing needs are met. We also need to provide the matched learning opportunities that they are ready for in each stage. This evolving process forms a backdrop to the two phases mentioned.

The first phase runs from conception to about twelve years of age. The second one runs from around thirteen to about 21 years of age. During the first phase the developmental sequence unfolds with predictable regularity with most children. During the second phase, by contrast, something else is added. While the stages continue to unfold predictably, young people start to recycle past stages, too.

Young people rework the experiences that they are carrying with them from earlier in their lives. During the seven years or so that their reworking takes, they review the past and modify its remnants. It is a wonderfully creative process. And parents have a very important part to play in this reworking and reviewing process.

The review gives our children a second chance. Of course, not all young people need a second chance. If things have gone well in their lives, then they may need to do very little. However, the more troubled, abusive, neglected, or unhappy their lives have been up to this stage, the more actively and obviously they will go through the process.

A second chance

When all goes well, our twelve-year-old children have grown into lovely, childlike, autonomous young people. Compared with the previous years, we offer them quite a degree of freedom and have fairly high expectations of their abilities. Many parents feel the relief of the greatly reduced demands their children make on them. However, these qualities do not usually last.

The beginning

Some time near their thirteenth birthdays, children usually change significantly. They revert emotionally to very young ages. It is as if they become babies in big bodies. They are not actual babies, of course, but they often feel like babies and act like them, too. This shift is the beginning of the second chance or review period.

Some common signs that this stage has begun are:

- Very large sons and daughters try to crawl into their mothers' laps for cuddles.
- They can become inclined to intense upsets, perhaps crying continually for hours with nothing seeming to console them.
- Tasks that they coped with easily before, become overwhelming to them.

- Their memories and sense of time seem to dissolve. They forget things they have agreed to do and are often late for things.
- Before going to school, or when arriving home, they may cry copiously about how, 'It's all too much'.
- Many become very dreamy. They may get halfway through an activity, such as dressing, only to stop and stand or sit in some sort of trance without any awareness that time is passing.

What was your experience of this time in your life? And what is your experience of your own children, if they have already turned thirteen? Here are some parents' responses to what we have just described.

- 'Oh, my children will never do that,' said one father of younger children. He learned otherwise.
- 'My children all did that. I wish I'd known about it beforehand, so I could have been prepared.'
- 'Our daughter just breezed through this time in her life. Everything was really easy.'
- 'It's such a relief now that I understand what was going on. I thought I was going crazy, or that they were.'

As already mentioned, some children go through this time very easily, so we don't expect everyone to recognise the beginning signs. In our experience, however, no matter what the children show externally, or do publicly at the beginning, they experience some level of regressiveness. Even those who are showing little overtly, can benefit from some of the suggestions we make about handling this time. The ones who show very clear signs will usually benefit from the much stronger application of the suggestions. (See particularly Chapter 21, 'Phases of childhood' for specific suggestions about what to do.)

Then what happens?

Having reverted internally to 'emotional babyhood' again, our young people experience their lives as if they are babies. This is one reason for the extreme dependency they demonstrate. As they do, they are reviewing the very earliest programs in their lives. When we provide the right support to them and help them to update these programs, they will start to grow up emotionally again. The sequence is very predictable with most young people.

Starting with emotional babyhood at thirteen, they progress to 'emotional two-year-olds at fourteen, and onwards through several other stages to 'emotional twelve-year-olds by the time they are about 21. The parallels between the actual and the emotional ages generally match the pattern in the graph.

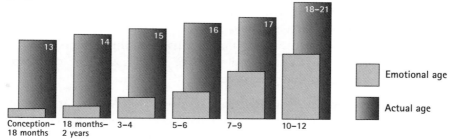

13	14	15	16	17	18–21

Emotional age

Actual age

Conception–
18 months | 18 months–
2 years | 3–4 | 5–6 | 7–9 | 10–12

Some specific changes

As they go through the review, they erase some old programs and modify others. Their current experiences are the basis of the reprogramming that they do. For example:

- One thirteen-year-old who was 'hushed' repeatedly as a baby is encouraged to cry openly to release unhelpful inhibitions on expressing her feelings.
- A fourteen-year-old is vigorously encouraged to listen to others and to do what he is told, whereas he was allowed to do whatever he chose as a two-year-old.
- At fifteen, a girl is encouraged to express her opinions, ask questions and discuss things, to replace parental criticism and impatience from when she was three and four years of age.

This is where we have a second chance. By identifying what we would have liked them to have experienced with us when they were younger, we can make it available to our young people when they go through adolescence. We can pay particular attention to those times in their earlier lives when we know things were less than we would have liked. The graph can help us to move from the ages of concern to the ages in adolescence in which we may get our second chance most obviously.

- Your five-year-old never completely dealt with her tendency to try and set up fights between other people. You can look at the graph and see that you will have another chance when she is about sixteen years of age.

At the same time, as they go through the adolescent years, our young people continue to learn many new things. No previous programming exists in many areas, so we need to remain active in helping them to learn about themselves, other people and the world. Their lives change and expand very quickly at times. They will need to learn:

- to adjust to bodily changes
- to learn how to manage rapidly-expanding school demands
- to master getting to know the boys and girls they like
- to take personal responsibility when they have no adult supervision

What you can expect

As we deal with our adolescent young people, we need to keep track of their emotional ages as well as their physical ages. If we don't do this, their development will be inhibited or blocked. And everyone is likely to have a much tougher time. If we do it, they will usually mature wonderfully over the seven years involved, into poised, well-balanced young adults. For example:

- When they are thirteen, we need to remember that they are emotional babies and take a lot of primary care of them, while we do all the other necessary things with them.
- When they are sixteen, we need to remember that they emotionally act like six-year-olds and manage them accordingly.

As they relive experiences from the past, they will often think, feel and behave as they did when young, although they may not have specific memories of the events that they lived through then. All that has gone well for them arises, along with all that has not. So, for example, if between seven and nine years of age, your child learned to follow through on jobs and take responsibility for himself or herself, then at seventeen, you are likely to have much less to teach and have a much more reliable son or daughter.

When they are dealing with troubled times from the past, their experience may involve the same levels of distress as they experienced then. This can be very disturbing for everyone. However, it is normal and we can deal with what is occurring and help all young people move on.

Do it while they are young

These prospects create a great incentive to provide what our children need in the first twelve years of their lives. If your children are pre-adolescent, we urge you to act now. Don't wait. (See Chapter 12, 'Knowing when and how to act', particularly the material on 'Imagining the future' for some of the value of doing this.) It is worth it from several points of view:

- The whole of their childhoods can be very much easier and happier.
- The momentum of undesirable behaviour and other patterns is minimised.
- Adolescent years are very much easier for all concerned.

'Everything' becomes easier

By doing what is needed when it is needed, children are generally much happier and more at ease. This makes them much more tranquil, satisfied, and easier to live with and manage. And we avoid the more intense repetition of the same issues during the adolescent review.

- Unloved, needy babies remain demanding. They continue to feel unloved and needy throughout their childhoods, until someone meets their needs. The neediness puts ongoing pressure on all involved with them.
- A disgruntled, suffering, unresponsive, or wilful two-year-old will turn into a disgruntled, suffering, unresponsive, or wilful child at all succeeding ages, unless something is done to interrupt the patterns.
- A happy, light-hearted, responsive, obedient child, someone we can all strive to create, is a joy to have close to us. And this style will travel with him or her throughout childhood, with the momentum getting stronger with every passing year, much to everyone's delight.

> Get it done now, while they are young, small and manageable. This is much easier than having to do it when they are older, bigger and beyond easy influence and control.

Momentum is reduced

The more children act in particular ways, the more inner momentum these actions develop. So, generally, the longer patterns go unchanged, the harder they are to change. During late childhood, or during adolescence, after all the previous years, the momentum of some behaviour will be considerable. Think of the extra intensity that doing something for three, five, ten or even fifteen years could add.

- A fourteen-year-old, rerunning his two-year-old experiences, is very much more difficult to handle than the original two-year-old ever was. Imagine handling the tantrums, pouts and suffering of nine- or twelve-year-olds. The same behaviour in a fourteen-year-old who is 175 centimetres tall and weighs over 65 kilograms, provides enormous challenges. It is much better to get these struggles resolved when they are 75 centimetres tall and only a fraction of the weight.
- If we insist from early in life that our children listen to us and respond immediately, it will be easier to have discussions with them in adolescence.

They get into a 'good habit'. The years of basic training pay off, so that even when spoiling for a fight in adolescence, they will keep talking to us rather than withdraw. Contrast this with allowing them when younger to ignore us, or to respond when they choose.

- It is much harder to change a pattern in a fifteen-year-old who has felt dejected for years, than to deal with its first appearance in a temporarily unhappy three- or four-year-old.

Adolescence is much easier

From their earliest years, it is well worth providing for children as fully and completely as we can, even if this means considerable disruption to our personal plans and preferences. Time well spent, this is a direct investment in future ease and satisfaction for all concerned.

- We had a family of five staying with us. The three boys were sixteen, fourteen and eleven. We have known the parents since the birth of the first. And it was a wonderful experience. The children were responsive and fun. They played cooperatively, listened to instructions and did what was expected (most of the time). They helped with meal preparation, joined in on activities with the adults, and generally impressed us as wonderful, reliable young people. Raised using most of the principles outlined in this book, they are living testament to the value of starting as early as possible.
- By contrast, we know another family who raised their son very differently. He was allowed to do whatever he felt like doing. From the age of two, he made such a fuss when expected to conform to his parents' wishes that they gave up. We told them at the time about how this kind of thing repeats in adolescence and is much harder to manage then. However, they preferred to define the problem as a combination of dyslexia and hyperactivity, rather than confront their lack of will to exercise control with him. Now at sixteen, he is even more uncontrolled. He is underperforming at almost everything, because he has little self-discipline. He is verbally abusive and physically threatening to both his parents whenever he feels like it. Had his parents done what was necessary to deal with what he was doing at three years of age and onwards, he would be a very different person now.

No exceptions. It will return.

What we do and don't do with our children when they are young, travels with us all into the future. We have never seen an exception to this.

Chapter 20

Four births, four bonds

Obviously, birth is a major event in our lives. What is not so obvious to many people is that we need to go through four different births, if we are to complete our development as human beings. The first three births are highly significant to our children's progress to full adulthood.

In this chapter we outline these four births and then discuss their importance. Note that our outline is 'ideal' and we recognise that many children may not complete the births as suggested. Knowing the 'ideal', nevertheless, can give us clear guidance on how to support the completions that they need.

The first birth – baby

During the first birth, the foetus moves from its mother's womb to the outside world. This *physical birth* occurs after about nine months of growth in the womb and can take up to several days. (See Chapter 21, 'Phases of childhood' for more on this.) Because we say our children are aged zero at birth, we can easily miss this growth and imagine that nothing has gone beforehand. The birth relocates babies physically with their mothers and fathers in the outside world, where they will continue to grow and develop. They learn through bonding that *they belong physically with their parents*. During the process they make a transition from foetus to new born baby.

Birth 'mother'

The mother is the physical mother of the child. The birth canal is the womb and the vagina.

Beginning

After nine months or so in the womb, the baby signals its readiness to be born and the contractions start.

Birth process

The birth is a physically interactive process between mother and baby. Both have important parts to play. On one side, the baby participates actively through its own physical movements and through chemical exchanges with the mother. On the mother's part, her own movements and the contractions are matched responses that provide what the baby needs for a successful birth. The contractions move the baby through the birth canal towards the world.

Delivery

The baby emerges into the physical world from the birth canal. A great sense of relief and release is often experienced by the mother and baby at this point.

Bonding

The birth process, when natural, is highly stimulating for both mother and baby. The stimulation primes them for bonding with each other. Immediately upon delivery, the baby is given to the mother with the father present. When she is ready, the baby is put to the mother's breast. The baby bonds with the mother and the father during this time. (See Chapter 21, 'Phases of childhood' for more.)

We cuddle our babies, look at them, talk to them, sniff and nuzzle them. We tell them how beautiful they are and how much we love them. We welcome them to our bodies and the physical world.

This bond is the baby's lifeline to its parents. It enables the baby to enter the parent–child relationship within which it will grow for about the next two years. Through this bond, babies know that they belong with their parents.

After a healthy and complete gestation, and a birth during which everything goes well, the outcome is a beautiful baby ready for the next stage of its growth. The miracle unfolds further from there.

The second birth – child

During the second birth, the baby moves from inside the womb of the parent–child relationship into the world of the family. This *emotional birth* usually takes about a year and begins at about two years of age. Babies do not relate to others emotionally in the same way as older children. This birth helps to reorient them so they can do the emotional learning they need for later life. It helps them to learn *to feel who they are in relation to others*. During the process they transform from babies into 'newborn' children.

Birth 'mother'

The 'mother' is the family of the baby, particularly the parents. The birth canal is formed by parents, their expectations and what they do with the baby. Other significant people – like siblings, and relatives and friends who spend time with the baby – may be part of the birth canal as well.

Beginning

At about eighteen months old, our children's behaviour generally changes. This is the signal that the child is ready to be born and the stimulus for parental contractions. Often becoming increasingly wilful and angrily self-absorbed, they also become less consolable and less easy to distract into enjoying themselves. On some days, they seem capable of producing misery, discomfort and struggle at the smallest provocation.

Birth process

The birth is an emotionally charged series of exchanges between the family and the baby. Parents are usually the most significant grown-ups in this. Babies dislike what they find uncomfortable in their lives and don't like some of what we expect. They push against these things. Their natural part in the birth process is to do this. What they want and don't want, what they feel, what they like and dislike, are all commonly at the centre of their struggles. Common statements are: 'I don't want to', 'I want to', 'I feel like ...', 'I don't feel like ...', 'I won't', 'You can't make me', and, of course, 'No!'

The families' primary job is to push back. Each push is a contraction that enables the birth to progress. The way we push is to set standards and limits that are properly matched with two-year-old children. What makes this easier is that we usually become increasingly determined or impatient with our children's behaviour at around this time. Feeling like this makes it relatively easy to persist or hold out with them over what they need to learn.

Through the months that follow, we will spend many hours doing this sort of thing. Expressing our feelings is a very important part of all of this. Not only is it normal and all right to feel upset, it is an important part of the process. Each time we do anything to meet their challenges, we help them to move a little more through the emotional birth canal. 'Standing to decide' really shows its value through this time. (See Chapter 11, 'Standing to decide'.)

Some days are fairly easy. We can thankfully rest between contractions. Whenever we have challenging, high-intensity exchanges with the children, the contractions have started again.

Delivery

We know that the child is delivered when our babies turn into young children in front of our eyes. The shift is usually obvious although sometimes gradual. Our somewhat unappealing, unhappy, demanding two-year-olds turn into lovely little people. These children are very different from the big babies with whom we have been engaging for the previous year. They become open, easy, cooperative and available in all sorts of ways. These children have a beautiful freshness and wholeness. The change is usually completed at about three years of age. Everyone generally feels great emotional relief and a sense of fulfilment, just like at the end of the physical delivery.

Bonding

The previous twelve months primes the whole family. All of us are usually affected by the antics of our two-year-olds doing their thing. The two-year-olds are usually just as primed and ready for a change when it comes too. They are not comfortable with the birth process either. After they shift, we all have a wonderful opportunity to come together in loving, friendly, companionable and cooperative ways.

We encourage newly delivered children to bond with the family as a whole. We tell them how beautiful they are, how well they are growing up and how wonderful it is to have them in the family. We welcome them as family members. We can give them jobs to do for their families and talk about these as their contributions to everyone in them. Through this, they know that they belong within their families.

The emotional bonds are lifelines to the family. The family forms the primary context in which the child grows and develops for about the next eleven years.

Babies who complete the second birth are true children. They are beautiful creatures. They have a self-contained poise, a balance and a maturity that is lovely. They can take the initiative and get what they want at the same time as having the capacity to wait patiently for what does not come immediately. They can think clearly, manage their own feelings, decide how they are going to act, and follow through. Usually doing what they are told to do, they clearly also make their own choices. These are very important results, as they mean our children are no longer subject to the whim of their feelings.

Having painted this wonderful picture, we hasten to add something important. These qualities are by no means fully formed in three-year-olds. It will be years before they are. However, when we handle the process well, a very firm foundation for all of this is laid during the second birth.

The third birth – adult

During the third birth the child moves from inside the womb of the family into the wider community. This *cognitive birth* usually takes about a year and begins when our children are about fourteen years of age. Children do not think in the same way as adults. They have much to learn about knowing and reality, and living life based on these. The third birth helps to adjust their ways of processing of reality so they can do this learning. It helps them learn *to know who they are in relation to others*. During the birth they transform from children to 'newborn' adults.

Birth 'mother'

The 'mother' is the community, particularly the young person's parents and other significant adults. The birth canal is formed by the community, its expectations (particularly adult expectations) and what key people do with the child. Parents and family members are still primary. Others might include teachers, family friends, employers, welfare personnel, the media, the police, and other young people.

Beginning

As thirteen-year-olds approach their fourteenth birthdays, they usually change in ways that signal the young person's readiness to be born into adulthood. The changes stimulate the necessary contractions from the community of adults with whom this 'big child' mixes.

Dependent and vulnerable at thirteen, as the change occurs, our children become increasingly disgruntled, wilful, argumentative, uncooperative, passionate and inclined to tantrums. For a while, they may go back and forth between this kind of thing and their vulnerable dependency. However, as the birth gets well established, these young people will spend much of the time dealing with life from an angry, disgruntled, wilful core.

Birth process

The birth is usually highly charged, with many exchanges about knowledge, how to know and perception. For example, 'You're wrong', 'What do you know?!' 'I know more than you', 'You can't teach me anything', and 'You don't know anything'. As they take their stands, our children are often filled with emotion and passion to do with what they think they know.

They often push and struggle and strain. They will do it with any handy adult who matters to them. Adults in the community have the job of pushing back. Each response is a contraction that helps the 'baby adult' to get born.

Our responses are much more than blind reactions to what they do, however. They are deliberately educational. We insist on them meeting our realistic and appropriate standards, and on them abiding by our clearly set limits.

While we parents carry a lot of the weight of the process, other adults definitely have their parts to play. School teachers are particularly important at this time. Joining forces with each other is a very good idea. The community as a whole needs to have an impact on the adolescent. The more united we adults remain in the process, the easier the transition often is. To help produce apparent unity, it is sometimes useful to limit or control the contacts our children are making outside the family.

They can struggle over almost anything in their lives, anything from making a bed, to doing homework, to staying out late at night, to leaving home. At their most intense, young people may yell and scream, throw tantrums, slam doors, physically assault us, or walk out of the house 'never to be seen again'. Much of the time, mercifully, they are more restrained than this.

Whatever they do, we need to remember that our job is to struggle back and to 'win'. Each time we do, the labour progresses. We may need to do our own shouting and yelling to engage with them effectively and to ensure that they hear what we are 'saying' above their own noise. Like with the two-year-old, this is a very emotional time, however, the issues are older and more grown up, and to do with their developing thinking capacities. By hanging in there until they are finished, we help to deliver them.

The delivery

At delivery, we observe a very obvious shift. Our difficult, argumentative adolescent children turn into lovely 'newborn' adults. This change may occur suddenly or gradually. Like the three-year-old, except that they are more experienced, the fifteen-year-old is open, available, cooperative, interested in others, attractive, curious about the world and happy. We can see the self-contained maturity that will continue to unfold. What a relief!

The bonding

By the end of the birth, everyone is usually ready for a break. The previous year can be very stimulating, even very upsetting. As the struggles end and our young people's developing maturity becomes obvious, we adults are primed for a change of pace. They are also primed and ready. They need to bond with the adult community. We help them do this by welcoming them into the adult world.

We talk to them as adults, thereby calling upon the maturity that is now available in them. We celebrate their talents and show them our love for them. By giving them grown-up things to do that make real and significant contributions to the community, we show them the increased respect in which we now hold them. They can be given expanded privileges and responsibilities in the home, too. We point out to them that these actions are a response to their entry into the adult community.

Their bonds with the community help them to know their place in the wider world in which they will continue to live. This also helps them to develop a sense of belonging in the world.

The 'newborn' adults who complete this third birth are powerful, creative, alive, self-contained, sensitive, and happy. Still very young and immature in terms of life experience and abilities, they are, nevertheless, beautiful young people who are ready to go on developing into wonderful adults through the next six years. They learn increasingly how to live in the grown-up world by taking expanding responsibility for themselves until they are ready to take over completely. They learn to relate to others with maturity and sensitivity, to contribute to the world around them, and to find ways of expressing their own meanings and purposes in the daily events of their lives. They grow into fine young adults.

Oh how wonderful!

We imagine that you are looking forward with breathless anticipation to the encounters you may have with your two-year-olds and fourteen-year-olds!

We want to reassure you that some children go through their emotional and cognitive births very easily, just as some physical births are fairly easy.

All the same, physical births do involve some effort, and so do these two. Whatever the effort involved, the miracle of the newborn from each birth is reward enough to make it all worthwhile.

The fourth birth – being

During the fourth birth, the adult moves from inside the womb of the world community and worldly life into the transcendent dimensions of life ('Life'). This *spiritual birth* can take the whole of life and may only end at death for some. While it starts with the onset of adulthood at about 21 years of age, the 'contractions' may take years to become obvious. Adults need to learn to think and perceive very differently, if they are to participate through 'being' while living with others. This birth helps them to change so they can do the necessary learning. It helps them *to be who they are with others*. During the process they transform from adults into spiritual beings ('Beings').

Birth 'mother'

The 'mother' is the spiritual realm that lies beyond physical sensory experience. The birth canal is formed by the presence of these realms and their impact on us as we live our worldly lives.

Beginning

This birth is a normal part of the whole of life. However, we may only know it is underway, when we become open and mature enough to recognise that there is more to life than the day-to-day routines with which we are familiar. If parents have alerted us to dimensions that lie beyond the sensory world, or to spiritual practices that help us to access those dimensions, we will find it easier to face the deeper meanings and purposes of life that arise during this birth.

Birth process

We live our lives, often out of balance within ourselves and out of balance with Life process. Because of the 'universal laws of life', our daily activities return to us what we do and show us replicas of ourselves. These returning consequences are the contractions from Life that prompt us to move on through the birth. They are the joys and sorrows, the achievements and challenges that we experience on a daily basis.

If we participate cooperatively in the process, we will continually progress through the birth. Our awareness will expand and our capacities in the world will transform. Wondrous potentials become increasingly routine. If we struggle against the process, however, our life energies get increasingly blocked and we run down until we die physically.

Delivery

If we are 'delivered' while physically alive, we experience a wonderful release and a continuing sense of light, joy, peace and love. We feel that we have 'come home at last'. We become transformed and will live in the world very differently from then onwards. Some people are delivered during what are called 'near death experiences'. Many had extraordinarily beautiful experiences when they died that they reported after being resuscitated. Their accounts are very consistent and interesting to read. If we are delivered during our physical deaths, the outcome is not a worldly experience and perhaps the texts of advanced spiritual practitioners are our best sources for what happens then.

Bonding

Once delivered, our consciousness is drawn to transcendent realms where we experience infinite light and love, and Life itself. We find ourselves blending with what we encounter in Eternity. It is an experience outside time and space, yet more real than anything worldly. The spiritual bonds that are established help us to find out who we are, to know our selves as deeply as we can. We end by knowing that we belong to and are part of the Ultimate (a synonym for God). We come to understand where we belong in 'the scheme of things' – and much more.

People who have completed this birth have a fulfilled, wholeness about them. They seem unified and present with themselves and others in beautiful, compelling and life-affirming ways. They spread life in everything they do.

The importance of completing each birth

Just imagine the impossible for a moment. Imagine that a baby got stuck partly in the womb and had to live in the world like that. Imagine the baby trying to suckle while caught between its mother's legs, or trying to explore the world with its hands, or to learn to crawl, all from partly within the birth canal. What a nightmarish prospect!

As impossible as this seems, it is a clear indication of the difficulties for children who do not complete their second and third births. All future development is blocked just as significantly as if they had been physically stuck. Because they do not fully arrive, they cannot learn what they need to learn.

The second birth

When the second birth is incomplete, babies get stuck in the womb of the parent–child relationship. Although more than two years old, they continue to live and feel as babies do, continuing to need mothers and fathers to care for them. They are extremely dependent and vulnerable, also often petulant, unhappy and difficult. They may remain perpetual babies.

They will not be able to live in the wider world easily, and are likely to have increasingly extreme problems as they get older. The demands of life automatically and inevitably will call on more abilities than they have and they can develop seriously disabling emotional and psychological problems, or can even become psychotic.

Knowing 'in the tissue of their bodies' that they need to be born emotionally, children persist in struggling with us until they are. Many is the baby who is still trying to get the struggle that he or she needs, even at nine or ten years of age. They have had to keep struggling, because their parents did not do what was needed at two years of age.

'Overgrown babies' are usually difficult for all concerned. They usually continue to suffer, to whine, to expect the world to revolve around them, to throw tantrums when thwarted and generally to expect others to take responsibility, both for finding out what they need and for providing it.

Now that you understand more about the serious consequences of not completing the second birth, we hope you are highly committed to doing whatever is necessary to complete it. In fact, what we need do is very simple. We do things like insisting our children help pick up their toys, that they choose milk or juice when asked, or that they accompany us immediately and easily to bed when we tell them it is time.

It is the little struggles over little issues that move the baby on through the second birth canal. This is not a big, complicated process. If you consistently back down or give up the struggle when your two-year-old wants his or her own way, realise that you stop the birth process at that point. To help our babies move to childhood from babyhood, we need to keep up enough pressure and do it often enough.

The third birth

When the third birth is incomplete, children remain stuck below the age of fourteen in the womb of the family. They will live with childlike consciousness and thinking processes. However, when expected to manage the world practically and independently as other adults do, they will not be able to do so. Grown-ups who are still emotional children are too young to manage alone in the grown-up world. They simply do not have the abilities. The usual outcome is that they live dependent lives, relying on the real adults around them to keep them on track and to take care of them.

Living well in the adult world relies on people having advanced ways of thinking and processing reality that only become possible after the third birth. People without them can sometimes manage by banding together to give support to each other. But they can't do this naturally and easily until they complete this birth. They 'play house' instead of living life as autonomous adults.

So the stakes are high and the way to act is simple. We set standards of behaviour to govern how they act and give them jobs to do around the home. They may not even matter very much to us, but as tools for completing the labour of the third birth, they are ideal. Every time we insist on them acting appropriately or completing a task, and doing it gracefully, we are providing more of the necessary contractions.

How wonderful that getting them to act pleasantly and with caring, to make their beds, tidy their rooms, help with the dishes and cooking, vacuum clean the house, clean toilets and bathrooms, do their homework on time, get up and go to bed when they need to, watch TV at the agreed hours, talk respectfully, wait their turn to talk in a group and a myriad of other things, is for their own benefit! We are sure they will love to hear this from us at the time, too!

Better for us to do it

Children know when they are not getting the contractions they need to progress. Their systems are designed to get them to correct the situation as quickly as possible. The way they generally do this is to do increasingly serious things until we act decisively. If they get stuck, our actions need to be strong enough to get our children moving through the birth canal again.

When they are two years old or more, they may bite, hit, kick, throw tantrums or do other fairly extreme things. In small children, these extremes are fairly manageable. But it gets increasingly more difficult as they get older. By then, too, they may have added behaviour like truanting, fire lighting, and bullying to their repertoires. In adolescence, they may also stop going to school, stay out late with friends, run away from home, get sexually involved, steal, assault people, or whatever they can dream up to get us to stand firm with them.

All of this is so we will say, 'No', or say, 'Do this' and insist that they do what we expect. It is not a lot to ask of us for the sake of getting them born.

The extended family

Our extended families can be a wonderful source of support and help. In recent times, the primary family unit has been getting smaller. Many people nowadays have less contact with brothers, sisters, parents, aunts, uncles and grandparents than families did in previous generations.

Some of the advantages

Here is a list of some of the advantages we see in our extended families or a strong social network.

- We can share the load.
- We can learn from each other.
- Children get a greater variety of people to imitate and learn from.
- The wisdom of experienced parents and grandparents is more on hand.
- Social contacts and emotional support are often more available.
- Material resources can be shared.

Developing contacts

What if we don't have an extended family? We can promote contacts with others. Make contact with:

- other parents with children of the same ages as ours (at school);
- people with similar interests, such as those with children (in clubs);
- older people who are available for warm, caring contact with others (in elderly citizens' clubs);
- the neighbours and people who live down the street or nearby;
- the people you meet when you go to the local shops, particularly those with children;
- parents in chat rooms on the Internet.

A little persistence every day or every week over several years can produce a wonderfully rich and emotionally satisfying network of people.

The four births – an overview

Physical birth is the first of four significant transitions, or births in our lives. Each one takes us from one way of living and being into another. The first three of these births are most directly relevant to child rearing. All the same, knowing that we are heading for a fourth birth may influence significantly what we teach our children and the way we teach them.

The 'newborn' baby comes from the first birth

It is a physical birth and occurs at age zero. The foetus is birthed by the mother from her physical womb. The contractions of the womb help to move the baby to the outside. The newborn baby is delivered into the physical world and immediately bonds physically with its mother and father. The parent–child relationship, particularly the mother–child relationship, forms the primary medium of learning until about two years of age. Babies learn that they belong with their parents.

The 'newborn' child comes from the second birth

It is an emotional birth that occurs at about two years of age. The baby is birthed by the family from the womb of the parent–child relationship. What parents and others do to enforce their expectations contracts the womb to move their babies into the feeling world of their families. The 'newborn' children immediately bond emotionally with their families and learn that they belong with them. They can feel who they are in relation to others. Family life is the primary medium of subsequent learning.

The 'newborn' adult comes from the third birth

It is a cognitive birth that occurs at about fourteen years of age. The child is birthed by the community from the womb of the family. The action of enforcing community expectations, particularly by family members and significant adults, creates the contractions that move the child into the world of the adult. The 'newborn' adults are delivered into the cognitive world and immediately bond with the community. They know who they are in relation to others and learn that they belong in their communities. The community is the primary medium of subsequent learning.

The 'newborn' being comes from the fourth birth

It is a spiritual birth that occurs some time during adulthood or at death. The adult is birthed from the womb of the community by the spiritual demands of Life. The impact of 'universal laws of Life' moves the adult into the world of spirit. The 'newborn' beings are delivered into the spiritual world and immediately bond with the Ultimate, where they, as Beings, learn how they belong there. Adults learn to be who they are with others. The spiritual realm is the primary medium of subsequent learning.

Implantation of **embryo** in physical womb

Physical womb is world of growing foetus

Physical mother

1st birth (0 yrs)

Newborn **baby** bonds with mother/father

Parent–child relationship is world/womb
of growing baby

Parent–child
relationship

2nd birth (2 yrs)

Newborn **child** bonds with family

Family is womb/world of growing child

Family

3rd birth (14 yrs)

Newborn **adult** bonds with community

Community is world/womb of growing adult

Community

4th birth (21+ yrs)

Newborn **being** bonds with Spirit/Ultimate

Spiritual realm is world/womb of growing being

Spiritual realm

AGES AND STAGES

Children move through a predictable sequence of stages as they grow up. While these stages blend into each other, each is also quite distinct in ways that are easy to recognise. In each stage, our children need us to respond to them so that they do the learning and changing that they need to do then. This paves the way for the stages to come. If parents provide what they need, this will usually lead to a systematic progression in their learning and to producing the inherent maturity and beauty they can have as adults. By contrast, incomplete learning in one stage interferes with the smooth passage of later stages and can result in considerable disadvantages in adulthood.

Section

Chapter 21

Phases of childhood

This chapter lists the ages and stages of a child's development and provides a brief summary of the different phases of childhood as they arise. We include brief statements of the issues that go with each stage and suggestions about what our children need from us so they can complete each stage. The ages given are approximate. While they are generally accurate, some children go through the stages earlier and some later than the 'average' child. Also, when children do not complete a stage, they can continue to act at later stages in ways that are consistent with earlier stages. This tends to confuse some people; however, once you realise that you may be seeing two-, three- or four-year-old behaviour in a five-year-old, for example, clarity is restored.

The suggestions about what to do at each stage are well tested, they have worked well with many children. While briefly stated here, you have the content of the rest of the book to fill out the detail of what you might need to do. When your child is dealing with mixed stages at the same time, we suggest that you blend the approaches of the stages that are involved. So, for example, you might deal with tantrums as you would with a two-year-old, the requests for information as you would with a three-year-old, and the fears as you would with a four-year-old, all in the five-year-old you are actually living with.

The embryo and foetus

Conception

What's going on

- sperm meets ovum, new life begins, implantation in the womb follows
- beginnings of a new person composed of the genes from both parents
- feelings, emotions, thinking and spiritual heritage passed on too

- some men and women are aware of the conception
- some aware of arrival of baby as a person
- every part of the conception forms early programming

What they need

- physically healthy men and women to produce healthy sperm and ovum
- healthy mothers for strong healthy wombs to sustain growing embryos
- happy, contented, loving and fulfilled parents to create best climate for future of the children

Helpful hints

- when planning conception, promote physical health and emotional balance
- get practical advice on how to do this
- stay grounded and express all feelings, whatever the circumstances of conception
- use grounding and expressiveness to release effects of unwanted, unexpected or imposed conceptions

Gestation

What's going on

- about 40 weeks of growth to birth
- mother's bodily processes, feelings, thoughts and spirituality all affect growing foetus
- physical and emotional climate around mother significant, too, particularly father's processes
- foetus learning the foundations of abundance, love, acceptance, belonging
- sounds, physical contact, feeling tones all have effect

What they need

- physically healthy mothers who eat and rest well, and exercise regularly
- loving acceptance from mothers and fathers
- much deliberate interaction: talking to them, thinking about them
- love and welcome them
- involving the other children: looking, touching, talking
- mothers staying grounded and expressing feelings
- preferably happy, contented mothers who celebrate pregnancies
- preparation for birth, including exercise to produce physical fitness

- create suitably gentle and loving birth environment
- fathers make arrangements for dealing with possible crises during birth
- fathers prepare to attend birth and provide support for mothers during the birth

Helpful hints

- yoga helps stretch and strengthen bodies and helps with relaxation
- childbirth classes for information and support for parents
- lots of discussion about feelings, thinking, and planning for the future
- arrange for friends and relatives to cook extra after baby arrives so you don't need to do this for a couple of weeks

Birth

What's going on

- baby triggers birth, then mother and baby coordinate to move baby through birth canal
- mother and baby highly stimulated which prepares for bonding
- all aspects imprinted, including sequence, laying foundation for later transitions
- affects initiative, persistence, completion, managing pressure and meeting challenges

What they need

- practical support for mothers to produce successful deliveries
- birth as natural as possible
- no or minimal medication or surgery
- fathers to participate as well as mothers
- fathers available for important decisions with support team
- fathers keep track of situation to produce best environment for mothers and babies
- a welcoming, gentle atmosphere: soft lights and sounds, and delicate fragrances
- birth team of calm, nurturing, loving and grounded people

Helpful hints

- moving about during birth often promotes the passage of the baby
- support team can rub backs, make drinks, talk soothingly, and get information
- previous physical training provides the stamina necessary
- intervene medically as little as possible, provided mother and baby stay safe

The baby

One to two hours (Bonding)

What's going on

- intense stimulation of birth readies parents and baby, particularly mother and baby, to connect
- babies bond with whatever they physically contact in first two hours
- first hour most crucial, restrict contact to parents and immediate family
- bond forms the foundation for all future relationships
- imprinting everything around it
- first impact of physical world at this time, foundation of future perceptions of environment

What they need

- need gentle, loving environments, that include soft lights and sounds, lovely fragrances
- time to bond with their mothers: to nestle, rest, suckle and be with their mothers immediately
- after mother and baby bonded, time to bond with father skin to skin

Helpful hints

- suggested order and timing for bonding
  - mother first, she is the most important, puts baby to breast when ready
  - father with mother as they bond, then father takes baby alone
  - others follow, including brothers and sisters
- choose soft music and fragrances you like for birth and bonding time
- only do medical procedures necessary for survival during bonding time

Birth to four months (Sponging)

What's going on

- babies absorb everything around them like sponges
- completely reliant on mothers to provide, filter, and balance their energies
- totally dependent on adults
- crying is signal that they need something
- express everything the moment they feel it
- learning complete self-acceptance from complete acceptance of parents
- connecting their initiative with results: crying gets help, smiling gets love
- learning about physical world as they suck, grasp, look and listen

What they need

- whatever keeps them safe, warm or cool, well fed, clean and dry
- complete acceptance and love creates secure foundations for whole of life
- lots of holding and touching, give baby massage and do baby yoga
- talk to them to lay good foundations for language
- babies not comfortable with everyone, select the people who hold them

Helpful hints

- suggest all newborn babies have at least one session of cranial osteopathy
- avoid dummies so feelings are expressed, not plugged in
- set up a 'sleep beautifully button' (See 'Notes and references')
- get visitors to help with washing up, folding nappies, cleaning bathrooms
- rest when the baby rests

Four to nine months (Exploring)

What's going on

- on the move, they roll, slither and crawl everywhere
- everything goes in the mouth, all senses explore the world
- teething begins
- ready increasingly for solid foods
- physical activity preparing for later walking, running, reading and writing
- more aware of and involved with others outside family

What they need

- space and freedom to move their bodies and learn about their environments
- lots of stimulation: talking and singing to them, playing peek-a-boo and other games, fun in the bath, reading books
- protection by 'baby proofing' the house and watching them closely all the time
- continued love and celebration of their expanding prowess

Helpful hints

- give them safe things to tear and pull apart: paper, old toys
- soothing naturopathic or homeopathic remedies relieve the pain of teething
- take their nappies off at times to leave them free to kick and move freely

Nine to twelve months (Weaning)

What's going on

- teeth increasingly make breast-feeding uncomfortable, a natural time to wean

- growth spurt and greater demand for nutrition, need more than milk
- eating more solid foods
- some start walking at this time, most are crawling very actively
- very social beings and love interacting
- more tolerant of short separations from mothers
- become clingy and cry, too, so keep the separations short
- can become rough: biting during feeding, pulling hair

What they need

- gentle persistence with weaning, allow time (about three months)
- mothers celebrate increased freedom and their developing independence
- lots of baby games: crawl with them, play hide and seek, dance with them, roll balls
- read stories to them daily
- protect and watch them, very quick and more at risk

Helpful hints

- give the baby solid foods before offering the breast
- start with simple foods, gradually increase variety, if rejected initially try again later
- find ways other than the breast for soothing and encouraging sleep

Twelve to eighteen months (Extending the world)

What's going on

- most babies walking
- becoming much more vocal, experimenting with sound, using some words
- often understand lots of words, and respond to directions and questions
- choose their activities, who to go to, and what foods and drinks they want
- still exploring lots and get further faster
- learning bodily mastery

What they need

- lots of talks with us
- need to name things and use words describing what we do
- telling them what to do and not do
- encourage word use and celebrate partial or complete success
- opportunities to experiment physically: climbing, running, walking, rolling, jumping

- continued alert protection
- time with other babies of their own age

Helpful hints

- when very excited about all they are doing, they can find it difficult to settle down to sleep; use the 'sleep beautifully button' (See 'Notes and references')
- make instructions simple: 'Hands off', 'Come here', 'Keep quiet'; *avoid*: 'Don't touch', 'Don't shout', and 'Don't cry'

Eighteen to twenty-four months (The turning point)

What's going on

- preparation for second birth
- much more definite and assertive, marked likes and dislikes
- determined to do things their way, inclined to be upset when interrupted
- many using multiple words, some using short sentences, others not talking much
- ready for short periods with well-known adults
- inclined to frustration
- others more real and begin noticing others' reactions
- starting emotional and social learning, how to use feelings
- beginning learning about instructions, decisions to obey or not

What they need

- begin teaching 'standing to decide'
- patience and acceptance, still not ready for discipline
- some stronger action from us to match their increased passions
- expressing our feelings about what they do, gently at first
- continued protection, gentle yet definite guidance, lots of stimulation
- exercise, games with big balls, playground games
- lots of contact with other children, though play is largely a solo thing

Helpful hints

- give little jobs using their love of helping
- supervised water play is great fun, especially in summer
- pets are great teachers but always need to be supervised

The child

Two-year-olds (Me, my and mine)

What's going on

- second birth from baby to child
- lots of energy and activity, some are very easy
- many throw tantrums and struggle, become very demanding, resistant and unhappy
- parents often feel frustrated and angry
- learning to control themselves, to manage intense feelings
- change 'Me–Me' experience to 'I–You'experience with others
- gradually develop basic idea of time – tonight, yesterday, tomorrow
- meaning of words comes from feelings and action

What they need

- love, time and our pleasure in their company
- enjoyment of their intensity and curiosity
- simple standards and limits set and enforced
- parents to show and express feelings
- give body instruction with words
- parents to win most struggles
- fathers to support mothers as they separate from their children

Helpful hints

- you are in physical control, even if they seem like emotional giants
- what you don't get done now, will repeat at fourteen and before, so get it done now
- husbands and wives may struggle with each other like two-year-olds, too
- when struggling, avoid life-changing decisions; two years of age passes

Three-year-olds (Little prince, little princess)

What's going on

- bonding with family
- trusting, open, vulnerable and loving
- lovely little people with wholeness about them
- curious about world and people; helpful
- discovering power of words and of 'Why?'
- discovering sexual difference, play horsey games, undress

What they need

- lots of family contact so bonding can complete
- jobs that really contribute to household
- inclusion in family activities like cooking, washing up, visiting people
- praise for growing up and discussing our expectations of them
- training in how to do things and how to act with people
- play with other children
- safe places to explore, like backyards and playgrounds

Helpful hints

- they love going out and about to museums, art galleries, playgrounds, zoos, farms, walks
- get your children to talk to you about what they are thinking; you'll probably love it

Four-year-olds (What if?)

What's going on

- stronger sense of self, maturing little people
- love to build things, cubby houses, toys
- love language, experiment with words, make small jokes
- learning to think, using fantasy, separating fantasy from external reality
- learning about fear
- can make real friendships, some have imaginary friends
- love creating and listening to scary stories (monsters, ghosts and bogey men)
- awareness of others increased, love caring for younger children
- strong sense of responsibility to others, often concerned

What they need

- rules for how to act with people; rules about truth
- talk about doing one thing here and something else there
- discuss feelings and thoughts, teach them to think
- teach how to use thought to produce pleasure
- teach the difference between what is 'made up' and what is 'real'
- remind them of past experiences to help them connect past and present
- talk about the future – going to granny's in two sleeps

Helpful hints

- they thrive on stimulation, so kindergarten is great

- encourage concentration on happiness and fun
- have lots of play things so they can create (constructor sets)
- at times, let them take over the living room or yard for playing house

Five- to six-year-olds (Playing with triangles)

What's going on

- often beginning school, much to learn about people and situations
- ready to explore wider world; excited about it
- want to be 'grown up' and imitate adults
- experimenting with triangles; combining, dividing, disrupting, joining others
- manipulate information to get own way
- often into a 'know it all' stage
- increase in single sex (boy–boy, girl–girl) play
- childlike seductiveness with parents, 'I'll marry Mummy/Daddy when I'm big'

What they need

- learning about 'You-Me-Us'
- to be given helpful rules and guidance; more rules about truth
- challenge their manipulations of information
- lots of encouragements for success
- lots of physical exercise to develop coordination
- close supervision in the streets
- lots of time with parents, especially just after school; time to reconnect and process day
- share their excited discoveries

Helpful hints

- adults need to have clear communication guidelines
- have two clear kinds of rules for living: general ones like 'Act gently, no hitting', and qualified ones like, 'Do what adults tell you to do (but not strangers)'

Seven-year-olds (Who am I?)

What's going on

- making deep inner shift from learning by taking in, to learning by putting out

- wonder 'Who am I?' 'Who are those others?'
- often make decisions that stick for life
- thinking expanding more, capable of simple analysis
- observe their own feelings with greater detachment
- intensely interested in how everything works

What they need

- parents to stay alert to decisions they make
- unhappy kids probably need support to change their decisions
- happy kids often need support to keep doing what works
- watch how they manage school, friends and others
- encourage feeling expression when they are not feeling happy
- help them learn to manage feelings with effective action
- parents to show that we are with them and available

Helpful hints

- a good time to start pocket money to teach about saving and spending
- saturate them in beauty, love and fun; helps them decide to feel happy
- at least once a day tell them how wonderful you think they are
- give them one important job to do for the whole family and show you appreciate it

Eight- to nine-year-olds (Us and them)

What's going on

- kids' clubs with entrance rules, secret passwords
- upsets about 'who's in and who's out'; who decides is a hot issue
- often very nasty, prejudiced or abusive
- thinking very concrete and legalistic; find ways around rules and try to catch others out
- lying to get around restrictions or to create impressions
- may start stealing
- learning to complete repeated chores at home and school (very important)

What they need

- adult oversight of group activities and intervention to stop bullying or nastiness
- support to stand up for what they value and not just go along with others
- 'nagging' helps so they learn about sustained effort over time
- rosters, charts and lists for memory; can often prepare these themselves

- support doing more self-care alone: brushing teeth, finding their clothes, dressing
- increased household jobs
- make consequences more situational
- help to learn tolerance and acceptance of others

Handy hints

- family meetings are great; they love having a turn at running them, under parental guidance
- whiteboards in the kitchen for rosters and messages are great

Ten- to twelve-year-olds (Little mum, little dad)

What's going on

- pulling early years together, practising being grown-up
- caring, nurturing, sometimes bossy and controlling
- practising parenting
- often show great insight and understanding
- a good time sense, past/future real, planning ahead
- may make binding decisions about life
- can judge speed and distance on the roads
- strong sense of justice, right and wrong, take action in good causes
- want to join clubs/classes: Scouts, dance, karate

What they need

- lots of listening/discussion
- stay alert for life-changing decisions
- expose them to good adult models
- monitor what they are exposed to in media and school
- teach them to plan backwards from future (school assignments)
- avoid invitations to squash their 'parental positions'
- offer guidance to soften their rule-based certainty
- give extra responsibilities and rewards
- remember they are 'more mature children', not yet 'grown up'

Helpful hints

- get together with other parents and find out what each other is doing
- realise that 'everyone else's parents' probably don't 'let them do it' either
- a great time for separate outings: men and boys, women and girls
- when moving to secondary school, visit the new school with them

Adolescence

Thirteen-year-olds (Baby)

Emotionally recycling the ages of conception to eighteen months.

What's going on

- often have major bodily changes and hormonal shifts
- concerned about body image
- may be very dependent, needy, cry a lot, forget things, unable to concentrate and dreamy
- stop doing things they were capable of doing previously
- often very sensitive to criticism
- going to secondary school
- want to appear capable, but often can't
- challenged by greater demands at school

What they need

- lots of primary, loving, gentle nurturing
- complete acceptance
- tell them what to do, walk with them through their schedules
- remove consequences for nonperformance until later in year
- allow for rapid shifts between dependency and independence
- someone to greet them after school, may need help to get to school
- practical advice on handling situations

Helpful hints

- put tidbits in their mouths – like feeding young birds; they love it
- modify your schedules for a few months to manage what they need; it's worth it
- organise a regular cuddle time

Fourteen-year-olds (Dissenter)

Emotionally recycling the ages of eighteen months to two years.

What's going on

- the third birth from child to adult, usually lots of passion
- arguments, tantrums and anger
- self-centred, 'I want' and 'I know' dominate
- parental passion necessary, appeasement and reason have little impact

- struggle over everything or nothing
- often confuse rebelliousness with independence
- often struggle about wanting more freedom to go out more
- passion often takes over thinking

What they need

- clear expectations and limits, consistently enforced by adults
- defined consequences when limits are broken
- duty schedules created, to teach time management and to plan ahead
- active, passionate involvement of parents and other adults
- as parents prevail, adolescents learn what is needed
- discussion is important along with high emotion
- increased responsibility at home, somewhat negotiable
- some areas absolutely not negotiable
- freedom needs to match proven ability to manage

Helpful hints

- encourage them to do 'three' small things a day that they may struggle over
- form support network of other parents to act as backstops
- bring in the adults as a group when necessary to impress things on the fourteen-year-olds

Fifteen-year-olds (Fledgling)

Emotionally recycling the ages of three to four years.

What's going on

- bonding with community
- often calm, happy, friendly, cooperative
- open to others' needs, feelings, intentions etc.
- expanding friendships
- love learning and discussions, curious, crave explanations
- learning to think and reason
- managing increased demands at school
- sorting out superstitions and magical thinking
- later on, enjoy horror movies, scary funpark rides
- can develop crushes on older people: teachers, movie stars, musicians, family friends
- looking for role models

What they need

- easy availability of adult world for bonding
- limits on behaviour, social outings, money etc
- teaching of time management, planning, thinking backwards from future
- more jobs in family
- can begin part-time work, like paper rounds
- give some money from wage to family, if they work
- expand financial responsibility (buy own clothes)
- train them socially through contact with nonfamily
- discussion of future work, do work experience, volunteer work

Helpful hints

- have a special ritual to welcome fifteen-year-olds to the community
- encourage talk with adults about their work, and seek work visits

Sixteen-year-olds (Sweet and sour)

Emotionally recycling the ages of five to seven years.

What's going on

- outrage common; 'How dare you interfere in my life!', 'I'm in charge of me!'
- primary issues: 'who is in control', 'who is responsible'
- 'I know everything' also common
- righteously take moral high ground
- expanded thinking and reasoning
- values developing, sorting 'right from wrong'
- sexuality explicit, still formative
- sexualised, naive 'crushes' on older adults (teachers, family friends)
- triangulation common, set up fights between teachers, parents, friends, siblings
- challenging power arrangements; parents often feel very intense feelings
- others love them; they are very different outside home
- parents may want to 'kick them out'; child may want to leave

What they need

- strong exchanges to teach them balance and moderation
- calm discussion when possible
- direct, clear feedback
- help to claim power and responsibility without fighting

- increased contributions to family, not ready for adult load
- need limits, consequences, now through withholding services
- lots of guidance from parents, teachers, adults
- talk about fears of responsibility for adult life
- parent of opposite sex confirms and 'applauds' emerging sexuality
- coaching in proper behaviour from the parent of the same sex
- parents to manage any sexual response we feel about them
- parents not to allow them to bulldoze us
- parents to talk to partners and others to manage the triangles

Helpful hints

- parents need to support each other
- act together as much as possible
- they are almost there; pull back from trying to do it for them
- the strength of our feelings is normal
- remember to do things together for fun

Seventeen-year-olds (Romantic)

Emotionally recycling the ages of seven to nine years.

What's going on

- threshold into more mature adulthood is crossed
- delightful maturity mixed with excitement about adult world
- often very friendly, responsible and respectful of others
- peer group important, often spend more time together
- time full of romantic fantasies
- values and ethics obvious in thinking and decisions
- answering question: 'Who do I want to be?'

What they need

- encourage their maturity
- act more as consultant and interested friend
- mothers/fathers to appreciate son's/daughter's blossoming sexuality
- teaching on how to be sexually attractive and appropriate, how to be with a partner
- grown-up discussions on all sorts of issues; ask thought-provoking questions
- increased responsibility for themselves and family
- talk about adult life, preparation
- support their work or school work, without taking responsibility

Helpful hints

- mutual decision-making is great
- have fun and help plan heroic adventures with your seventeen-year-olds
- keep discussing need for work and training; the time is approaching

Eighteen- to 21-year-olds (World leader)

Emotionally recycling the ages of ten to twelve years.

What's going on

- almost adult, they know – excited, frightened
- everything coming together
- most have finished school, some in tertiary study
- move into larger world through working, studying, or leaving home
- may have legal status as adult
- values, rights and wrongs, how to run the world – all prominent
- much basic evaluation, everything thrown into question
- often assume there is one right way to live
- family values and approaches tested in the outside world, then adapted

What they need

- give lots of consultative support, they decide
- celebrate with them and love them
- encourage them to live as adults in the community
- chance to move in and out of family home to become accustomed to independence
- if they stay, they need full adult responsibilities in home
- learn about parents as people, no longer mum and dad
- enjoy their departure and encourage on-going contact

Helpful hints

- do adult things with them: outings, special events, fun
- celebrate twenty-first birthdays with a splash
- enjoy their friends and give them space to learn
- we didn't know everything then, nor do they – they will learn, too

Useful one-liners . . .

Keeping to your 'no'

You've said, 'No', but your child is determined to sway you with drawn-out hassles.

You say, **'The more you go on like this, the more determined I am not to do what I'm not going to do anyway'.**

Ending the hassle

You have given the reasons and discussed them. Your child still hassles, whinges, whines, or acts cutely so as not to comply.

You say, **'No more discussion, (explanation etc.). Just do it'.**

A nag for all occasions

'Oh you're always nagging. Why can't you just be quiet (leave me to myself, let me decide)?' our children say (mutter, shout). Often we are uncomfortable about the nagging ourselves and they are counting on it.

We can say, **'As soon as you do what you're supposed to do, I'll stop nagging. Until then, I will keep doing it. You are supposed to do certain things. This is one of them. Do it now'.**

Managing lies

Your child lies to cover up something (having forgotten a message, broken something, got into trouble at school...).

You say, **'Always tell the truth; you will get into far more trouble from me, if I discover that you are lying than if you honestly tell me that you have done something wrong'.**

TOOLS

In this section we present four 'tools' that have great value in many different situations. They can provide daily benefits to your lives and those of your children.

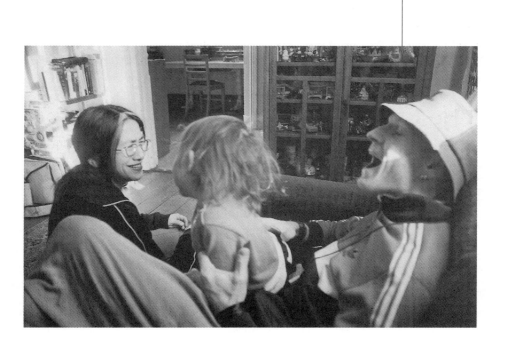

Chapter 22

Grounding

Grounding is a great tool to use when children and young people are upset or overexcited. It helps them to calm down and get in contact with what is going on so they can deal with it. At the same time, they can keep thinking and feeling – something that is very important.

What does it do?

By getting our children to ground themselves regularly, they usually become balanced, responsive, energetic and aware much of the time. Grounding also removes anxiety, as it is not possible to be grounded and anxious. Because they become more aware of the inside and outside, they often have more realistic views of situations.

When well-grounded, children usually feel calmer and more balanced, alert and relaxed. The process of grounding produces two very useful results. It helps to dissolve and release discomfort; it also helps to intensify comfort and pleasure while it spreads through the body. Very importantly, it makes our children much more available to us. What magic is this?

The basics

To get our children well-grounded we get them to pay attention to what is going on physically. The basic thing is to get them to concentrate on physical awareness; on what is going on inside their bodies physically and on what is around them. This means two things:

- They notice their physical sensations: hot, cold, tight, loose, bright, dark, loud, quiet, fragrant or foul; and they notice where these sensations are in their bodies.
- They notice the physical things and events around them through their five senses: what they can see, hear, touch, taste and smell.

There is no effort involved in any of this. Staying grounded is also something human beings are designed to do naturally.

Grounding exercise

Notice what is going on physically in your body right now. What sensations are in there and where are they? If you notice 'nothing', realise that 'nothing' is a sensation. Just pay attention briefly to what you notice anywhere in your body. Do this for about one minute.

Now pay attention to what is going on around you. Look at what is around you. Listen to any sounds you can hear. Reach out and touch things and notice the textures and temperatures of what you touch. Notice any tastes in your mouth. Notice any fragrances around you. Do this for about a minute, too.

Now practise doing both together: notice the inside and outside. If you don't find that easy, do one after the other. Repeatedly go back and forth between the inside and outside, for a while. Do this for about a minute too.

Now notice any differences in what you are experiencing. Are you calmer, more relaxed, more alert, feeling more intensely? What do you notice has changed?

Various ways of grounding

We can use grounding from the moment children begin to understand words. Whenever they are ungrounded, they have unbalanced awareness of what is occurring. They become overconcentrated on their feelings and upsets, or overconcentrated on the things, situations and events around them. The way to handle this is to give them simple instructions that get them to correct the imbalance.

For example, let's imagine that children are upset. They are very aware of what is happening on the inside. Perhaps they are sad and crying, angry and shouting, frightened and not responsive to what we are saying, or something similar. Or, perhaps they are happy and jittery with excitement. They don't need help to notice this, but they do need help to notice the outside. Here are some things you can say:

- 'Feel your feet on the ground', if they are standing.
- 'Feel the seat under your bottom', if they are sitting.
- 'Look at me in the eyes and really see me', and point to your eyes.
- 'Look over there at (name something). What do you see?' Get a reply.
- 'Listen to what I'm saying. What did I just say to you?'
- 'Can you hear that (name something)?'
- If you say something and they don't listen, say, 'I'll tell you again. Listen to what I'm saying this time'. Say it again, then pause and say, 'What did I say?'

- Squeeze a hand or an arm and say, 'I am here. Now pay attention to me'.
- Take their hand and say, 'Come with me. Let's go for a walk and you can tell me what's going on'. As they walk, they have to notice the outside.
- Take their hand and say, 'Come over here, sit on my lap and tell me what's going on'.
- Ask, 'What's happening?' or say, 'Tell me what's happening'.
- Ask, 'What are you feeling inside right now?' Then ask, 'Where is that and what does it feel like?'
- Ask, 'What are you thinking right now?' Then ask, 'Where is that in your body, and what does it feel like?'
- Ask, 'What are the sensations in your body right now?'
- Say, 'Pay attention to what is going on right here. What can you see?' Pause, 'What's that sound?' Pause, 'Feel this', and hand something to them or touch something within their easy reach. Pause, 'Can you smell anything (or name something)?' Pause, 'Have you got a taste in your mouth?' You can do all of these, and may only do one or two, particularly if the early ones work quickly.

These ways of acting are designed to help move our children's awareness to the outside. The idea is not to distract them from what they are feeling, but to help the energy from their excitement or upsets flow as they need to. (See Chapter 14, 'Paying active attention' for more on how to draw our children out when they need to talk.) When well-grounded, they will generally express themselves more easily and reach calm resolution much more readily than when not grounded.

Children and young people sometimes also become very focused on the outside. At these times, they are very aware of what is going on around them. They forget themselves and their current feelings. Typically, they do this when overexuberant, or very upset and not letting themselves feel the upset. The way we approach this is to get them to pay attention to themselves. Things to do:

- First we need to stop the action. We may go to them and touch them, or take a hand to get their attention, or we may call them over to us. Using the name of the child is a good idea, as what we say usually has much more impact when we do. Compare, 'Come over here for a moment', with 'Andrew/Sarah, come over here a moment'.
- When you have their attention, say, 'Now, just stand still and feel your feet on the ground'. Getting them to stay physically still is an important part of this, as their agitation or casting around is part of how they stop noticing the inside. Then say, 'Calm yourself down and feel your feet on

the ground'. When you notice they are a little calmer, say, 'That's good, now keep going. Keep feeling your feet on the ground'. Some of our children will respond faster by getting them to look, listen, taste or smell. Choose what works.

- When stationary and calmer, ask them what is going on inside them. 'What are you feeling?', 'What are you thinking?', or 'What's going on inside you?' If they don't seem able to connect to anything, ask specific questions that guide their attention: 'What's happening in your belly?', 'Do you notice anything in your chest?', or 'Are your legs cold or hot?'. As they start to pay attention to the inside, things will change and they will either calm down, or will begin to talk about what they are experiencing.
- The next step is to give instructions, to make suggestions and/or get them to make decisions about what to do next. What you do will depend on the ages and issues involved.

Movement often helps

When children are ungrounded it often helps them to tune in to both the inside and the outside by getting them to move. For example, we can get them to walk around, go for a run, ride a trike or bike, or go for a swim. Select an activity that encourages them to notice their bodies and that also requires them to pay attention to the outside. Movement is not usually helpful when they are already jumpy, agitated or rushing around.

Older children and young people

Once they know the ropes, we don't usually need to go through the process in as much detail. Although, at times of great challenge, we may still need to remind them to do it with a comment such as, 'Feel your feet on the ground'; mostly it is enough to say to them, 'Just pause and get yourself grounded'.

Many uses

The process becomes part of everyday ways of coping. Whatever they are doing, or thinking of doing, getting grounded will help them do it much more easily and effectively. It becomes an easy, effective way for them to manage themselves, for example, in:
- resolving specific upsets (arguments, disappointments)
- anticipating the future (going somewhere, upcoming exams)

- dealing with current challenges (taking exams, talking to the teacher)
- releasing the hold of the past (old arguments, frightening experiences)
- intensifying enjoyment (watching movies, relaxing with a boyfriend or girlfriend)

Parents can learn too

Why let the kids have all the fun? We can learn, too, and it is very easy. In fact, one of the easiest ways of teaching it is to do it ourselves. Then, when our children are very challenging, we can use grounding to keep our own balance, to keep thinking clearly and to act effectively. We imagine that this would be a rare event in most families, of course!

Audio recording

We have produced a recording of the process (called the 'Grounding Meditation') that explains the way it works and how to do it. Once our children reach four to six years of age, we can put the recording on in the background to help to keep everyone well grounded. Children and young people take to the process very well, and will often ask for the recording when they are challenged and wanting to take care of things themselves. (See 'Biame Network' on page 230 for contact details.)

Grounding works in groups

Jenny, a primary school teacher, learnt grounding. She found it so useful that she decided to try it with her pupils.

The children loved it. They asked for it whenever they thought they needed it, and reminded each other about doing it when someone was upset.
The class had a reputation as a happy, settled group. The children learnt well and parents pressed for their children to have her as their teacher.

What to do when you feel you are losing control

Many parents face this. We experience a build-up of intensity on the inside and have difficulty acting calmly and safely with our children. These are the times when parents may shout abuse, shake, hit, kick, beat, or injure their children. Children are harmed by parents acting in any of these ways. So what can we do?

Three simple steps help:
1. Stop and get grounded.
2. Move away.
3. Talk to someone as soon as you can.

Stop and get grounded

Stop talking and stop moving. Stay still and get grounded. Usually it is best just to notice your feet on the floor. (See Chapter 22, 'Grounding' for more on this.) This will often help you to calm yourself and help you to act appropriately.

Move away

If your feelings are very strong and you are uncertain that you will control yourself properly, physically move away so you cannot touch your child. If your child is a babe in arms, carefully put him or her down in a safe place, then move away. If necessary, go to the next room, or sit on the verandah, until you are calm enough to resume directly caring for your child. How far away you can go is dictated by ensuring your child stays safe. If someone else is there who is competent to take over, ask him or her to do so.

Talk to someone as soon as you can

Ring someone to talk out your feelings and get yourself settled: a friend, your parents or a brother or sister, the local GP or health sister, a telephone help line. Do this both to deal with the immediate situations and to get more long-term help if you need it. Then return and continue caring for your child. If you need to take a long time, make arrangements for someone else to care for your child until you are ready.

Chapter 23

Relaxation

Relaxation is important for everyone, including our children. We use a simple relaxation technique that you can teach your children from a very young age. It will assist you in helping them to stop when they need to, and to go to sleep as well. We have also developed one to use with babies.

The technique

Older than eighteen months

With children older than about eighteen months, the approach we use is as follows. It has four simple steps:

1. *Grounding*: Get your children to pay attention to what is supporting them, so they feel the ground under their feet (standing), a wall behind their backs (leaning), a chair underneath them (sitting), or whatever they are lying on (lying). (See Chapter 22, 'Grounding' for more information)

2. *Breathing*: Have them notice their breathing. Encourage them to stay relaxed and just notice the way their breath is going in and out. You might even breathe with them for a short time, just to show them what you mean. Keep your breathing relaxed, if you do.

3. *Releasing*: Have them let go a little, each time they breathe out. Watch them and when you see them breathing out, you can say, 'Now let go, just relax. Let your muscles relax; let yourself go quiet; allow yourself to go transparent'. You might even take a deep breath in, encouraging them to do the same, then breathe out in an exaggerated way, allowing your body to go loose and floppy as you do. This shows them what to do in a way they can imitate.

4. *Persisting*: Return to the earlier steps, if you see the children getting ungrounded or not concentrating on the breathing. Keep going, particularly with Step 3, for as long as is helpful.

Timing

We can do the relaxation in a matter of seconds.

- Denise is about to do something and she is a bit wound up about it. She needs a quick relax to calm down. Say, 'Denise, stop for a moment'. When she has, say, 'Feel the ground under your feet'. As she does, say, 'Good. Now, notice your breathing'. As you see her doing this, say, 'Good, keep noticing your breathing'. After a couple of breaths, say, 'Great. Now take a deep breath in and as you let it out, just let go completely'. Perhaps breathe out with her, then say, 'Good. Now go to it!'

Or we can do it for a lengthy time.

- Jean-Claude is trying unsuccessfully to go to sleep. So you go into his room, sit down on the bed beside him and take him through the four steps. Say slowly and with the necessary pauses, 'Okay, now open your eyes and look around, listen to everything you can hear, notice the bed underneath you and the sheets on top of you, notice any smells you can smell. Now let your eyes close and keep listening to the sounds and feeling the bed and bedding. Great.' (Let him do this for a minute or so.) 'Now notice your breathing. Notice it going in and out.' (Do this for a minute or more.) 'Now each time you breathe out, relax. Each time you breathe out, just let go. It's really easy and you're doing well. Just keep relaxing each time you breathe out.' (Do this for a few minutes, too; you don't need to talk all the time.) 'Now, as you feel yourself relaxing, you can go to sleep any time you need to. Just keep relaxing each time you breathe out and allow sleep to come when it is ready.' (If he has a 'sleep beautifully button', press it at this point. Then you get up and leave quietly.

Younger than eighteen months

Babies also need to relax at times. They sometimes get very unrelaxed and seem unable to let go. Noticing how powerfully influenced they are by their mothers, we developed a way of helping babies relax, by helping their mothers relax. Fathers can do it, too. It also has four steps.

1. *Grounding*: Hold your child in your arms, whether you are standing, sitting or lying. The more comfortable you are and the more physical support you have, the better. Get yourself grounded by noticing the contact of your body with what is supporting you. At the same time, notice your contact with your baby. Just accept any wriggling and keep concentrating on your own grounding.

2. *Breathing*: Notice your breathing for a while, by noticing your breath going in and out for a few minutes.

3. *Releasing*: Each time you breathe out, relax deliberately. Consciously let go and release. Release everything, every time you breathe out. Obviously you don't let go of your baby! As you continue to breathe and relax like this, your baby will probably start to settle down, too. Stay aware of your baby as you keep releasing yourself with each outward breath. Keep reminding yourself to stay grounded.

4. *Persisting*: Keep doing this, returning to the first or second step as you need to, until both of you are relaxed and calm. You might even find this a good way to go to sleep together.

We heard the following story from one astounded mother.

'The other day I lay down alone to do the relaxation. Joel was far too busy to lie still, but he needed a rest. Anyway, as I lay there relaxing, I kept feeling him and thinking about him too. When I got to the relaxing with each breath part, he started to go quiet. I had my eyes closed, so I did not see what he was doing. But within a minute or so, I felt him beside me. Then he crawled half on top of me and went to sleep with his head on my belly. We had a wonderful rest.'

The results

The three most obvious results from relaxation are that it helps to calm people, produces generalised happiness and enables them to rest. In addition, children who are anxious and doubtful about themselves can become secure and confident.

Audio recordings

We developed a relaxation meditation recording many years ago. Using it with children of most ages enables us simply to put it on and leave them to it. It has been used in kindergartens, so quite young children manage it easily.

With regular use, we have witnessed change with chronic anxiety, depression, insecurity, 'panic attacks', persistent pain and poor health. In addition, many hyperactive, ADD or ADHD children have changed significantly by using the recording.

A similar recording is the 'Loving Bond Meditation'. This is for use by parents with children up to about eighteen months old. It is beautifully relaxing and mutually restoring for both parents and babies.

(See 'Biame Network' on page 230 for contact details.)

Chapter 24

Family meetings

Regular family meetings make a wonderful difference in many families. They help us to achieve things as families much more easily than is otherwise possible.

Getting the family together

Basically, the idea is to get together regularly as a whole family. The following general recommendations have worked well for many others. We suggest that you consider them and develop your own, if these don't look as if they will suit your family.

- Choose a time when everyone can be there.
- Have the meetings at least weekly.
- Make them compulsory for everyone (including boarders, extended family members who live in the household and visitors.)
- Make one parent the chairperson, possibly rotating between the two of you occasionally.
- Have them as short as possible and as long as necessary.
- Keep these meetings separate from entertainment.
- Start them from the time your oldest child is about two.
- Get everyone to have a say, no matter how simple that say may be.
- Parents stay in control of the meeting, although children may have special jobs to do for the meeting, including being the chairperson, once they are old enough.
- Keep the talk practical and related to practical results.
- Have a list of items prepared for each meeting. Children who are old enough can take responsibility for preparing this.
- Have every member say at least one affirming and friendly thing to each of the others.

- Encourage the 'quiet ones' in the family to have a say and the 'active ones' to hold back a little to give others a go.

Family meetings can be used for many purposes. We see them as largely administrative and suggest the following are worth including in what you do. Use the meetings to:

- keep track of particular jobs and of how things are going in the family generally;
- plan jobs and work out who will do them;
- sort out the basic running of the house;
- encourage everyone generally and reward individuals for good performance;
- identify problems and work out solutions; these may involve emotional issues;
- review previous decisions to make sure what was planned is working;
- thank each and every person for his/her contributions when they make them;
- collect ideas about proposals;
- share information.

Great outcomes

Many wonderful results can come from these meetings.

- They highlight the importance of the family unit as a unit. The family is much more than a collection of individuals who happen to live in the same house.
- They give the family the chance to run things systematically.
- Children often feel much more secure, because they see that we are on the job, watching, monitoring, and running things.
- Children learn how to participate in shared tasks, how to discuss them, how to resolve difficulties, how to make group choices, how to think about the family as a whole and many other things.
- Everyone learns how to negotiate and cooperate with each other.
- The meetings emphasise the contribution that every family member is making and provide a place for that contribution to be acknowledged.
- All members have a chance to learn to resolve emotional issues with each other, partly by watching others do it, partly by doing it themselves.

Everyone generally gets so much benefit and learns so much from these meetings, that they are worth any extra effort they may seem to take.

Chapter 25

Couple time

Parents are people. We are husbands and wives, lovers, friends, or lone adults. We are much more than mothers and fathers. Whether we live alone or with other adults, we have needs and desires as adults that cannot be satisfied through the filter of family activities. We have to respond specifically to these needs, if we are to meet them.

When we live in a couple, we have the opportunity to take time together each day as a couple.

Time together

If couples take regular time with each other, they have regular opportunities to grow together. This is important, because everyone matures and develops other interests, changes perspectives and evolves through the years. These changes can enrich us both if we share them. Also, love and pleasure in each other's company arise with union and sharing. We need time together for this. If we don't make the time, we may end up having little or nothing in common once the children have left home. Some parents, when their children leave, find that they are strangers with familiar faces.

Making the time

We suggest that you make time in two general ways. One is spontaneous and the other is planned. Here are some suggestions for busy people who are attracted by this idea.

Spontaneous

Look for opportunities for quick connections with each other.
- Take five minutes to share a cup of tea or coffee. Actually sit together to have it.
- Go outside and look at the garden together. Hold hands.
- Turn off the TV and talk to each other for ten minutes.

- Arrange for a friend to provide childcare, so you two can have a walk together.
- Go to a movie, during the day if that is the only time you can arrange childcare.
- Get a baby-sitter and go out for dinner once in a while.

Planned

Make a half-hour, couple time appointment each day. Making an appointment is helpful, because it emphasises its importance. Various alternatives are available. Do it:
- over breakfast
- when the children have gone to school
- at lunch
- after the paid workers arrive home from work
- after the children are bathed
- immediately after the children are in bed
- at a specified time during the evening
- while the children are doing their homework

Remembering your purpose is to connect as people, not as mothers and fathers, the way you use this time will influence the outcome. We have several recommendations.
- Make the place you meet and what you do as pleasant as possible for you both.
- Having a drink and something to nibble is enjoyable for many people.
- Concentrate on pleasures and enjoyment.
- Use the opportunities to talk about things you like about each other and about your hopes and plans for the future with each other.
- Emphasise loving, enjoyable and satisfying things, whatever the topics.
- Avoid conversations about the children. This is your time.
- Leave talk about problems and difficulties until another time.

Handling the children

Making practical plans for the children during your couple time is obviously important. So:
- organise for them to be in another part of the house
- younger ones can entertain themselves with you, but do their own thing as much as possible
- older ones don't need to be in the room

- babies need more actual attention than older children, although even they don't have to be the complete centre of attention
- if you can't organise to meet while the babies sleep, try getting on with your own conversations and interests while caring for them.

As you take time with each other, your increasing strength and balance as a couple transmit into the rest of your family and all benefit. This will be a natural motivation. Also, children adapt quickly to consistent expectations and to regular events. As you set the pattern with each other, your children will adapt. This will become 'Mum's and Dad's time' and they will respect it, if you expect them to.

Lone parents

Men and women who are parenting alone are people, too, not just fathers and mothers. They benefit from regular social contact with other adults. These contacts give them the chance to exchange with people about adult issues and interests. Also, they open up opportunities for grown-up friendships and intimacy. Sharing our time with other parents, whether they are lone parents or coparents, is one way of doing this. Setting out to make new friends and staying in contact with old friends are two other options and well worth the extra effort involved. Making this a priority can pay off beautifully.

A final word

Our basic message to all parents is very simple: 'We do make a difference to our children. We are making a difference to them through everything we do'.

So we hope that what we have written will help you. We hope that knowing some of the effects we have on our children and how we can plan to affect them deliberately, will help you to raise your children well. This is both for their sakes and your own.

At the same time, through our children, we are helping to shape the world to come. The way they are when they reach adulthood helps to form the world they will live in. By looking forward to the future that we would like our children to have, we can begin to prepare them today, to produce the kind of world that future includes and to be able to live well in it as they create it.

The journey of childhood is 21 years long. Much of it is filled with joy and delight, and other aspects can be difficult. The vast majority of parents find certain parts of the journey very challenging. The whole range of experiences from great joy to heavy challenge is completely normal. We hope that this book will help you to expand those parts of the journey in which you delight and help you to deal more easily with the challenges.

Acknowledgements

This book is the culmination of many years work. We thank the hundreds of people who have contributed to it, and a brief acknowledgement cannot do justice to the significance of their help. Even so, we do thank everyone who has contributed directly and indirectly.

Given the subject, it is fitting first to thank our own parents, Allan and Betty, and Alfred and Phyllis. We appreciate all the love, time, effort, dedication and commitment that they showed over the years.

We also thank Jacqui Schiff who introduced Ken to both the orientation we have used in the book and many significant observations about people. Many hundreds of parents and children have also contributed significantly. We thank them for allowing us to observe them, for making themselves so wonderfully available to us and for their willingness to try our suggestions and find out if they worked.

Averil Coe kept things going while we did the writing. As the Network's office manager, she took significantly more weight than usual to allow us the time to get on with the very enjoyable job of writing. Sara Parsons also spent many hours typing tens of thousands of words from tape transcripts of our lectures. This work formed the basis of significant parts of the book and saved us inestimable amounts of time. To both of them our thanks.

We thank all our colleagues and friends for their ongoing encouragement and support for the project. Their excitement at the prospect of the book and their delighted feedback at what they read were abundant sources of nourishment. We include in their number Rex and Vicki Finch, of Finch Publishing, who are significantly responsible for the form and shape of the book. The four of us spent many happy hours discussing, planning and shaping the final product that you now hold in your hands.

Our thanks also to Steve and Shaaron Biddulph, friends of many years. Over the years we have shared much, including discussions of our own children, and have switched between the roles of teacher/mentor and trainee on several occasions. Their open-handed help and generosity in both talking about their thinking as they wrote their own books and their willingness to link us to people like Rex and Vicki Finch have been a very great help.

Finally, we thank everyone who contributed by reading the manuscript in various stages of completion. We valued all their feedback.

Recommended reading

A New Start for the Child with Reading Problems: A Manual for Parents, Carl H. Delacato, David McKay Company, Inc., New York, 1970

Baby Massage, Amelia D. Auckett, Hill of Content, Melbourne, 1981

Becoming the Way We Are: A Transactional Analysis Guide to Personal Development, Pam Levin, Levin, Berkeley, 1974

Beginning Fatherhood: A Guide for Expectant Fathers, Warwick Pudney and Judy Cottrell, Finch Publishing, Sydney, Australia, 1998

Being Happy: A Handbook to Greater Confidence and Security, Andrew Matthews, Media Masters, Singapore, 1988

Born to Win: Transactional Analysis with Gestalt Experiments, Muriel James and Dorothy Jongeward, Addison-Wesley, Reading, 1971

Boys in Schools: Addressing the Real Issues Behaviour, Values and Relationships, Editors: Rollo Browne and Richard Fletcher, Finch Publishing, Sydney, 1995

Discipline That Works: Promoting Self-discipline in Children, Thomas Gordon, Plume, USA, 1991

Facing Death and Finding Hope: A Guide to the Emotional and Spiritual Care of the Dying, Christine Longaker, Random House, London, 1997

Father Time: Making Time for Your Children, Daniel Petre, Pan MacMillan, Sydney, 1998

Fathers After Divorce: Building a New Life and Becoming a Successful Separated Parent, Michael Green, Finch Publishing, Sydney, 1998

Fathers, Sons & Lovers: Men Talk about Their Lives from the 1930s to Today, Peter West, Finch Publishing, Sydney, 1996

Girls Talk: Young Women Speak Their Hearts and Minds, Edited by Maria Pallotta-Chiarolli, Finch Publishing, Sydney, 1998

Life after Debt: Women's Survival Stories, Sue Wells, Scarlet Press, London, 1997

Life after Life, Raymond Moody Jnr., Bantam Books, New York, 1975

Magical Child: Rediscovering Nature's Plan of Our Children, Joseph Chilton Pearce, Paladin Books, London, 1979

Making Friends: A Guide to Getting Along with People, Andrew Matthews, Media Masters, Singapore, 1990

Manhood: A Book about Setting Men Free, Steve Biddulph, Finch Publishing, Sydney, 1994

More Secrets of Happy Children, Steve and Shaaron Biddulph, HarperCollins, Sydney, 1994

Motherhood: Making It Work for You, Jo Lamble and Sue Morris, Finch Publishing, Sydney, 1999

New Passages: Mapping Your Life across Time, Editors: Gail Sheehy and Joel Delbourgo, Ballantine Books, New York, 1996

Now that I'm Married Why Isn't Everything Perfect? The 8 Essential Traits of Couples Who Thrive, Susan Page, Bookman Press, Melbourne, 1994

Passages, Gail Sheehy, Bantam Books, New York, 1984

PET: Parent Effectiveness Training, Thomas Gordon, New American Library Trade, New York, 1990

Pregnancy and Childbirth, Sheila Kitzinger, Michael Joseph Limited, London, 1980

Raising Boys: Why Boys Are Different – and How to Help Them Become Happy and Well-balanced Men, Steve Biddulph, Finch Publishing, Sydney, 1997

Silent Knife: Cesarean Prevention & Vaginal Birth after Cesarean, Nancy Wainer Cohen & Lois J. Estner, Bergin & Garvey Pubishers, South Hadley, USA, 1983

Talking to Kids ... with Feeling: A Book for Adults and Children, Dr Nora Duffield, Random House, Auckland, 1995

The Money Tree, Diana Mathew, Money Tree Management Service Pty Ltd, Adelaide, 1996

The Secret of Happy Children: A New Guide for Parents, Steve Biddulph, Bay Books, Sydney, 1984

The Puberty Book: A Guide for Children and Teenagers, Wendy Darvill and Kelsey Powell, Hodder and Stoughton, London, 1995

The Cycles of Development, Pam Levin, *Transactional Analysis Journal*, vol. 12, no. 2, pp. 129–39, 1982

The Making of Love: How to Grow in Today's Family and Find Fulfilment, Freedom and Love, Steve and Shaaron Biddulph, Doubleday, Sydney, 1988

The Soul's Code: in Search of Character and Calling, James Hillman, Random House, Sydney, 1996

The Tibetan Book of Living and Dying, Sogyal Rinpoche, HarperCollins Publishers, London, 1992

The Crying Baby: Why Babies Cry, How Parents Feel, What You Can Do About It, Sheila Kitzinger, Viking, London, 1989

The Cathexis Reader: Transactional Analysis Treatment of Psychosis, Jacqui Lee Schiff, Aaron Schiff, Ken Mellor, Eric Schiff et al., Harper and Row, New York, 1975

Toughlove, Phyllis and David York and Ted Wachtel, Bantam Books, New York, 1983

Toughlove Solutions: Runaways, Sex, Suicide, Drugs, Alcohol, Abuse, Disrupted Families, Community Indifference, Phyllis and David York and Ted Wachtel, Bantam Books, New York, 1985

Understanding Men's Passages: Discovering the New Map of Men's Lives, Gail Sheehy, Random House, New York, 1998

Within Me, Without Me – Adoption: An Open and Shut Case? Sue Wells, Scarlet Press, London, 1994

Biame Network

Biame Network Inc. is an international, non-profit, educational organisation. It is an incorporated association with members in many countries. Founded in 1984 by Ken and Elizabeth Mellor, its primary purpose is to take a spiritually based approach to helping people integrate personal awakening with their day-to-day activities. The approaches developed within the network are down-to-earth, practical and easily used by people living everyday lives in the modern world. They have origins in a variety of traditions, but owe no allegiance to any.

The network's varied activities and programs enable people to use it as a resource for many different purposes to do with self-management, personal development and spiritual awakening. The wide-ranging techniques are drawn from many parts of the world in both the East and the West. Areas include personal health and wellbeing, self-management, parenting, teacher education, relationship development, financial and business management, community development, personal growth and change, spiritual evolution and practices, and advanced spiritual awakening.

All enquiries are welcome:

Biame Network, PO Box 271, Seymour, Victoria 3661, Australia

Telephone: +61 3 5799 1198, Freecall (in Australia):1800 244 254

Fax: +61 3 5799 1132

Email: biamenet@eck.net.au

Website: www.biamenetwork.net

Notes and references

1 Your job as a parent

Page 3 **'Keeping children safe'** Contact your local children's hospital for information about how to protect children from common hazards around the home.

Page 4 **'... cross roads safely'** The neurological developments necessary for children to make safe and accurate judgements about approaching vehicles are only completed at about nine to ten years of age. They cannot handle the simultaneous judgements of distance, speed and their own positions until then.

Page 5 **'... go to a cranial osteopath'** Osteopaths gently readjust the body so it functions optimally. They correct mis-alignments in the skeleton that are creating difficulties. Cranial osteopaths concentrate on the head and neck as well. Osteopathy is a cousin of chiropractic.

Page 11 **'If separated or divorced ...'** As our children take in each of us as their parents, they are also recording the way we get along with each other. So you can think of you and your partner lodged inside your children, continuing to parent them internally the way you have both parented them externally, as well as interacting with each other just as you do. When parents separate or divorce, it creates a similar rupture between the parents inside the children. Parents who make it their business to develop a good working relationship with each other (at the very least) help their children heal these ruptures and so contribute a great deal to the future wellbeing, balance and inner security of their children.

Page 13 **'Money and other resources ...'** *The Money Tree* by Diana Mathew is a wonderfully clear and simple book. It spells out how to plan and organise personal and family finances to make the most of the money available to us. You can get it from PO Box 501, North Adelaide, South Australia 5007. Telephone: 1800 686 008 and Facsimile: (08) 8340 2888.

2 Being a successful parent

Page 19 **'Make time ...'** **Making time** is different from **having time**. With 'making time', we actively and deliberately set it aside, perhaps leaving other things undone. By doing this, we program in, or schedule the time that we need. With 'having time', we generally don't. 'I just

don't have the time,' is a common result of not planning. We tend to wait for time to appear, as if it will magically manifest by itself. Experience shows, of course, that it often doesn't.

Page 20 **'... time just for play ...'** Have a look at *When Will the Children Play?* by Angela Rossmanith. She has some refreshing ideas on how to live in balance with the variety of our children's needs for time and attention.

Page 24 **'... not passive observers ...'** See *Magical Child* by Joseph Chilton Pearce for the idea of 'body knowing'. (Paladin Books, London, 1979.)

3 Your experience of families

Page 32 **'... produce a replay'** This is a phenomenon noticed by many people. It is part of the literature of several forms of psychotherapy. Transactional Analysis, in particular, has explored it. TA is a simple system for understanding people. These recordings are called 'ego states'. See *Born to Win: Transactional Analysis with Gestalt Experiments* by Muriel James and Dorothy Jongeward (Addison-Wesley, Reading, 1971.)

Page 33 **'... responses to our own children ...'** See the video called *Kangaroos: faces in the mob* – Green Cape Wildlife Films (Tel. 02 9875 1066 Fax 02 9484 9261) This shows that even kangaroos do it. A lovely video shows two years in the life of a mob of kangaroos in New South Wales. In particular, two mothers and two joeys were followed through from birth until about weaning time. One thrived on the care of her mother, a female in a line remarkable for its good parenting. The other died from a dingo attack before being weaned, because his mother had neglected to teach him the basic survival skills he needed. She had been neglected by her own mother.

Page 34 **'... early experiences ...'** If you don't know anyone who has had some effective help who can give you a personal recommendation, look in your local *Yellow Pages*. Several categories are helpful: Marriage Guidance, Counselling, Psychotherapy, Family Therapy, Psychologists, Mediators, Family Welfare (Organisations), and Pregnancy Counselling. Also, contact your doctor for referral to medically trained people, such as psychiatrists. Local councils, hospital social work departments, local libraries, citizens' advice bureaus, and community health centres are often helpful for referrals or for offering the services themselves. Local libraries often have good information, too. Emergency services are usually also listed in the front of telephone books, including Life Lines, Personal Emergency Services, Parents' Crisis Lines, Child Protection Crisis Lines and several others.

4 Your own family patterns

Page 37 '... **developing our ideals** ...' Here are some more that we think are important:
* criticism is offered along with options for what to do instead
* intuitive awareness is important
* mutual caring and support are important
* contributing to the family in some productive way is expected
* everyone likes having fun as a family
* respect for property is encouraged
* assertiveness and directness are valued
* facing things as they are and dealing with them are very important
* staying practical and down to earth in all things is helpful
* meeting obligations is expected
* taking personal responsibility is encouraged
* acting adequately is supported
* everyone's strengths and vulnerabilities are respected.

Page 37 '... **thinking of a motto**' As you think about your family as a whole, you may get some fun from thinking of a motto that covers most things. Some examples are:
* 'Everyone is uniquely important'
* 'Follow in your father's/mother's footsteps'
* 'On with the revolution'
* 'There's never enough'
* 'Family always first'
* 'Loving, caring, sharing'
* 'Anything goes'
* 'Kids rule the roost'
* 'Everything has a place; everything in its place'
* 'Parents come first'
* 'Mother knows best', or 'Father knows best'
* 'Men are okay/not okay', or 'Women are okay/ not okay'
* 'Don't tell me what to do'
* 'Us against the world'
* 'You can't push us around'
* 'Happy to help'

5 Family dynamics

Page 43 '**The Drama Triangle**' This idea was developed by Steve Karpman in the sixties. It is known in Transactional Analysis circles as 'The Karpman Drama Triangle'. You can find an excellent presentation in *Born to Win:*

Transactional Analysis with Gestalt Experiments by Muriel James and Dorothy Jongeward (Addison-Wesley, Reading, 1971.)

6 Balancing work and family life

Page 51 '... **if the fathers are not around**' Of course, throughout history, large numbers of men and women have raised their children alone. Widows and widowers have often had to do this. We are considering current, general trends.

Page 53 '**Childcare centres** ...' See the continuing research done by Jay Belsky (Professor of Human Development and Family Studies, Pennsylvania State University, University Park, PA, USA) with over a thousand children. Some are or have been in childcare and some have not. This work is highlighting some very interesting findings that are consistent with our position.

Page 54 '**Job pressures**' Read *Father Time: Making Time for Your Children* – Daniel Petre (Pan MacMillan, 1998)

Page 55 '**Health suffers** ...' Think of all the information now available about the need to live a balanced life. The connections between sustained stress and ill-health are obvious. Living an unbalanced life is now seen as a direct contribution to physical conditions, such as heart attacks, strokes, and cancer. Recovery from these diseases and conditions is seen as greatly enhanced or even completely effected through lifestyle changes.

7 Working as a team

Page 64 '**Lone parents**' Various organisations exist for this purpose, for example, in Victoria, Big Brothers/Big Sisters (169 Dandenong Rd., Windsor, Victoria 3181. Tel. 03 9525 2500) If you look around, you can also find parenting groups for lone parents where the emphasis is on parenting rather than on finding a mate.

8 Handling parental conflict

Page 67 '... **so everyone benefits**' Working out the assets of our styles, we can decide who will do what according to who is most likely to succeed with the children. For example, one is better at staying calm under pressure, another at getting children to do uncomfortable things, one at settling things down, another at getting kids thinking clearly, one at thinking of creative consequences for actions, another at following through on setting those consequences.

Page 68 '... **descriptions of final outcomes**' You will find detailed discussion of this way of setting goals and its advantages in two publications. *Maximising Performance & Well-being at Work* – Ken Mellor, a small booklet, and *Creative Release Meditation* – Ken Mellor, an audio recording, one side of which has step-by-step instructions for setting goals. (See Biame Network, page 230.)

Page 70 '**Grounding helps us ...**' Several sources are available for exploring grounding further: The *Grounding Meditation* – Ken Mellor, an audio recording; *Personal Well-being Course Notes* – Ken Mellor, extensive notes from a nine-session course on self-management; and *Personal Balance at Home & Work* – Ken Mellor, a small booklet. (See Biame Network, page 230.)

Page 73 '**If you disagree ...**' All the same, if you tend to react regularly with disagreement, practise saying 'Yes' as your first response for a while. By the same token, if you tend to react with agreement regularly, practise saying 'No' as your first response for a while. These changes can help you to develop more choice over your responses.

9 Parenting with love

Page 74 '**Well-loved children thrive**' Babies who are not touched lovingly have stunted growth. They were called 'failure to thrive babies' years ago and were diagnosed with a condition called marasmus. Older children who are starved for affection and love show us the cost in their adulthood through their pinched looks, the yearning chasm they often feel inside and their unavailability to love, even when it is offered in abundance. For all of them, the solution is love. Love them enough and in the right way and they thrive.

Page 76 '**Body love ...**' 'Body love' is associated with our urge to have children and, once they arrive, our physical drive to keep them alive and well. Parents seem naturally to experience a distinct physical bond with their biological children. The saying 'blood is thicker than water' probably comes from this distinctiveness. Our bonds with other children do not have this same quality, although they can be powerfully pleasurable and loving.

Many step-parents, foster parents, and adoptive parents know this wonderful connectedness. Our bodies are very responsive to the biological imperatives we have to care for the young. We know of one mother who powerfully demonstrated this. She was able to breastfeed her adopted son, because she started to lactate spontaneously very soon after his arrival from the hospital.

Page 77 '**Feeling love ...**' Some people will not experience love like this. We are all in various stages of openness. The more open we are, the closer our description of the feeling is to what people experience. We have worked for many years helping people to open up their capacities to feel their emotions, so we know that a wide variety of experience is possible.

Page 80 '**... the whole person inside ...**' James Hillman in *The Soul's Code: In search of character and calling* (Random House, Australia, 1996) discusses the very interesting idea that everyone is born like an acorn. If we look at the acorn only, we do not see the full potential into which people can grow. He suggests that we practise seeing the tree in the acorn that our children are, so we support their personal development in ways that are in harmony with the person they are pressing to become.

Page 81 '**We experience "being love" ...**' Other words for 'being' are 'soul', 'higher self', or 'I Am Presence'.

Page 81 '**... spiritual practice**' This is different from adopting a set of beliefs. We are talking about daily routines that will help you to realise the being that you are. Many opportunities exist for this these days with a large number of religious, secular or other groups. Contact us if you would like to know what we do. (See Biame Network, page 230.)

10 The discipline sequence

Page 93 '**... an agreement from your children**' An advantage of making commitments is that our children convert **external motivation and commitment** into **internal motivation and commitments**. Much of our guidance, urging, expecting, pushing and rewarding naturally comes from our own understandings. We know what our children need to learn and we set about helping them do this. But they are often not interested in what we take as important. It is only our insistence that gets them interested. Getting them to make commitments gets them increasingly to take an interest in and responsibility for what we are wanting them to learn.

Part of the frustration that many parents experience when disciplining their children is to do with this very thing. The parents seem much more motivated and committed than their children. Realise that this is very probably true. An effective way to deal with this is to get them to decide to act differently and to make agreements with you about what they are going to do. We can save a lot of parental wear and tear by doing this.

'I don't like such and such. You are to do X from now on. Rant, rant, rave, rave ...', turns into 'I don't like such and such. You are to do X from now on. What are you going to do from now on?' This is generally much easier and it is a simple thing to do.

11 Standing to decide

Page 96 '... a powerful tool' Like many people who lived in the 1940s or before, Ken was introduced to 'standing to decide' in school. Then, however, it was called 'standing in the corner'. It was also often used, it seemed, to ridicule and berate the unfortunate children who were the butts of poor teaching practices. Like many people, he decided never to use it himself. However, when training with Jacqui Schiff at Cathexis Institute in the USA in the early 1970s, he was reintroduced to an entirely different, refreshingly systematic and sensitive method of using the technique. Still called 'standing in the corner' then, Jacqui used all the basic guidelines outlined in this chapter. You will find more material on the process under the title of 'Stand and Think' in Steve and Shaaron Biddulph's book *More Secrets of Happy Children*, HarperCollins 1994. Steve was first exposed to 'standing in the corner' also at Cathexis Institute in 1980 when there on a Churchill Fellowship. He and Shaaron 'got more inspiration about it' during the mid-1980s when we taught it at a workshop that they organised for us. We use 'standing to decide' as the name, because we wish to emphasise the decision-making that takes place near the end of the process.

Page 105 '... Harry was completely transformed ...' When we realise that this kind of child is likely to end out on the streets, in the prison system, in a psychiatric hospital, or the victim of violence he has provoked, doing something mild, like struggling physically with him for a few hours, is well worth it. All parents need to realise that what their children are doing 'today' is what they are very likely to do 'tomorrow' unless someone acts effectively enough to change it somewhere between 'now' and 'then'.

13 Communicating clearly

Page 122 'Young children are "body minded".' Ken first encountered this idea in a different form in *Magical Child: Rediscovering Nature's Plan of Our Children* – Joseph Chilton-Pearce (Paladin Books, 1979). He called it 'body knowing'. The physical and concrete ways children understand themselves and the world has been known for a long time. It was explored in detail by Jean Piaget, a Swiss biologist and psychologist early this century.

Page 123 '... by changing the words ...' Be alert both to the general words people use and the specific expressions. Here are some to avoid: 'I would kill for a drink', 'You little devil', 'I'll kill you kids if you don't all shut up', 'You're all hopeless', and 'I won't take "No" for an answer'. We are sure you can come up with many of your own.

Page 124 'Mother is still programming ...' The general point applies more than just the words we use. It applies to seeing, feeling, tasting and smelling as well. Two visual examples illustrate this.

* Some friends of ours had a 'wonderful' safety poster pinned to their dining room wall. It had a picture of a home with little cartoons of a family in various places, such as on the roof, at the sink, and using power points. The only trouble was that every one of the pictures showed people getting into trouble. They pulled it down soon after we pointed this out.
* Jeff was having many problems studying at home. He was fine in the library at school or at friends' homes, so this was puzzling. When we checked his room, we discovered a very large red road sign attached to the wall above his desk. It said, 'STOP'. We suggested that, if he was going to steal road signs, and we recommended that he didn't, then we thought 'GO' would be better. He took the sign down and studied well at his desk from then on.

Page 129 'The level of compulsion ...' They usually translate into something akin to the original meaning of the word 'please', however. 'Please' is a contracted way of saying 'If you please', or 'If it pleases you'. With 'okay', the translation is 'If you are okay with this', or 'If it's okay with you'. Both shift the responsibility for deciding to the person 'being asked'.

15 Repeating ourselves

Page 137 'Learning relies on repetition' Many years ago, Glenn Doman and Carl Delacato became aware of this link and developed a regime for helping children to re-pattern their neurological systems. Their work stimulated many wonderful developments in the treatment of brain injury and in how to enhance learning. One reference is *Diagnosis and Treatment of Speech and Reading Problems* – C. H. Delacato, Out of Print, Published 1963.

16 Developing self-esteem

Page 141 'Good self-esteem ...' Grown-ups with good self-esteem manage well in most situations. They are able to handle criticism and use it well. They can deal with difficult circumstances and end up in good shape. Disagreements with others may challenge them, however, they retain a sense of proportion about the issue and stay balanced within themselves. Generous with their praise of others, they generally also lend active support unstintingly to those in need. They make great team members and leaders, because their sense of self worth is not dependent on the opinion of those around them. At the same time, they take note of what others think and use those thoughts to make adjustments, if they are necessary. They value themselves and others as people and as people with talents.

Page 142 **'We will love them forever ...'** Notice how the four types of love, 'body love', 'feeling love', 'person love' and 'being love' are all involved in this. (See Chapter 9, 'Parenting with love'.)

17 Managing brothers and sisters

Page 149 **'... families with one child ...'** Get together with your extended family so your child can spend a lot of time with cousins. Have friends to play and stay regularly. When they are pre-school age, play groups, family visits to friends and others, and kindergarten are all possibilities. As they get older, getting them involved in team sports, and group activities like Scouts or Guides, will all help.

Page 149 **'While they get along well ...'** A very important principle is behind this. **What you notice or put energy into is what you get.** What we pay active attention to with our children they will tend to repeat. And they tend to repeat it in proportion to the duration and the intensity of our attention. So if we spend more time concentrating on what they are doing that we like, then we will tend to get more of that behaviour. If we pay more attention to what we don't like or want, then we will tend to get more of that behaviour. Naturally, we need to pay attention to both at times, but we are wise to keep the overall balance as we would like it to be. So by making sure we spend more time laughing, celebrating, loving, shouting and, even, getting angry about the things we want them to be doing, we are going to get much more of what is important to us, than otherwise.

Page 156 **'Repeated patterns of difficulty ...'** A very powerful way of doing this is to use a procedure that we have developed called the 'Unifying Meditation'. It helps us to get ourselves clear inside, so we can handle what we and they do with each other, and to ensure that we arrive at the most desirable outcomes that we can. You can obtain a recording with step-by-step instructions from the Network. (See Biame Network, page 230.)

18 Natural transitions

Page 166 **'To make the necessary decisions ...'** One of the ways of thinking about this is to think of our children as living in a box. Inside the box, they are free to do whatever they decide. But they are only allowed out of the box under some sort of supervision. As their capacities expand, we expand the size of the box. If they manage the expansion, we expand the box further. If they don't manage it, we keep it the same or contract it temporarily, until they can manage. Throughout childhood, we keep the box as big as we can, but we ensure it is no bigger than they can manage. Assuming all has gone well, by the time they reach adulthood, the walls of the box will no longer exist, because the box will be the world and they will be capable of living well in it.

19 A second chance

Page 169 **'Two general phases'** These phases are different from and much more general than the specific developmental stages we consider in the next section.

Page 169 **'... from conception to ...'** It does not stop at the end of childhood. Adults continue to unfold developmentally. In the middle 1980s many of us first became aware of this from the work of Gail Sheehy. She has several books that are very informative in this area. They include: *Passages* – Gail Sheehy (Bantam Books, 1984), *New Passages: Mapping Your Life across Time* – Gail Sheehy, Joel Delbourgo (Editor) (Ballantine Books, 1996), and *Understanding Men's Passages: Discovering the New Map of Men's Lives* – Gail Sheehy (Random House, 1998)

Page 170 **'... reworking and reveiwing ...'** Adults do these reviews, too. We seem to upgrade ourselves cyclically about every fourteen years. We may also begin an upgrade in response to a major crisis or challenge.

During each upgrade, we keep on with the day-to-day events of our lives. The beginning is usually signalled by regression. We start to perceive, feel, think and behave as if we are much younger. People often want to curl up alone, to have others look after them again, to enjoy childlike play and be free from responsibilities, and to act in other 'young' ways.

These periods commonly occur in our late twenties, early forties, mid-fifties, late sixties, mid-eighties and late nineties. Usually times of major reevaluation, we deeply reconsider who we are and where we are going in our lives.

A primary shift in inner energy is responsible for these reviews. The shift and the regressive pull of earlier experiences, stimulates a major update of the programs that we laid down earlier in our lives that still bind and guide us. We update them by bringing them into the mature light of our current lives. During this very creative time, we gradually grow up again emotionally, rewriting and upgrading our previous conditioning as we do. The upgrading usually takes about seven years.

This phenomenon has been observed by many people. You will find various aspects of it mentioned in the following references. *Becoming the Way We Are: a Transactional Analysis Guide to Personal Development* – P. Levin (Levin, Berkeley, 1974), *The Cycles of Development* – P. Levin (Transactional Analysis Journal, vol. 12, No. 2, pp. 129–39, 1982), and *The Cathexis Reader: Transactional Analysis Treatment of Psychosis* – Jacqui Lee Schiff, Aaron Schiff, Ken Mellor, Eric Schiff et al. (Harper and Row, 1975, p. 45)

Page 170 '... a second chance' With this statement we are not implying that parents are solely responsible for any trouble in their children's lives. Children are running their own programs and make their own decisions throughout their lives. These influence outcomes very powerfully and are out of our control as parents. For example, a difficult birth or a visit to hospital when very young; a child's decisions not to cooperate or feelings that they are unloved and unlovable all influence later attempts on our parts to give our children the best we can. What children take from each encounter is always a blend of what is occurring around them and what they are making out of it.

Page 170 '... the more troubled ...' Children who missed out a lot, who had significant problems that were not resolved, or who were traumatised and harmed during the first phase of their lives, generally relive all those experiences during the upgrade. They may not have memories of the past events, but they will act in the same sorts of ways as they did then. This naturally adds to the challenges in their lives. It challenges us, too, of course, because it is our job to help them deal with all of this.

Page 170 '... quite a degree of freedom ...' Twelve-year-olds are still children, all the same. So we need to keep track of them accordingly. They are not adults in little bodies, regardless of how much they may think they are, or how much they would like us to think they are. Because they are still children, we continue to keep a close eye on their activities and to make sure they are protected and are fulfilling their responsibilities.

Page 170 '... near their thirteenth birthday ...' Some may start a bit earlier and some a bit later. Also, as far as we can determine, the process is not triggered solely by puberty, so that some children who begin puberty well before or after thirteen years of age have still started the upgrade at about thirteen.

Page 171 '**Many become very dreamy ...**' If you get any of these signs, relax. Your children are going through a completely normal, very creative and very important process. We make specific suggestions about what to do at this time to respond to their needs, so that everyone moves through the process as easily as possible. Unless there are other problems, these are not signs of deep psychological problems requiring psychiatric attention.

Page 172 '**... those times in their earlier lives ...**' In our work as psychotherapists and as parent educators, we have witnessed a seemingly miraculous transformation through this time. Deeply troubled young people have transformed into well-balanced, mature, happy and fulfilled young adults. We explain in general what is involved in the process in this chapter. We give specific descriptions and guidelines in Chapter 21, 'Phases of childhood'.

Page 173 '**This can be very disturbing ...**' If you find that you cannot manage, get help. The people to look for are those who understand the normal corrective process that is occurring and know how to support it in your child, while helping you manage things as a parent. Other parents whose children have already grown up are often very helpful.

Page 175 '**From the age of two ...**' Even if dyslexia, retardation, hyperactivity, ADHD or some other physical or emotional condition is affecting what our children do, we still need to teach them to manage themselves. In our experience, it is even more important with these children that we use discipline. We may modify the way we use the procedures, but we need to persist until the children have learned to adapt. We have found many children were able to make very much more of their lives than they otherwise might have. They manage and control themselves well, because they have learned from us how to do it.

20 Four births, four bonds

Page 176 '**The birth relocates ...**' We include the bonding process as part of the complete description of birth, as you will see. Until they are bonded, they have not fully arrived in the new world that awaits them at the other end of the birth.

Page 177 '**... bonds with the mother and father ...**' Increasing numbers of fathers are attending the births of their children. This gives them the wonderful opportunity for a bonded involvement with their children that was mainly the province of mothers in the past. This paves the way for wonderful and deeply meaningful involvement with children as they grow up.

We recommend that you make it your business to be conscious and available at this time. Realise that the baby will bond with whomever and whatever is there during the crucial hour or so after birth. The medical worker doing painful procedures, the crib he or she is left in – whatever is there. And this bond forms a fundamental basis for all later relationships and the outcomes of all later transitions. We give some recommendations in Chapter 21, 'Phases of childhood', about this.

Page 180 **'Birth mother'** Our children's contacts with the wider community are generally expanding by this time. In fact, many adolescents spend more time away from home in their waking hours than they do at home. We are wise to keep track of who is influencing them and the nature of the influence.

Page 180 **'Beginning'** This is similar to the change we observe in the eighteen-month-old child before the second birth. We describe this as the birth of the 'newborn adult'. However, while they are adults, they are at the very beginnings of adulthood and have at least a further seven years of development ahead of them before we would describe them as adults in a mature sense.

Page 180 **'As they take their stands ...'** During the second birth, the struggles and passions are about wanting, feelings and desire. This is different from the struggles about knowing, although they can seem very similar in many ways.

Page 181 **'The more united ...'** Adults do not necessarily agree on everything. So we are usually faced with having to deal with some adults who want to respond to our young people in ways that we do not think are good for them. This may require that we take stands with other adults as well as with our children.

We can often get help and relief at times by developing friendship groups. Some people also create teams of like-thinking adults who are willing to come and visit their homes at times of high-level crisis. Their job is to throw their weight behind the parents who need support. They show our adolescent children that we and other adults share the same attitudes values and expectations, and that we will take a stand to ensure that they accept them.

Page 181 **'... limit or control the contacts ...'** One family took their son away from a high school where the teachers did little to confront dishonesty, disrespect, bullying and lack of application to work. After finding a school that supported honesty, mutual respect and caring, and concentration on satisfactory work, their

child started to adopt the same standards. Prior to that, his parents had been amongst the few significant adults in his life to support these sorts of things.

Page 181 **'At their most intense ...'** Stimulated by the distress these antics often cause, some adults get between young people and their parents during the birth process. This is very unhelpful. They interrupt the process and can hinder the development of the young people in ways that will influence them for the rest of their lives. Under some circumstances, of course, actual intervention may be necessary for the real protection of young people whose parents are actually abusive. However, we adults do well to recognise that fourteen-year-olds are skilful at getting others to believe the worst of their parents. We should always check the actual state of affairs at home before intervening.

Page 182 **'... entry into the adult community'** In *Magical Child* (Paladin Books, London, 1979) Joseph Chilton Pearce gets close to a similar realisation. It interests us that many initiation rites used to occur between thirteen and sixteen years of age. It is as if children are at their most impressionable (thirteen), are educated and are gestated by the community (of men or women) until they are ready to be born and then to bond with the adult world as adult men and women in their own rights.

Page 182 **'... a sense of belonging ...'** By staying actively engaged with our young people through this time, we adults make ourselves available for young people to bond with us. Because the need to bond with a group is imperative, we can be sure that young people who don't bond with us will bond with the next most available group. This is usually the group of their peers. From then on the peer group becomes the major reference for what they do and how they learn. Remember that this is a group of people who, in worldly terms, are immature, inexperienced, inclined to impulse-driven behaviour and in need of about five more years of guided maturation before they will be fully adult.

Page 183 **'We become transformed ...'** This delivery results in states that some people call Illumination, Enlightenment, or Awakening. Experienced people and spiritual practices that help us to keep expanding and embracing these 'non-worldly' dimensions are increasingly available, should you be interested in exploring these possibilities. Contact us at the Biame Network, if you want further information. (See Biame Network, page 230.)

Page 183 **'... interesting to read'** Lots of books on this issue are available these days. A beautiful, spiritual text that considers many of the issues of the fourth birth, although not as we have here, is *The Tibetan Book of Living and Dying* – Sogyal Rinpoche (HarperCollins Publishers, 1992). One of the early writers who collected stories 'of near death experiences' is Raymond Moody Jnr. His book *Life After Life* (Bantam Books, 1975) was the first or one of the first to do this.

Page 185 '... even become psychotic' After many years of working with people with severe disturbance, it is clear to us that completing the second birth is crucial for good mental health. People who don't get well started in life are prone to much more serious problems than those who do. This birth seems to us to be the boundary between what can turn into psychosis and normal or relatively normal development. People who get stuck part of the way through frequently end with what are technically called 'borderline personality structures', or with 'personality disorders'.

Page 185 '... had to keep struggling' Some keep struggling well into adulthood. Many adults act just like two-year-olds and have much more limited lives than they would have had, if they had resolved these issues when they were young.

21 Phases of childhood

Page 193 'love and welcome them' A lovely recorded meditation – the *Loving Bond Meditation* – is available that helps to deepen the welcoming process. It also helps profoundly with mothers and fathers who are not completely happy or accepting of the growing child, and with mothers who have to deal with miscarriages. (See Biame Network, page 230.)

Page 194 'Birth' See Chapter 20, 'Four births, four bonds' for more on the birth process.

Page 195 '... contact in first two hours' Babies imprint mothers, fathers, nurses, doctors, operating tables, cribs – whatever they are exposed to at this crucial time. It is crucial that the mother and father are the primary people with whom the baby bonds. Only in serious emergencies should this process be interrupted. Many people have their lives very seriously affected by this not being done.

Page 195 'first impact of physical world' If the world is warm, welcoming and friendly, the child will have a basic confidence about life that will form a wonderful foundation for it. If it is painful, intrusive, rough, harsh, unfeeling or something similar, then the child will develop a basic expectation that this is what life is like fundamentally. This is not a good beginning.

Page 195 'choose soft music' Choosing music that is soothing and relaxing is important. Also, parents can influence the atmosphere with fragrances that they like and think will be mellowing and relaxing for the baby.

Page 196 '... foundations for whole of life' See Chapter 9, 'Parenting with love', Chapter 10, 'The Discipline sequence', Chapter 16, 'Developing self-esteem' and Chapter 18, 'Natural transitions' for more information on this.

Page 196 '... holding and touching ...' A wonderful way to recharge and spend beautiful time with babies is to do a simple meditation that brings you deeply into contact with each other through simple relaxation. It is called 'Loving Bond Meditation'. (See Biame Network, page 230) See also a lovely little book called *Baby Massage* – Amelia D. Auckett (Hill of Content, Melbourne, 1981) This has a very simple and tested system of baby massage that can delight and soothe both parents and babies.

Page 196 '... at least one session ...' Cranial osteopathy is very gentle. Many problems in babies result from the misalignment of the cranial plates during birth. By gently realigning these, many babies have been spared months of discomfort and pain. We highly recommend this as a corrective measure and as a way of preventing later difficulties.

Page 196 'a sleep beautifully button' When your baby is about to fall asleep, run your finger or thumb from the space between his/her eyebrows to the hairline, saying as you do, 'Sleep beautifully'. This can be a wonderful bonus in the years to come. Repeatedly doing this establishes the 'sleep beautifully button'. When they are tired and needing to sleep, but are not relaxed, simply repeating the movement and the statement helps to induce sleep.

Page 197 'can become rough' They don't intend to hurt, but we still need to deal with it. We stop them doing whatever is causing the problem and say things such as, 'Suck gently', or 'Let go', or 'Be gentle'. When we can, we take them physically through the motions of what we are describing as we say the words.

Page 197 '... solid foods before ...' If they are full of breast milk they won't feel hungry and ready to try other things.

Page 197 '... use words ...' We actually recommend that parents do this from the very beginning. The general input of words over time lays a wonderful foundation for this stage when they get to it. Mentioning it here highlights the particular significance it takes on at this stage. They are primed and ready for words at this stage.

Page 198 '... **their own age** ...' Playgroups are great for them and for their mothers.

Page 198 '**make instructions simple** ...' See Chapter 13, 'Communicating clearly' for more on how and why this works.

Page 198 '... **second birth**' See Chapter 20 – 'Four births, four bonds'.

Page 198 '... **other's reactions**' Instead of pouring their milk on the floor to see what happens to the milk and the floor, they pour it on the floor to see how we respond.

Page 198 '... **"standing to decide"** ' See Chapter 11, 'Standing to decide' for simple instructions on how to introduce this way of managing children at this age.

Page 198 '**games** ...' All sorts of games are possible, depending on what is there. They can go down the slide or on the swing sitting on Dad's legs.

Page 198 '**give little jobs** ...' Maybe you have a small wastepaper basket that could empty, or they could help feed the pets, or have a bit of pastry to play with as Mum or Dad cooks, or wash dishes that are unbreakable. See Chapter 18, 'Natural transitions' for more on this.

Page 199 '... **from baby to child**' See Chapter 20, 'Four births, four bonds' for an expanded description and explanation.

Page 199 '**give body instructions** ...' If you give an instruction that they don't obey, go to them, give the instruction again and, as you do, firmly put them through the physical motions. This gives them a body base for knowing the meaning of the words. It also gives them a body base for knowing what an instruction is. For example, 'Come over here', as you take the child by the hand and walk him/her to where you were sitting; 'Pick up your toys', as you reach down and put her/his hands around a toy and put it in the box.

Page 199 '**parents to win** ...' See Chapter 20, 'Four births, four bonds' and Chapter 11, 'Standing to decide' for the reasons why it is so important for us to 'win'.

Page 199 '... **get it done now**' See Chapter 19, 'A Second Chance', where the way this works and the advantages are spelled out in detail.

Page 200 '... **family contact** ...' See Chapter 20, 'Four births, four bonds' for information on this.

Page 200 '... **teach the difference** ...' If they come to us and say, 'There's something under the bed', we suggest several things. Avoid going and checking, unless you think there is a high probability that there is. Going to look, merely convinces most thinking children that there could be something under the bed; why else would a fully grown adult go and check? We say something like, 'If you're going to make up things, I suggest that you make up something that you enjoy, rather than something scary. Why not pretend that it's a lovely warm and friendly animal, or something like that?'

Page 201 '**lots of physical exercise**' Ball games, and running, jumping, climbing games that develop a good sense of rhythm are all great. Schoolyard games like skipping, hopscotch and hand clapping games are ideal.

Page 201 '**close supervision** ...' Children do not have the neurological development to judge the progress of oncoming vehicles at this age. It is only at about nine years of age that they do. This is surprisingly old to many people, yet experience of school age children does confirm this.

Page 201 '... **communication guidelines**' We cannot always rely on our children to give clear, truthful information. Make sure you check everything with each other before you say what they can and cannot do. 'It's all right, I've asked Dad/Mum' can actually mean 'and he/she said, "No", but I'm not going to tell you because you might say, "No" too.'

Page 202 '... **decisions that stick** ...' They think deeply and draw conclusions that make sense to them. They can decide who they are, how they will act and what they will do with the rest of their lives. These decisions can be very powerful and can 'stick' for the rest of their lives. Because they have limited information and experience, their decisions can be very limiting: 'I'm hopeless', 'I'll never succeed or be happy', 'I just know no-one will like me'; just as limiting, 'I'm always right', 'I'll beat everyone I have to prove it', 'I'll always get what I want no matter what'.

Page 202 '**encourage feeling expression** ...' We can teach them that their feelings are not who they are: 'You are not what you are feeling. You are a wonderful person who is feeling sad at the moment. You are not a sad person.'

Page 202 '... **pocket money** ...' Give them, for example, fifty cents a week. They have twenty-five to spend and have to save twenty-five. Start a bank account for them, or keep the money in a safe place. They love watching it grow.

Page 202 '... **to feel happy**' We can use anything for the job that will work. Naturally, living in happy ways and affirming their happiness is very powerful. We can also expose them to happy, loving books, movies, people, songs, paintings, and games.

Page 202 '... who's in and who's out' This is a very tough time for excluded children, who need support to handle the exclusion. If schoolyard bullying or other unpleasantness is involved, talking to teachers may be very important. Children often bully in gangs at this time.

Page 202 'may start stealing' They are learning about ownership, stealing and lying. How is ownership determined? What is the difference between sharing and stealing? If I say something is true, how come it isn't? How do I get something, if it is not mine and I want it? All good questions.

Page 202 '... complete repeated chores ...' We need to ensure they learn this. We do so by repeatedly following them up and making sure that they do their jobs. The process lasts about three years or more and is worth every minute. By following up, we help them learn to complete repeated daily tasks and to complete long-term goals that might take many days, weeks or months to finish. Much of later adolescence and adulthood is filled with these kinds of demands. This learning needs to be supported strongly by parents and teachers with reminders and consequences.

Page 203 '... household jobs ...' They are capable of a great deal at this age: cleaning, vacuum cleaning, washing dishes, cooking. We can also encourage them to look after living things, such as plants or pets. This is a great way to teach them about the responsibilities of caring for life. We need to supervise this, of course.

Page 203 '... consequences ...' We would expect children of this age to undo what they have done, rather than just 'stand to decide'. For example, we expected two children to clean the ball marks off the wall as well as to decide that they would throw balls outside, not inside. If children steal, they need to face the person they have stolen from, return the goods, apologise and tell the person what they will do in future. We also encourage the person to set a consequence – in our presence. We need to give them strong messages that it is wrong to steal.

Page 203 '... tolerance and acceptance ...' Many future prejudices and patterns of nastiness and unpleasantness can become set at this age. Wise parents check out what the children are thinking, interrupt when necessary, and discuss, educate and set consequences when important.

Page 203 '... whiteboards in the kitchen ...' Each person in the family could have a special colour so that they can see their messages easily.

Page 203 'practising parenting' They act primarily from parental positions: 'I am responsible for you', or 'You are responsible for me'. They are learning about personal power, control 'over' others, and about the reality and limits of this control.

Page 203 '... decisions about life' Now that they have a clearer idea of time, they start to think ahead and make plans. Their thoughts about their futures are more realistic than when they were seven. They can see the results of things that they did earlier and apply what they learnt from these experiences.

Page 203 '... life-changing decisions ...' We can support their useful decisions and intervene in those that are not useful or that may be harmful to them or others. Examples of useful decisions are 'I am a happy person', 'People like me', 'I will be a ... doctor/mother/artist/carpenter/good person'. Decisions that we would like to modify include 'I won't ever succeed', 'I'm hopeless', 'Life isn't worth living', or 'No-one will ever like me'.

Page 203 '... what they are exposed to ...' Notice what they are reading, watching on TV, seeing at the movies, playing with on the computer, listening to on the radio or on cassettes and CDs, and learning at school. If we don't like what is being said, sung or shown it is a good idea to intervene and to stop them doing it. We can explain why we are doing this. See Chapter 2, 'Being a successful parent' for more on this.

Page 203 'offer guidance ...' Discuss issues with them. They need us to support and guide them and are generally open to this. This 'little parent' stage is a foundation time for strong future parenting skills. Affirm them.

Page 203 '... not yet grown up' They are not ready to be treated as adults. They, of course, might dispute this. The primary process is to replay the recordings that they made of us, their parents, so that they can check that what we taught them still works. If it doesn't, they can modify what they have learnt with our help. This is mimicry, not real adulthood. They are not yet ready to go out on the town alone!

Page 204 'Emotionally recycling the ages...' In Chapter 19, 'A second chance' we outline the way adolescents regress emotionally so they can rework and update their early programming. This is a predictable sequence. Chapter 19 contains a graph that matches the 'emotional ages' to actual ages of our adolescent children.

Page 204 '... gentle nurturing' They need to be held, fed and accepted, sometimes just as babies do. Don't let their big bodies put you off.

Page 204 'complete acceptance' You will find more on how to do this in Chapter 9, 'Parenting with love'.

Page 204 'tell them what to do ...' They often need high involvement early in this time. If we provide it, much of the emotion is managed more easily. For example, we take them by the hands when they arrive home and tell them what to do, perhaps accompanying them, as we would a small child. 'Give me a kiss. Now put your lunch box on the sink, now come to your room with me and get undressed. Now go to the shower. Now put these clothes on.'

Page 204 '... cuddle time' Physically holding them is easy. Sit on a couch, have them face you and lie curled up across your lap. Have the head at shoulder level. Support some of their weight with a cushion or two, and put your arms around them. You can get your very large thirteen-year-olds to lean against you while you stroke their hair. Alternatively, they can lie with their heads on our laps. This is not as nurturing. The nurturing usually helps deal with the lost feelings and neediness that they experience.

Page 204 '... lots of passion' See Chapter 20, 'Four births, four bonds' for more information on what is going on and how to handle things.

Page 205 'often confuse rebelliousness ...' Rebellious people act **against** other people's expectations, stated intentions and desires, or against their fantasies of what others expect, intend or want. Rebellious people usually think that they are acting powerfully. However, because they act against something, it is what they are acting against that has the power. Without that, they would not act. So, they actually depend on another person taking a stand, before they know what to do. They are very predictable.

All of this means that they are very dependent. They are also very easy to manipulate. All we need to do is to say the opposite of what you want them to do. So when your rebellious children are not cooperating, say something like, 'I know you won't agree with this, but ....', then add what you want them to agree with. Or you can say, 'I know you won't do this, but ...'.

People act with true independence or autonomy when they think about themselves, other people, the situation that brings them

together, and then make decisions based on the balance of what is going on.

Page 205 ' "three" small things a day' This enables you to choose the areas of struggle, rather than waiting for your child to choose. If you decide that housework has to be done and they struggle about it, then join in the struggle and win it. This is better than them having to choose serious issues to get attention. All the same, if they struggle spontaneously about something, join in and win. Obviously, if we become clear that they are right, then we give way gracefully, but beware of the desire to give way, just to avoid the hassle.

Page 205 'bring in the adults' Two books are particularly helpful at the ages when children struggle. They recommend that parents support each other, particularly when their children are adolescent. They are *Toughlove* – Phyllis and David York, and Ted Wachtel (Bantam Books, 1983) and *Toughlove Solutions* – Phyllis and David York and Ted Wachtel (Bantam Books, 1985)

Page 206 'adult world for bonding' See 'The third birth – Adult' in Chapter 20, 'Four births, four bonds' for information on what to do at this time.

Page 206 '... special ritual ...' Have special privileges that are given at fifteen in your family. You could have a special dinner party for them. Get some adult friends together and do a simple review of the young person's childhood successes. You might also give them a key to the house to signify your trust in their increased maturity.

Page 206 'righteously take ...' One parent said, 'They have a fourteen-year-old's determination, the assurance that they are right, plus the indignation of the sixteen-year-old'.

Page 206 'parents may want ...' Red Alert: This is not a good time for them to leave home. Most sixteen-year-olds need the active presence and involvement of their parents for at least another two years. The struggles they are engaging in are to do with responsibility – whether they take it or not – not to do with where they should live.

Page 207 'need limits ...' When they are calm, we can talk with them about the consequences they will find helpful for getting them to act as expected. They can become more committed to adhering to the rules through this approach.

Page 207 'lots of guidance' The idea is to talk to them as if they are adults. In the context of the other behaviour, this can be a challenge. However, part of them is very grown up, while another part is involved is a deep struggle about taking responsibility. So when things are relatively quiet, attempt calm, reasoned discussions that are like information-sharing sessions, rather than high-level power struggles.

Page 207 **'coaching in proper behaviour ...'** Everyone needs to abide by very clear limits. While apparently mature in many ways, their sexual maturity and seductiveness is more mimicry than real readiness. We need to nurture this carefully and appropriately.

Page 207 **'... manage the triangles'** Remember that clear communication is the way out of triangulation. Check with each other before making assumptions, or taking action. Your sixteen-year-old may be setting you up.

Page 207 **'... romantic fantasies'** Boyfriends and girlfriends often appear at this age but this is only one way that romance may be seen. They may read and write poetry, or read romantic novels. They love heroes performing feats of valour, or heroines tackling wondrous challenges. It is an age for heroic feats and journeys, both enacting them or reading and writing about them.

Page 207 **'... to appreciate ... blossoming sexuality'** This helps to launch their children into sexually mature adulthood. 'Wow you look great!' 'If I was your age, I'd think you were a real hunk.' 'You look so beautiful.' The guys/girls will be queueing up for you.' Of course, all of this is very embarrassing for the youngsters, but they love it and appreciate the intention.

Page 208 **'Mutual decision-making ...'** For example, we can talk with seventeen-year-olds about what they think they are capable of doing around the house. This could include what they think they still need to learn. Then, together we can work out what jobs they will do that both matches their capacities and extends them. For example, John was able to organise the clean-up after dinner really well, but was still not confident about preparing the meal. So, he and his parents decided that he would cook at least three times a week and be completely in charge of the meal on those nights.

Page 208 **'... legal status ...'** In Australia, they can vote, get married, drive a car, drink alcohol and sign contracts.

Page 208 **'... one right way ...'** They can adopt styles of life that they think will help them to live with integrity. They may become, for example, sages, missionaries, good citizens, acolytes, renegades, rebels, terrorists, police, or philosophers.

Page 208 **'if they stay ...'** If we are supporting our teenagers, it is a good idea to think about the years ahead and to discuss with them what we will be expecting of them as they reach eighteen to twenty-one. For example: 'We expect that you will be fully financially independent by twenty-one, so you need to be thinking about how you will do this. We are happy to talk to you about it if you would like our ideas'.

Page 208 **'celebrate ...'** This is a great way of marking the end of adolescence and the beginning of full adulthood. We can send our 'children' off with a great launching party.

22 Grounding

Page 212 **'... helps to intensify comfort and pleasure ...'** At times, grounding may also result in an increase of intensity. It doesn't remove feelings, it helps the body to digest them. As it digests them, it takes the 'energetic nutrients' out of them and allows the rest to be released as 'waste material'. So, the feelings will diminish in the long run, even if they do increase for a while in the beginning.

23 Relaxation

Page 219 **'sleep beautifully button'** See note on p. 238 (Page 196 'a sleep beautifully button') for how to install one of these in your children.

25 Couple time

Page 224 **'... couple time appointment ...'** Some friends of ours introduced us to this practice years ago and we have done it and passed on the idea ever since.

Other Finch titles

Life Smart: *Choices for young people about friendship, family and future*   Vicki Bennett gives advice to young people (13 to 19) on the challenges of adolescence – how to develop positive thoughts, relate to their friends and families, believe in themselves, make the best choices and develop a vision for their future. ISBN 1876451 130

Fathering from the Fast Lane: *Practical ideas for busy dads* (Dr Bruce Robinson) A book to help dads understand what children need. Over 75 men interviewed for this book (from pig farmer to prime minister) talk about ways they spend their limited time with their children more effectively. ISBN 1876451 211

Online and Personal: *The reality of Internet relationships*   With the boom in Internet dating services and chat rooms, the authors, Jo Lamble and Sue Morris, offer guidelines for Net users to protect themselves, their relationships and their children from the hazards that exist online. ISBN 1876451 173

Kids Food Health: *Nutrition and your child's development*   The authors, Dr Patricia McVeagh – a paediatrician – and Eve Reed – a dietitian – present the parents of children from newborns to teenagers with the latest information on the impact of diet on health, growth, allergies, behaviour and physical development. **Kids Food Health 1:** *The first year* ISBN 1876451 149 / **Kids Food Health 2:** *From toddler to preschooler* ISBN 1876451 157 / **Kids Food Health 3:** *From school-age to teenage* ISBN 1876451 165

Side by Side: *How to think differently about your relationship*   Jo Lamble and Sue Morris provide helpful strategies to overcome the pressures that lead to break-ups, as well as valuable advice on communication, problem-solving and understanding the stages in new and established relationships. A marvellous book for young people. ISBN 1876451 092

Stories of Manhood: *Journeys into the hidden hearts of men*   Steve Biddulph presents his selection of the best writings from around the world on the inner lives of men. Powerful, funny, and heart-rending, these stories show that men are infinitely larger than the narrow stereotypes they are given. ISBN 1876451 106

Girls' Talk: *Young women speak their hearts and minds* (Edited by Maria Pallotta-Chiarolli) Girls want a book that gets real about the issues in their lives. Here 150 young women tell it like it is. A riveting read – credible, direct and heartwarming. ISBN 1876451 025

Manhood: *An action plan for changing men's lives* (2nd edn) This bestseller by Steve Biddulph has changed the lives of tens of thousands of men and women. It tackles the key areas of a man's life – parenting, love and sexuality, finding meaning in work and making real friends. ISBN 0646261 444

Bullybusting: *How to help children deal with teasing and bullying*   Evelyn Field reveals the 'six secrets of bullybusting', which contain important life skills for any young person. Activities introduce young readers to new skills in communicating feelings, responding to stressful situations and building a support network. An empowering book for parents and their children (5-16 years). ISBN 1876451 041

On Their Own: *Boys growing up underfathered*   (Rex McCann) For a young man, growing up without an involved father in his life can leave a powerful sense of loss. *On Their Own* considers the needs of young men as they mature, the passage from boyhood to manhood, and the roles of fathers and mothers. ISBN 1876451 084

Fathers After Divorce: *Building a new life and becoming a successful separated father* (Michael Green)   'Comprehensive, beautifully clear, fair and friendly ... a separated man's best friend.' *Steve Biddulph* ISBN 1876451 009

Raising Boys: *Why boys are different – and how to help them become happy and well-balanced men* This bestseller by Steve Biddulph looks at the most important issues in boys' development – and the warm parenting and guidance that boys need. ISBN 0646314 181

Motherhood: *Making it work for you* Jo Lamble and Sue Morris provide useful approaches for mothers to deal with difficulties in everyday family life and to help make motherhood a rewarding, enjoyable experience. ISBN 1876451 033

Boys in Schools: *Addressing the real issues – behaviour, values and relationships* (Edited by Rollo Browne and Richard Fletcher) A positive and encouraging book for parents and teachers who are concerned about the poor performance of boys in schools. ISBN 0646239 589

Dealing with Anger: *Self-help solutions for men* (Frank Donovan) Focussing on emotional healing and practical change, this book includes case studies from clients of the author's (a psychotherapist) and a program of exercises for the reader. ISBN 1876451 05X

Chasing Ideas: *The fun of freeing your child's imagination* Christine Durham teaches thinking skills to children, and in this book she encourages parents and teachers to see how discussing ideas with their children (aged 4 to 14) can be an enjoyable and creative activity for everyone. ISBN 1876451 181

The Body Snatchers: *How the media shapes women* Cyndi Tebbel examines the rampant conditioning of women and girls by those who push starvation imagery. She challenges our preoccupation with the 'ideal' body. ISBN 1876451 076

Fear-free Children Dr Janet Hall provides solutions to conflicts in a wide range of family ages and situations, from young children through to adolescents. ISBN 1876451 238

Fight-free Families (Dr Janet Hall) This book draws on real-life case studies to help parents overcome specific fears and anxieties that their children have, such as fear of the dark, fear of being alone or fear of animals. ISBN 1876451 22X

Index

abilities, 108, 143-44, 166
acceptance, 50, 77, 79, 100, 105, 203
  complete, 6, 87, 141-42, 147, 160-61, 204
  conditional, 142-43, 160-61
access, 53
accidents, 55
acting out, 122-26
action
  stopping the, 151-52
  taking, 21, 50, 107-19
activities, 25, 42, 57, 62, 200, 203
ADHD, 236
adolescence, 101-2, 162, 164, 166, 169-75, 204-8
  see also children, adolescent
adoption, 10-11
advice, 26, 27, 204
affection, 23-24, 37, 42, 91, 204
agreement, 67, 69, 72, 73
agreements, 73, 89, 92-93, 151, 153-55
alcohol, 4
anger, 44, 46, 49, 78, 87, 157, 204, 213
anxiety, 212, 220
apologies, 151, 153, 156
appeasement, 49, 204
arguments, 39, 43-48, 216
arithmetic, 138
aromas, 132
arrogance, 146
assertiveness, 46-48, 127
asthma, 49
attention
  getting, 100, 128
  paying, 100, 128, 131-36
  seeking, 49
  span, 103
Auckett, Amelia D., 238
awareness, physical, 212-15

babies, 42, 86-87, 111, 137, 141, 160, 162
  needy, unloved, 174
  phases in development of, 195-98
  reading to, 196
  relaxation for, 219-20
baby massage, 196
balance, 12, 41, 51-57, 70, 110, 144, 168, 206
bed time, 88
behaviour, 112-13, 138
  acceptance of, 160-61
  bad, 15-16, 22, 84, 100

caring, 46-48, 50
changing, 15, 22, 100, 124-26, 156
childlike, 169
patterns, 138
proper, 50, 142, 207
risk-taking, 110, 113-15
seductive, 46, 105, 201
'being love', 76, 78, 80-83
being stream, the, 161-62, 164-65
belonging, 145-46
Belsky, Professor Jay, 232
Biddulph, Shaaron, 234
Biddulph, Steve, 234
birth
  cognitive, 180-82, 188
  emotional, 177-79, 188
  four births overview, 188-89
  'mother', 176, 178, 180, 183
  physical, 176-77, 182, 188
  process, 177, 178, 180-81, 183, 192-94
  spiritual, 182-84, 188
biting, 197
blackmail, 65
blame, 16, 19, 33, 34
boarding schools, 11-12
'body love', 76-77, 82-83
'body-mindedness', 122
body stream, the, 161-63, 165
bonding, 176, 179, 181, 184, 194, 195, 199, 205, 206
boredom, 119
bossiness, 127, 203
brain damage, 5
breast feeding, 196-97
breathing, 218-20
bullying, 30-32, 143, 186
busyness, 37

camps, 24
caretakers, 54
caring behaviour, 46-48
cartoons, 24
censorship, 24-25
changing, 22, 39-40, 41, 100, 124-26, 156
chat rooms, 25, 27
childcare, 11-12, 53-54
childhood
  phases of, 169-70, 192-208
  transitions of, 160-68
  the twenty-one years of, 52, 226
children
  ADD and ADHD, 220, 236
  adolescent, 42, 101-2, 111, 163, 164, 166, 169-75

comparing, 17-18
contributing to household, 40, 41, 110, 116, 144-45, 166-68, 200
different needs of, 168
eighteen-month-old, 86, 87, 101, 160, 162, 166, 178, 197-98
eighteen-year-old, 208
eight- to nine-year-old, 202-3
emotional ages of, 171-73
fifteen-year-old, 181, 205-6
five- to six-year-old, 201
fourteen-year-old, 161, 162, 174, 180, 182, 188, 204-5
giving love to, 6, 74-83
living together, 149-57
making time for, 19-21
meeting the needs of, 173-75
needing discipline, 114-15, 116-17
and parental conflicts, 73, 156
passive, 104
protecting, 3-4, 110, 165
at risk, 113, 118-19
seventeen-year-old, 207-8
seven-year-old, 201-2
sixteen-year-old, 173, 175, 206-7
suicidal, 41, 118-19
talking to, 117, 120-30
ten-year-old, 203
thirteen-year-old, 161, 162, 166, 170, 171, 173, 180, 204
three-year-old, 179, 199-200
twelve-year-old, 170, 171, 174, 203
twenty-one-year-old, 171, 208
two-year-old, 174, 178, 179, 182, 185, 186, 188, 199
unhappy, 202
uniqueness of, 17-18, 108, 150
  see also babies; toddlers
choice, 125-29
chores, 37, 40, 41, 109, 116, 144-45, 166-68, 202
  for toddlers, 198
  see also tasks
clarity, 124, 126-27
clinginess, 197
clubs, 202
coaxing, 87, 88, 127

commands, 125-29
commitments, 22, 61, 93, 138, 156
common sense, 103
communication, 46-48, 68, 120-30, 198, 201
communities, 29
 bonding with, 181-82, 188, 205
companions, 25
comparisons, 17-18
completion, 184-86
compromise, 72
computer games, 24-25
conceit, 146
conception, 9, 192-93
confidence, 85, 100, 126, 143-44, 220
conflicts
 children's, 31-32, 94, 149-57
 parental, 61, 66-73, 156
confrontation, 88
consequences, 15, 48, 88-89, 91-92, 100, 102, 161, 203
consistency, 39, 41, 209
consultation, 61
contact, physical, 40, 42, 76-77, 163
contractions, 176, 177, 178, 180
contributions, 61-63, 116, 144-45, 207, 222
control, 45, 49, 114, 165-66, 206, 217
conversations, 25
cooperation, 41, 50, 156, 222
coordination, 42, 137, 201
correction, 41, 50, 138
counselling, 34
couple time, 60
courtesy, 50
cranial osteopathy, 5, 196, 231, 238
crawling, 196-97
creativity, 18, 201
creches, 11-12
crushes, 205, 206
custody, 11
cuteness, 46, 105, 209

dangers, 3-4, 40-41, 110, 165
day care, family, 12, 54
death, 10, 53, 55, 56, 110, 188
decisions, 34-35, 41, 84, 92-93, 96-106, 138, 143, 202
 life-changing, 203
dejection, 148
Delacato, Carl, 234
delivery, 177, 179, 181, 183-84, 186-88
dependency, 46, 161, 168, 169, 171, 204
depression, 41, 110, 118, 220

deprivation, 74
destiny, 7
detachment, 9, 11
development, 162, 169-75
developmental sequence, 169-70
disagreements, 154-56
discipline, 84-94, 96-106, 116, 143, 209
discomfort, 92, 100, 104
discussion groups, 27
discussions, 41, 61, 62, 205, 207
 class, 25
disputes, 43-44
distraction, 87
divorce, 11, 53
Doman, Glenn, 234
dramas, 43-50, 106, 169
Drama Triangle, The, 43-48
dreaminess, 171, 204
driving, dangerous, 4, 110
drug use, 4, 114, 115
dyslexia, 5, 175, 236

embryo, 192, 193
encouragement, 138
ethics, 161, 162, 164, 207
exaggeration, 147
exercise, 70, 201
expectations, 50, 88, 94, 112-13, 161, 178, 205
experiences, 24, 200, 216
 near-death, 183-84
 recycling, 170, 173
experts, 26, 27
exploring, 196, 197, 200
expressiveness, 61, 67, 117, 120-29, 134, 138, 193
eye contact, 22-23, 104
eyesight, 5, 6

fairness, 50, 157
families
 activities for, 57
 blended, 50, 52
 bonding with, 179, 188
 extended, 187
 management of, 13-14, 60-64, 221-22
 membership of, 157
 patterns in, 36-41
 your experience of, 30-35
fantasy, 200, 205, 207
fathers, 10, 51, 53, 199
 bonding with babies, 176, 177, 188, 195
 role in birth process, 193-94
fear, 49, 78, 157, 200, 216
feedback, 148, 206
'feeling love', 76, 77-79, 82-83
feelings, 49, 83, 93, 94, 100, 161-62, 163

expressing, 37, 41, 47, 50, 104-5, 134, 148, 193, 202
 see also expressiveness
feeling stream, the, 161-63, 165
fighting, 37, 115, 206
finances, 14, 51-52, 206
foetus, 176, 192, 193
follow-up, 94, 148
food fads, 49
force, 91
foster parents, 10-11
freedom, 101, 165-66, 205
friends, 124, 200, 205, 208
fulfilment, 5, 7-8, 47, 111
fun, 37, 42, 57, 201, 207, 208
future, the, 107, 111-13, 200, 206, 215

games, 42, 57
 baby, 197
gaps, emotional, 33-34, 113-14
gay parents, 11
genetic links, 10
gestation, 193-94
goals, 36, 61, 67-69, 111
good intentions, 92-93
grief, 10
grounding, 62, 67, 69-71, 100, 104, 156, 193, 212-17
 technique, 218-20
guessing, 155
guidance, 113-14, 138, 142-43, 147, 207
guidelines, 50, 85, 86, 103-6

happiness, 5, 6-7, 47, 78, 157, 201, 220
hassles, 107, 209
health, 5, 12, 193
hearing, 5, 6
Hillman, James, 233
homeopathy, 196
homework, 136, 181
honesty, 148, 209
hormonal changes, 204
househusbands, 51
hyperactivity, 175, 220, 236

ideals, 37
illness, 49, 55
 making allowance for, 106
imitation, 24
impatience, 87
inactivity, 21, 49, 110, 115
inadequacy, 105
incentives, 91, 152
inclusion, 61
independence, 102, 204, 208
individuality, 79, 156
inequality, 156
infants, 42
initiative, 50, 107-10

insensitivity, 146
insistence, 88
instinct, 25-26
instructions, 97, 124-29
intensity, 127, 129, 163, 217
interests, 61, 91
interference, 42
Internet, the, 25, 27
intuition, 25-26
involvement, 9-10, 19, 20, 41

James, Muriel, 231, 232
jealousy, 150, 157
Jongeward, Dorothy, 231, 232
justice, 157, 203

Karpman, Steve, 232
kindergartens, 200, 220

language, 22-24, 79, 92-93,
    120-29, 200
'latch-key kids', 52
learning, 5, 27, 41, 114, 137-
    40, 205, 216
    opportunities, 169-70
    the streams of, 161-65
    tasks, 9
leaving home, 181, 206, 208
leniency, 106
lesbian parents, 11
Levin, Pam, 236
life skills, 8-9, 84-85, 102
lifestyle, 52
limits, 7, 85-86, 89, 114-15,
    143, 161, 181, 199
listening, 61, 131-33, 203
living well, 5-8, 85
lone parents
    see single parents
looking, 131-32
loss, 9-12, 118
love, 6, 37, 47, 74-83, 84, 87,
    106, 141-42
    tough, 145-46
lying, 114, 202, 209

manipulation, 48-49
    of information, 201
Mathew, Diana, 231
maturity, 181, 182, 207
media, 25, 203
meetings, 63-64, 203, 221-22
memory, 138, 171, 202
messages, 65, 122-29, 139, 142
    negative, 122, 125
misbehaviour, 15-16
money pressures, 51-52
    see also finances
monitoring yourself, 35
moods, 123-24
Moody, Raymond, Jnr, 238
mothers, 10, 53
    bonding with babies, 176,

177, 188, 195
    role in birth process, 193-94
    separating from toddlers,
        199
motivation, 104
mottos, 37, 232
movement, 215
movies, 25, 205

nagging, 137, 140, 202, 209
name-calling, 45, 49, 72
nastiness, 105, 156, 202
negotiation, 222
neural pathways, 137
nicknames, 23-24

obedience, 97, 100, 126
observation, 107, 117, 118, 166
'only child', the, 149
openness, 46-48, 77, 199
orders, 125-29
outings, 4, 200, 203, 206, 208
ovum, 192, 193

panic attacks, 220
parent groups, 27
parenting, 2-14, 107-10, 116-17
    active, 107, 108-9
    children's needs for, 53
    with love, 74-83
    patterns in, 33-35, 36-41
    proactive, 107, 108-9, 116
    reactive, 107, 108-10
    second chance in, 169-75
    skills, 59, 67
    successful, 15-27
    team, 60-64
    from the 'victim position',
        129
parents
    adoptive, 10-11
    biological, 9-12, 52-53
    gay and lesbian, 11
    job description for, 2-14
    loss of, 10-12, 118
    networking, 27, 203, 205,
        207
    nonbiological, 10-11
    responsibilities of, 3-4, 39,
        50, 61
    self-care for, 12, 41
    separated, 19-21, 53
    single, 11, 51-52, 64, 225
    working, 12, 19, 51-57
passion, 169, 180, 204, 205
Pearce, Joseph Chilton, 231,
    234, 237
peers, 42, 207
penalties, 94
perfection, 16-17
persecutor, the, 43-48, 105
perseverance, 9-10
persistence, 20, 21, 67, 71, 104,

139-40, 218, 220
    the power of, 105
personal mastery, 143
'personhood', 80
'person love', 76, 78, 79-80, 82-
    83, 88
Petre, Daniel, 232
pets, 134-35, 198
petulance, 105
Piaget, Jean, 234
pin-ups, 25
playtime, 42, 57
pocket money, 167, 202, 206
politeness, 37, 41, 125-26, 128-
    29
posters, 25
posture, 104
power, 45-46, 96, 206
practicality, 39
praise, 41, 91, 147, 160
prejudice, 202
principles, 164
privileges, 91, 101, 156
problem solving, 7, 41, 148,
    153, 222
professional people, 26, 27
programming, 21, 23-24, 32-
    34, 124, 147, 171-73
provocations, 107, 113-15
proximity, 20
punishment, 49, 92

questions to ask about your
    family, 38

radio, 25
reading, 138, 196
realism, 146, 148, 212
reality, 200, 205
reason, 161-62, 163, 204, 205,
    206
reasons, 88, 90, 130, 164
reassurance, false, 147
rebellion, 120, 168, 205
recordings, life, 32-34, 69, 127
recycling experiences, 170, 173
regression, 161, 170-73, 204,
    205, 206, 207, 208
reinforcement, 22-23
rejection, 9, 74
relating to others, 7, 143, 177
relatives, 10-11, 54
relaxation, 218-20
repetition, 41, 94, 137-40
replaying the past, 32-35, 69
requests, 125-29
rescuer, the, 43-48, 105
resistance, 96, 100, 102, 156
resolution, 66-73, 91-92, 97-99,
    103-6, 150-57, 209
resources, 27
respect, 7, 37, 41, 50, 91, 128,
    134, 157

between parents, 61, 72
responses, 123-24, 142
responsibility, 34, 39, 100, 140, 153, 200, 207, 208
restraint, physical, 105
reviews, 64, 222
rewards, 41, 91, 94, 203
road hazards, 4, 110, 165, 201
role models, 21, 24, 205
roles, clarifying, 62-63
romance, 207
Rossmanith, Angela, 231
rosters, 202
rules, 41, 113, 152, 161, 164, 200
    household, 65
running away, 49

sadness, 78, 157
safety, 3-4, 40-41, 107, 110, 120, 165
saying 'No', 4, 186, 209
schedules, 205
Schiff, Jacqui, 234, 236
school, 138, 203, 204, 207
    assignments, 24-25, 203
    books, 25
    pressures of, 111, 173, 204, 205, 216
    starting, 201
security, 47, 78, 142, 220
seductive behaviour, 46, 105, 201
self-care, 12, 41, 203
self-control, 86, 105, 143
self-doubt, 148
self-esteem, 7, 34, 141-48, 234-35
self-evaluation, 146
self-importance, 146
selfishness, 146
self-management, 98, 127, 215-16
self-sufficiency, 102
senses, the five, 5, 131-32, 212
sensitivity, 41, 148, 182, 204
separation, parental, 53
separation, the quality of, 11, 75-76, 199
sexuality, 199, 206, 207
sexual predators, 4
sharing, 60-61, 78, 157, 222, 223
Sheehy, Gail, 235
shouting, 127-28
sibling rivalry, 149-57
signals, conflict, 73
single parents, 11, 51-52, 64, 225
skills
    physical, 138, 144
    social, 8-9, 138, 206

'sleep beautifully button', 198, 219, 238
smelling, 131-32
social turmoil, 115
Sogyal Rinpoche, 238
songs, 24-25
soothing, 87, 88
sperm, 192, 193
spiritual dimensions, 7, 8, 81, 182-84, 188, 193
sports, 24
squabbling, 37, 150, 151
standards, 6, 50, 85-86, 143, 156, 161, 181, 199
'standing to decide', 38-39, 95-106, 128, 155, 156-57, 198
statements, 'I' and 'You', 72-73
stealing, 114, 186, 202
step-parents, 10-11
stories, 24
'straight communication', 46-48
strength, 88, 100, 106, 115
stress, 55
struggle, 94, 106, 107, 145, 181, 185
    physical, 105
    toddlers, 87, 178
    where to, 115-17
styles
    family, 36-37
    parenting, 66-67, 107-10, 168
suffering, 46, 105
suggestions, practical, 148
suicide, 41, 118-19
support, 10, 61, 62, 73, 117, 207, 208
swimming, 4, 110

talents, 18, 108, 117, 146, 182
talking
    to babies, 196, 197
    between children, 153
    to children, 117, 120-30, 200
tantrums, 15, 49, 112, 143, 174, 180, 181, 199
tasks, 9, 97-98, 103
    see also chores
tasting, 131-32
teachers, 115, 181
teamwork, 60-64
teeth, 5
teething, 196-97
telephone calls, 20
television, 24-25, 99-100
therapy, 34
thinking, 138, 156, 202
    development, 162
    magical, 205

value-based, 164
thinking stream, the, 161-62, 164, 165
threats, 37
time, 19-21, 41, 54, 56, 154
    couple, 60, 223-25
    management, 205
    out, 69-71, 104, 224
    sense of, 171, 203
tiredness, making allowance for, 106
toddlers, 86, 87, 101, 160, 162, 166, 178, 197-98
tolerance, 203
touching, 76-77, 131-33
tough love, 145-46
training, 84, 90, 160
    toilet, 95
train surfing, 110
transitions, 160-68, 186-88
treats, 37
triangulation, 43-48, 201, 206, 207
truancy, 114, 186

Ultimate, the, 184, 188
understanding, 77, 79, 161-65, 203
union, 75, 77, 79, 81, 223
uniqueness, 17-18, 108, 150
unity, 62, 181
upsets, 87, 88, 98, 113, 123-24, 212-16

values, 35, 94, 162, 164, 206, 207, 208
victim, the, 43-48, 105, 129, 152
video games, 24-25
videos, 24, 27
violence, 24-25, 37, 99, 114
visits, drop-in, 20
vulnerability, 46-48, 49, 161, 199

Wachtel, Ted, 241
wants, 7
warnings, 97
weaning, 196-97
whingeing, 46, 119
wilfulness, 161, 174, 180
withdrawal, 49, 118
work
    children, 206, 207, 208
    parents, 12, 19, 51-57
writing, 138

yoga, 194, 196
York, David, 241
York, Phyllis, 241